# *Textbook of*
# *MARINE FISHERIES*

## *Fisheries of World Oceans and India in Perspective*

# *Textbook of*
# *MARINE FISHERIES*

## *Fisheries of World Oceans and India in Perspective*

**Alok Kumar Upadhyay**
**Bhuwan Chandra Joshi**

BIOTECH
2014
BIOTECH BOOKS®

ISBN 978-81-7622-302-7



*Published by*: **BIOTECH BOOKS®**
4762-63/23, Ansari Road, Darya Ganj,
New Delhi - 110 002
Phone: +91-011-23262132
E-mail: biotechbooks@yahoo.co.in

*Printed at*: **Chawla Offset Printers**
Delhi - 110 052

PRINTED IN INDIA

भारत सरकार
कृषि अनुसंधान और शिक्षा विभाग एवं
भारतीय कृषि अनुसंधान परिषद
कृषि मंत्रालय, कृषि भवन, नई दिल्ली 110 001
GOVERNMENT OF INDIA
DEPARTMENT OF AGRICULTURAL RESEARCH & EDUCATION
AND
INDIAN COUNCIL OF AGRICULTURAL RESEARCH
MINISTRY OF AGRICULTURE, KRISHI BHAVAN, NEW DELHI 110 001
Tel.: 23382629; 23386711 Fax: 91-11-23384773
E-mail: dg.icar@nic.in

सत्यमेव जयते

डा. एस. अय्यप्पन
सचिव एवं महानिदेशक
**Dr. S. AYYAPPAN**
SECRETARY & DIRECTOR GENERAL

# FOREWORD

The world oceans have great resource and potential for enormous supply of food. This potential is obvious when one realizes the ocean occupy the far greater area of about 70 per cent to that of land about 30 per cent from planet earth. The exploration of ocean for the production of protein rich food is taking place from prehistoric times. However with the passage of time, advent and improvisation of modern sophisticated methods of fishing there has been great increase into the landing of fish from the world oceans. In the last five decades, the world fish food supply is therefore has outpaced global population growth and thus at present fish constitute an important source of nutritious food and animal protein for much of the world's population. The major contribution to the extent of 63.76 per cent to the world fish production is realized from marine fishery sector. However due to subjection of constant relentless fishing activities from coastal inshore waters the future of marine fisheries is at risk with the declining share from marine capture and thus the fish production from world ocean instead of maintaining progress remained almost stable for last one decade. It is therefore many experts believe that the extent of the level of exploitation up to the continental shelf of world oceans is already being fished to the maximum.

In today's world of globalization with increased demand of fish and advancement into technologies of fishing, it is a challenge to reduce the fishing activities. A more rational approach in formulating fishing regulation to curtail the fishing activities from the continental waters, diversifying and extending the fishing range in offshore waters, limiting to marine parks and reserves for the conservation of endangered fish species and above all the implementation of the international principles enshrined in the code of conduct for responsible fisheries are some of the measures to reduce overfishing.

I am happy to see the commendable work of Dr. A.K. Upadhyay for the book *"Textbook of Marine Fisheries: Fisheries of World Oceans and India in Perspective"*. I am sure the students, teachers and scientists from different Fisheries Colleges in the country would benefit from this knowledge-base as a handy literature in the discipline of marine fisheries.

***Dr. S. Ayyappan***

# PREFACE

The world oceans apart from more and more use than just an abstract of curiosity are the largest repository of life on planet earth and therefore are visualized as great reservoir of protein rich food resource. The increased knowledge and understanding lead to the increased exploration of sea food resource from all the oceans. The food from ocean continues to grow in importance as with the passage of time; efforts are made to produce more to feed the multiplying world population. The improvisation of fishing effort from ocean has resulted in the significant growth in terms of production from marine sector up to the nineties. However owing to undue concentration, intense exploitation of coastal waters in pursuit to capture more and more premium quality fishes, from the past one decade the situation of marine fisheries sector in the world oceans crippled with the effects of over-fishing and stalemate at the production level. It is therefore that the monitoring the harvest of different marine fishery resources is very much essential for planning and implementing policies for the sustained production from the oceans.

The global overview of marine fisheries, the state of prominent marine fish resources overall fisheries development in the world are therefore immaculately documented in this book according to different FAO Recognized International Fishing Zones of the world oceans.

Fishery is also the emerging sector in India. India as being second largest producer of fish in the world, the fisheries sector plays pivotal role in alleviating the shortage of protein rich food resource for its ever increasing population. The fisheries sector in India beside being significantly contributing to the food security, puts its most valuable share to the national economy through seafood export and most essentially provides employment to millions of people. However just as from the world oceans, the fate and future of Indian Marine Fisheries sector is also in doldrums since from last decade due to stalemate and even sometimes decline in production due to over-fishing.

Therefore in the Indian context the book also contains the comprehensive account of development of fisheries sector, critical analysis of the production data, individual appraisal of top prominent Indian Fisheries, critical gaps and constraints ailing to marine fisheries sector and prudent management measures to be undertaken for the upliftment of fisheries sector in India are meticulously discussed.

The book is written keeping in mind the latest syllabus for the course of 'Marine Fisheries' as recommended by the 4$^{th}$ Dean's Committee of Indian Council of Agricultural Research. I am sure the Students, Teachers and Scientists from different Fisheries Colleges and other academic institutions would refer this book to add to their knowledge in the discipline of marine fisheries.

I would like to thank respected **Dr. S. Ayyappan**, Director General and Secretary DARE of Indian Council of Agricultural Research for providing his most valuable inspiration and blessing in forwarding this book. I also owe my sincere thanks to **Dr. Dilip Kumar** former Director of CIFE Mumbai for his constant encouragement. The affection and good will generated from my innumerable number of students who actually provided me the inner strength to write this meaningful book also deserve my worthy thanks. I also thank my co-author Dr. B. C. Joshi for his subject matter contribution and graphical illustrations which added value to this book. I am also highly impressed with the cooperation and efficiency of my publisher Mr. Sunil Mittal Biotech Books New Delhi.

I constantly derive my inner strength from the life of my father Late **Dr Uttam Chandra Upadhyay**, a great human being, scholar and academician of very high repute, who distinguishably served in different capacities like ADG and DDG ICAR, Vice chancellor for eight years respectively at Narendra Dev University of Agriculture and Technology, Faizabad and Assam Agricultural University, Jorhat. In the profound memories of his affection and learning out of his inheritance the teaching for high moral in life, I dedicate this book to him. I am indebted to my wife Neelam for her constant encouragement, immense patience, boundless understanding and her selfless assistance. I also sincerely appreciate the support I received from my grown up children Mitesh and Neha Upadhyay in bringing this manuscript. Finally the inspiring thought of appreciation towards big fellow 'The Ocean' that divides and yet unites mankind with its worthy attributes which blend elegantly my professional pursuit and interest.

***Alok Kumar Upadhyay***

# CONTENTS

# Chapter 1
# INTRODUCTION

## 1.1 IMPORTANCE AND INNOVATIVE USES OF THE OCEAN

Ocean environment is hostile and adventurous to common man and does not yield its secrets easily, due to its impounding vastness. However this very secrecy, lure and romance of the ocean has drawn many scientific persons and enthusiast to study the aspects related to ocean. This includes marine biologists, oceanographers, marine geologists, ecologists, etc. Within the sediment layers of ocean floor are recorded the geological and in fossils the biological history of the earth. Life on planet Earth undoubtedly began in the ocean a few billion years ago and since then the ocean has added vast quantities and varied forms of life through the process of evolution. In recent years, there has been increasing interest in to marine related activities. The human venture in to ocean started with hunting or exploitation of the Coastal Bioresource. After mapping of world Ocean when it was realized that the spread of oceans has been from continents to continents, the ocean was navigated for the purpose of spreading trade, commerce and increasing the territorial power. In later years many scientific discoveries proved ocean to be an enormous source of food through biological exploitation, as largest reservoir of mineral, oils, heavy metals and natural gases through its exploration, meteorologically ocean is the major supplier of oxygen and regulator of climatic pattern of planet earth. However though, unfortunately the ocean has also been used as the dumping ground for the mounting burdens of human waste material such as pollutants and nuclear wastes etc.

The world oceans covers an area of 361 million km$^2$ roughly forming about 71 per cent of the earth's surface and due to their vast spread and depth, they encompass about 300 times more habitable volume than terrestrial habitats on earth. Besides being abode for thousands of varieties of plants and animals, it forms immense resource of food, many pharmaceutical drugs, life saving drugs of rare quality for the treatment of dreaded diseases and variety of byproducts of human use.

## 1.2 OCEAN AS BIOLOGICAL RESOURCES

A large amount of life of earth exists in the ocean. Exactly how large proportion is unknown, since many species are still to be discovered. Marine life is a vast biological resource, providing food, medicines and raw materials in addition to helping to support the recreation and tourism all over the world. At a fundamental level, marine life helps determine the very nature of our planet. Marine organisms are widely spread right from shore, pelagic waters, at great depths and surprisingly there are marine organisms that even help in creating new land.

Marine life covers a great deal from microscopic including most phytoplankton, zooplankton, to organisms from almost all phyla of invertebrates, and many vertebrates to amazing collection of marine mammals including the largest huge cetaceans (Whales) which reach up to a reported 48 meters or 125 feet in length.

The habitats studied by marine biologist include everything from the tiny layers of surface water in which organisms and abiotic items may be trapped in surface tension between the ocean and atmosphere, to the depth of ocean trenches, sometimes over 10000 meters or more beneath the surface of ocean. It also include the most diverse habitats such as coral reefs, kelp forests, tide pools, rocky, sandy and muddy bottoms and open ocean pelagic zone.

There is no denying to the fact that life exists throughout the immense volume of ocean. The ocean constitutes the single largest repository of organisms on the planet earth. These organisms include representative of virtually all phyla and are tremendously varied.

There is growing emphasis on exploitation of plants and animals from the ocean for the requirement of easiest source of animal protein, nutrients and minerals. The importance of ocean as food resource is significant with the passage of time. Similarly rendering of exclusive value added and byproducts from the biological resource of ocean (mainly fish and shellfish) is gaining momentum. The advent of variety of seafood products include frozen fish, shell fish, canned and smoked fish/shellfish products, products in retortable pouches, masmine etc. Byproducts like fish liver oil, fish meal, fish silage, fish hydrolysate, fish protein concentrate, shrimp extract, isinglass, glucosamine, hydrochloride, chitosan etc. are fulfilling the basic requirement of protein and products of multifarious utility. Plants and macrophytes from ocean are also the useful source of production of Agar-agar, Alginic acid, China grass etc.

The ocean is the greatest supplier of food resource. Fish and shellfish explored from ocean are important to man as it alone provide 3 per cent of protein that human body need and shares about 10 per cent of all animal protein consumed.

The commercially important biological resources from the ocean can be grouped under invertebrates comprising mainly the crustaceans and mollusks, while bony and cartilaginous fishes and marine mammals as vertebrates. The sequential details of composition of each group of commercial sea food commodities from world oceans, based on the tonnage production are given as below.

## Crustaceans

Penaeid and non penaeid shrimps, others include crabs, lobsters and cray fish are the important crustaceans contributing the sea food.

## Molluscs

In terms, of tonnage, squids and cuttle fish, bivalves such as oysters, mussels and clams are the molluscan resources of the ocean.

## Fishes

Based on the tonnage production, there are mainly three or four groups. The first largest group is clupids or members of clupidae family from surface pelagic waters such as sardines, herrings, anchovies and menhaden. They mostly venture in surface waters and graze on low tropic level phytoplankton and zooplankton like copepods. The second group is of Gadoids which mainly comprise of demersal species of Cod, Haddock, Pollock and Hake. The third group is occupied by Scombroid fishes which include Mackerels, Tunas, Seer fishes etc. They are mostly fast swimmer and occupy warmer surface waters.

There are also some important members of flat fishes such as Sole, Plaice, Halibut and Flounders which have considerable importance because of their demand.

The list of commercial fishes which are very important, high to moderate in demand but are produced in less quantities, include Whiting, Perches, Pomfrets, Snappers, Sciaenid's and Croakers, Carangids, Ribbon fishes, Silver bellies etc.

The shark and elasmobranches cartilaginous fishes even though not preferred for eating due to high urea content are in demand due to extraction of oil and other byproducts like skins, fins, fin rays, shark teeth etc. The salmonids, which are very important food fish, however they from a very minor part of world landings.

### Marine Mammals

The dominant fishery of marine mammals is of whale but they are endangered in recent time due to their persistent fishing and over exploitation. The other marine mammals from point of view of demand are mainly the pinnipids seals and comprising of sea lions.

The other miscellaneous commodities which are not eaten but are exploited on commercial basis because of their high esthetic demand the list include Corals, Sea pens, Ornamental coral reef fishes, Sponges, Sea anemone, Star fishes, Sea cucumber, Octopus, Sea turtle, Dolphins etc.

The plants or sea weeds from the ocean are also exploited for the extraction of algin derivatives like agar-agar, alginic acid and carrageenanase. Few sea weeds like Ulva, Porphyra, Enteromorpha etc. are also harvested for their consumption mainly in Japan.

## 1.3 TROPHIC STRUCTURE IN MARINE ECOSYSTEM

It is most worthy to find that in the ocean just on land there are scientific principles that govern the organization and perpetuation of organisms and associations.

Since ecosystems are composed from one to many communities, each in turn composed of many populations of producers, consumers and decomposers. The transfer of energy in an ecosystem may follow several pathways. Each pathway that transfer energy from a given source of primary producers (autotrophs) passes through to different series of consumers called a Food Chain. The combination of all food chains in a given community or ecosystem called a Food Web. The food web thus is a summary of all the path ways by which energy moves from one level to another through community or ecosystem.

Based on this basic concept of trophic level, the marine ecosystem is principally no different. The energy is fixed in life process by the reaction of photosynthesis by phytoplankton and marine macrophytes, which passes on to the level of consumers of herbivores and carnivores and the part of energy gets recycled through the decomposers.

Even though communities and ecosystems have the same trophic levels and ecological principles apply equally, there have been some striking differences between the terrestrial and marine ecosystem.

One striking difference is the absence of large flowering plants, trees, forests in the marine ecosystem. In the marine ecosystem with the exception of certain kelp and macrophytes, the dominant autotrophs are small microscopic cellular entities called phytoplankton. The bloom of phytoplankton does not exist for long time (as long standing crop material) because by size and number they are small and that the marine herbivore by continuous grazing and consuming eliminate them regularly. At the time of existence, the high bloom of phytoplankton due to their continuous grazing by herbivore like zooplankton and primary consuming fishes, the phytoplankton cells come to the stage of complete elimination and unless the fresh supply of nutrients gets seasonally available to them they remain dormant. It means most of the herbivores have to face danger of availability of food to them. Most of the herbivores in the ocean are short lived. In marine ecosystem there are very less herbivore than terrestrial ecosystem. In the marine ecosystem there always is the danger of misbalancing of food chain due to limited number of autotrophs and their elimination and the resultant reduction in the number of herbivore. It is therefore from the point of view of capture fisheries management, it is imperative to carefully harvest the available fish resource that exist at the base of trophic level (primary consumers) so that this valuable resource is conserved possibly for maximum length of time.

In the marine ecosystem majority of large animals are carnivores. Large marine animals therefore exist at the higher trophic levels than large land animals. From the stand point of human beings harvestable food in the form of animal protein from the marine ecosystem is from the carnivores from third or fourth tropic level such as salmon, tuna, halibut, etc. Therefore any disturbance at any trophic level due to over exploitation may result into the collapse of entire food chain in the ocean.

## 1.4 OVER EXPLOITATION OR OVER FISHING

The situation of over exploitation of resource at any trophic level must be averted. There have been abundant examples of the decline of fish stocks of all types in all areas of the world ocean. The decline has been mainly due to exceeding the maximum amount of fishes that can be taken from that portion of ocean, in other words mainly due to over exploration of stock and mismanagement of fisheries. The signs due to the effect of over fishing or exploitation of stocks are very apparent like shortening of average fish size, increase in effort to land same amount of fishes than preceding fishing attempt, change in age structure of captured fish stock etc. The world is known from the temporary elimination of Peruvian Anchoveta from south east pacific water, complete decline of Californian Sardine from Central East Pacific, loss of North Atlantic Cod, great reduction to the stock of Whales from North Atlantic Waters are owing to overexploitation of stock. The decline in the landing of penaeid shrimps from Indian water is also due to over exploitation of stock from the continental waters.

## 1.5 MAXIMUM SUSTAINABLE YIELD

In order to overcome the situation of over exploitation it must be ensured that the stock of fishery should not sustain any damage from the ill effects of anthropogenic sources. The stock of aquatic animals, fish and other valuable resource from ocean are the renewable resource. The renewable resources have in support recycling of biological process of growth, reproduction; breeding and spawning which never allows the stock to diminish instead allow it to prosper more vigorously through sustained recruitment. It is therefore for the biological entity once the yearly recruitment is ensured and if the balance in the harvestable (fishing) effort and sustenance of stock on long term basis is maintained, the problem of overfishing would never occur. Thus the term maximum sustainable yield for fisheries refers to the long term yield of fish to a fishery that can be sustained indefinitely. It must therefore be assured that the level of maximum sustainable yield for every fishery must be respected and adhered with. It means under no circumstance the production level by increase in fishing effort should be increased than to the production level required for maximum sustainable yield. The fishery management needs the effort at the higher average fishing level over time that does not reduce a stock of abundance in balance with the stocks with reproductive and growth capacities under a given set of environmental conditions.

## 1.6 MEASURES FOR RESTRICTING OVER EXPLOITATION

The situation of overfishing can be easily averted by maintaining the balance in the effort and maximum sustainable yield. It can further be followed by rational fishing which include in harvest only adult forms which have already undergone the process of maximum growth and spawning stages. Limiting the fishing effort or reduction in number of fishing days or closed fishing season after realizing danger to any fish crops. Avoid the repeated fishing from same places of continental shelf. Introduction of rational fishing practices, maintenance of the correct mesh size of gears to exclude the juvenile younger ones from the harvest. The other measures to be undertaken for avoiding the over exploitation include diversification of the fishing to reduce the fishing pressure from one single fishery of high demand to be replaced by other. The enhancement and monitoring for fisheries database is highly imperative to obtain correct production figures for knowing the level of biodiversity. Further the assessment of fisheries information, framing of policy and legal framework for rational fishing are also necessary. Most importantly the community participation by fishery scientists, fishermen and government and private agencies is necessary to avert the chance of occurrence of over exploitation. Conservation of fish stock of importance through establishment of marine park and sanctuary, protection of coastal breeding and nursery area etc. are some very important measures to avert the danger of over expatiation.

# *Chapter 2*

# DETAILS OF WORLD FISH PRODUCTION

## 2.1 TRENDS OF WORLD FISH PRODUCTION

The world fish production has registered year wise increase between the years of 2004 to 2011 (except in 2009). This gradual increase into this landing was from 134.3 mmt in 2004 to 154 mmt in the year 2011. The major contribution to the world fish landing was realized from marine fishery sector with the average percentage of 68.28 per cent than inland fish production with the average production of 31.72 per cent (Table 2.1).

Even though the share of marine fishery sector was more to the world fish landing, the production remained fluctuating dwindling in between the years of 2004 – 2011, with maximum 100.5 mmt in 2006, marginally increased to 97 mmt in 2007 again declining to 95.5 mmt in 2011 and accounting for 98.2 mmt in 2011. The reason for this fluctuating trend into world marine fish production was mainly attributed for the continuous reduced share in the production from its capture fishery resources (world oceans) with catastrophic decline from 83.3 mmt in 2004 to 77.4 mmt in 2011 with slight increase in the landing of 78.9 per cent in 2011. The world marine fish production trend also suggested that the production from capture fisheries was accountable for 83.42 per cent while the share from culture production was just 16.58 per cent. Although the share from Inland fishery sector to world fish production was less but there has been significant increase into its landings over the years. In between the years of 2004-2011, the inland fish production in the world increased from 33.8 mmt to 55.8 mmt. Aquaculture contributed for the share of about 77.34 per cent, to the fresh water fish production in the world.

**Table 2.1: Year wise world fish and aquaculture production (in mmt)**

| *Resources* | *2004* | *2005* | *2006* | *2007* | *2008* | *2009* | *2010* | *2011* | *2004-2011* |
|---|---|---|---|---|---|---|---|---|---|
| **Inland Capture** | 8.6 | 9.4 | 9.8 | 10.0 | 10.2 | 10.4 | 11.2 | 11.5 | 10.13 |
| **Inland Culture** | 25.2 | 26.8 | 31.3 | 33.4 | 36.0 | 38.1 | 41.7 | 44.3 | 34.6 |
| Total Inland | 33.8 | 36.2 | 41.1 | 43.4 | 46.2 | 48.5 | 52.9 | 55.8 | 44.74 |
| **Marine Capture** | 83.8 | 82.7 | 80.2 | 80.4 | 79.5 | 79.2 | 77.4 | 78.9 | 80.26 |
| **Marine Culture** | 16.7 | 17.5 | 16.0 | 16.6 | 16.9 | 17.6 | 18.1 | 19.3 | 17.33 |
| Total Marine | 100.5 | 100.1 | 96.2 | 97.0 | 96.4 | 86.8 | 95.5 | 98.2 | 96.34 |
| Total world fish production | 134.3 | 136.3 | 137.3 | 140.4 | 142.6 | 135.3 | 148.4 | 154.0 | 141.08 |
| **Total capture (Inland+Marine)** | 92.4 | 92.1 | 90.0 | 90.4 | 89.7 | 89.6 | 88.6 | 90.4 | |
| **Total culture (Inland+Marine)** | 41.4 | 44.3 | 47.3 | 50.0 | 52.9 | 55.7 | 59.8 | 53.6 | |

*Source*: SOFIA, 2012.

The fate of marine fishery sector seems to be not fascinating as in previous years. World over the mariculture practice has just been at low level even though flourished in some counties like Japan, China, Taiwan and Korea, it has yet not got the beginning at many places. There has been continuous decline in the capture of marine fish from all world oceans from the turn of centaury year 2000 onwards. The main reason which could be attributed for the decline of capture from the marine fishery sector is due to extreme stress of fishing from the continental waters of world oceans leading to reduction of premium verities of marine fishes due to their over exploitation. Unless the fishing from the marine sector gets diversified by reducing the fishing effort from continental waters and shifting attention to the exploration of offshore pelagic and deeper waters in the high seas beyond and implementation and adherence to judicious

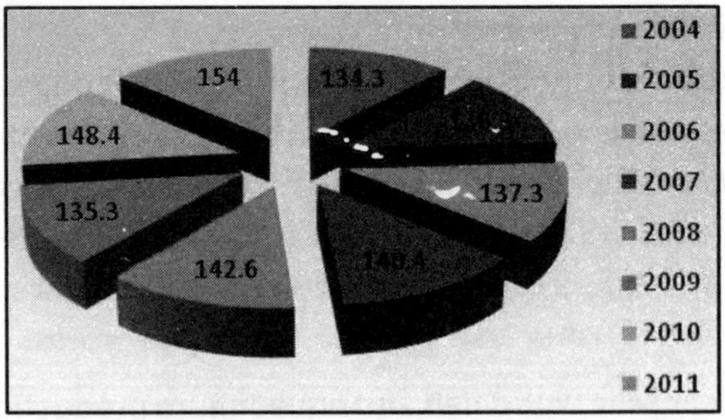


**Figure 2.1: World's Total Fish Production (mmt)**

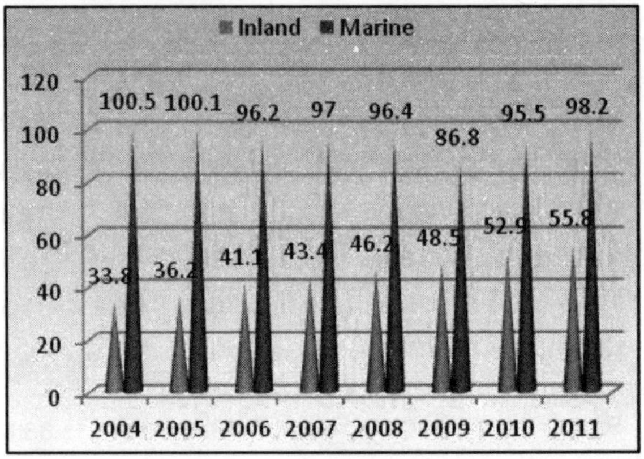


**Figure 2.2: World's Total Production: Marine and Inland (mmt)**

management practices, the future of marine capture fisheries seems to be bleak.

The production from Inland fishery sector seems more promising due to intensification of culture practices all over the world. Even though the capture from inland water bodies is reducing owing to the alteration of ecosystem, water abstractions etc. and the inland fishery sector enjoys great support of increase in production through aquaculture practices.

## 2.2 PRINCIPLE MARINE FISHING AREAS WITH CAPTURE FISHERIES PRODUCTION – 2008

Although during the period of 2006-2008 global marine production was practically stable and the individual fishing areas showed distinct catch trend (Table 2.2).

**Table 2.2: Capture Fish Production by World's Principle Fishing Areas**

| *Sl.No.* | *Fishing Areas* | *Fish Production by Capture (mmt)* | *FAO International Fishing Zone* |
|---|---|---|---|
| 1. | North West Pacific | 20.1 | 61 |
| 2. | South East Pacific | 11.8 | 87 |
| 3. | Western Central Pacific | 11.1 | 71 |
| 4. | North East Atlantic | 8.6 | 27 |
| 5. | Eastern Indian Ocean | 6.6 | 57 |
| 6. | Western Indian Ocean | 4.1 | 51 |
| 7. | Eastern Central Atlantic | 3.4 | 34 |
| 8. | North East Pacific | 2.6 | 67 |
| 9. | South West Atlantic | 2.4 | 41 |
| 10. | North West Atlantic | 2.0 | 21 |

*Source*: SOFIA, 2012.

The North West Pacific still leads by far the ranking of marine fishing areas with the production of about 20.1 mmt despite the revision of Chinas fishery statistics reducing reported catches by about 2.0 mmt. The South East Pacific having the production of about 11.8 mmt and Western Central Pacific with the production of about 11.1 ranks second and third respectively in region wise oceanic fish production by capture. This signified ever lasting dominance of Pacific Ocean in marine fish production by capture.

Among the six very large and highly diverse fishing areas into which the Pacific Ocean is divided, recent changes in catch trends have occurred in North East, South West and Eastern Central Pacific. In the North East Pacific, a catch decline has been noted since 2006 for both Canada and the United States of America, the only two countries catching significant quantities in this area. In the South West Pacific the catch has decreased since 2006, in this area New Zealand's share of total catch was 73 per cent in the period but it is noteworthy that 23 per cent of the catch was caught by European and North Asian vessels which travel to this distant area to target pelagic and demersal fish and cephalopods. Starting in the 1980's total catch in the Eastern Central Pacific has been fluctuating around an average of 1.6 mmt but a positive trend since 2005 has produced an overall 20 per cent catch increase.

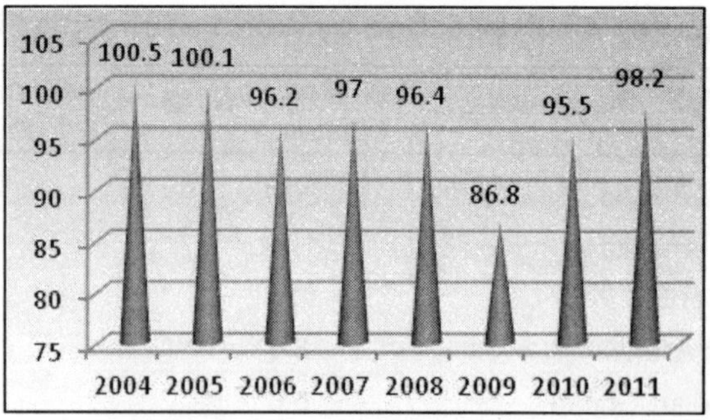


**Figure 2.5: World's Total Inland Production (mmt)**

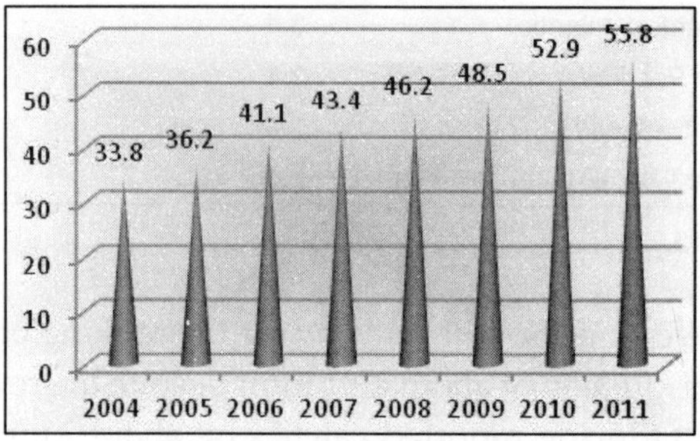


**Figure 2.6: World's Total Inland Production: Culture (mmt)**

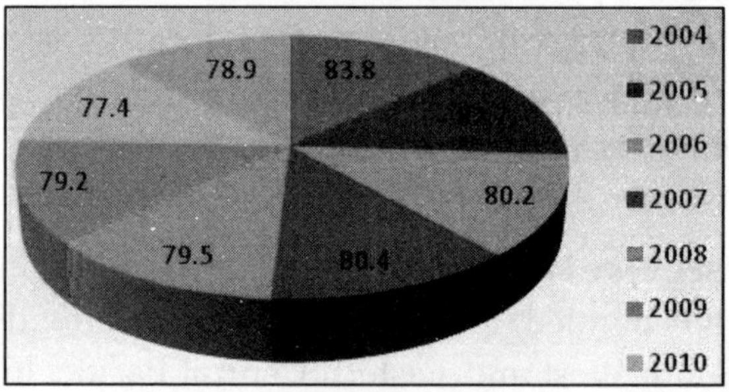


**Figure 2.3: World's Total Marine Production (mmt)**

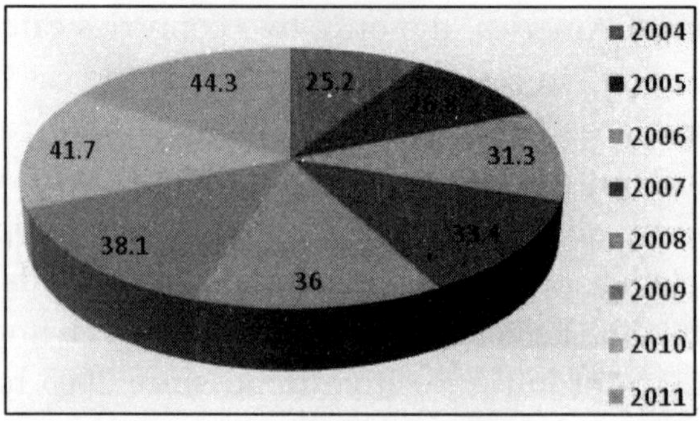


**Figure 2.4: World's Total Marine Production: Capture (mmt)**

The North East Atlantic occupies fourth place with the significant share in production of 8.6 mmt. In the North East and North West and Western Central Atlantic, the capture production reached peaks in 2004, 2001 and 2000 respectively but in the following years catches consistently decreased with the overall reductions of 13, 23 and 30 per cent respectively. Catch trend in the Atlantic areas did not very much in 2oo6 – 2008.

In the Mediterranean and Black Sea, catches decreased by 12 per cent in 2008 in comparison to the high catches of the previous year, a negative result shared by all five major fishing countries.

Fairly handsome share in world fish production by capture is also given by Indian Ocean. The Eastern Indian Ocean and Western Indian Ocean with the production of 6.6 mmt and 4.1 mmt respectively ranked at fifth and sixth places in principle fishing areas by capture in 2008. The growth in total catch in the Indian Ocean has been sustained since 1950 but in earlier years the contribution of Western Indian Ocean was more than Eastern Indian Ocean but in 2007 and 2008 this trend reversed in the Western Indian Ocean where as it kept its pace in the Eastern Indian Ocean. The catch decrease in the Western Indian Ocean is mostly due to a reduction in tuna catches from both local and distant fishing fleets.

## 2.3 TOP TEN FISH PRODUCING COUNTRIES IN THE WORLD

The content of Table 2.3 indicates that in 2007 - 2008 China is the leading producer of fish in the world with the total production of 47.53

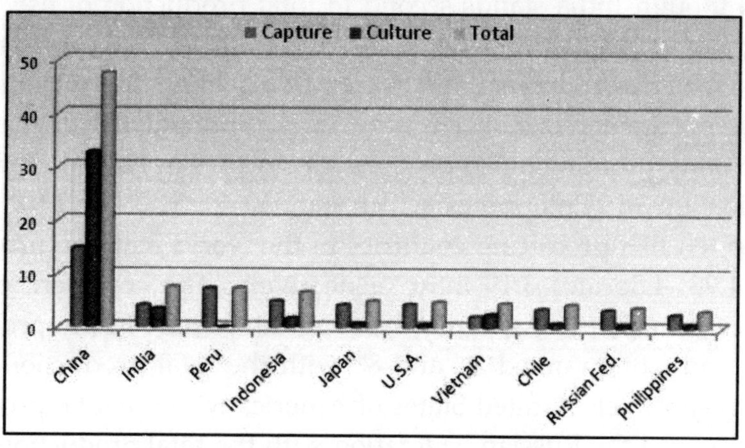


**Figure 2.7: Major Fish Producing Countries in the World with Production (mmt) 2007-2008**

mmt, with the high share from capture and culture fisheries, however the fish production from China was more in 2006-2007 with the total production of 51.529 MMT with the share 17.1 mmt from capture and 34.429 MMT from culture fisheries.

China is the only country in the world where the share from culture is significantly more to capture in the total fish production. In china there exist very strong base for culture especially from Inland fishery sector to the total fish production.

**Table 2.3: Major Fish Producing Countries in the World with Production (mmt)-2007-2008**

| *Rank* | *Counties* | *Capture* | *Culture* | *Total* |
|---|---|---|---|---|
| 1 | China | 14.79 | 32.7 | 47.53 |
| 2 | India | 4.16 | 3.48 | 7.58 |
| 3 | Peru | 7.36 | 0.04 | 7.41 |
| 4 | Indonesia | 4.96 | 1.69 | 6.65 |
| 5 | Japan | 4.25 | 0.73 | 4.98 |
| 6 | U.S.A. | 4.35 | 0.50 | 4.85 |
| 7 | Vietnam | 2.09 | 2.46 | 4.55 |
| 8 | Chile | 3.55 | 0.84 | 4.40 |
| 9 | Russian Federation | 3.38 | 0.50 | 3.88 |
| 10 | Philippines | 2.56 | 0.63 | 3.19 |

*Source*: SOFIA, 2012.

Even though India stands second in total production of fish there is yawning gap in production when compared to china. India stands second in culture fisheries and overall 6$^{th}$ in capture fisheries. The major share to world fish production is realized from Asian continent, beside China and India the other prominent fish producing countries in Asia are Indonesia, Japan, Vietnam and Philippines, which stand at 4$^{th}$, 5$^{th}$, 7$^{th}$ and 10$^{th}$ placing in the top ten fish producing countries in the world with the production of 6.65, 4.98, 4.55 and 3.19 mmt respectively. The continent of Latin America stands next to Asia with the substantial share in fish production by Peru, and Chile ranked 3$^{rd}$ and 8$^{th}$ with the total production of 7.41 and 4.40 respectively. United States of America with the total production of 4.85 mmt and the Russian Federation with the total production of 3.88 mmt stand at 6$^{th}$ and 9$^{th}$ positions respectively. A close look at the table also suggests that as like in China and India, in Vietnam also there is major contribution to the fish production through inland fish culture than the capture fisheries. The pattern of fish production from countries other than China suggests that the production through capture is more than the culture fisheries; the contribution from capture is mainly from the marine fisheries sector.

**Table 2.4: List of Capture Production by Principle Species (2008)**

| *Rank* | *Species* | *Production (in MMT)* |
|---|---|---|
| 1 | Peruvion Anohoveta | 7.43 |
| 2 | Allaskan Pollock (*Theragra chalcogramma*) | 2.65 |
| 3 | Atlantic herring (*Clupea herrings)* | 2.48 |
| 4 | Skip jack tuna (*Katsuwanus pelamis*) | 2.42 |
| 5 | Chub mackerel | 1.88 |
| 6 | Large head hairtal | 1.37 |
| 7 | Blue Whiting | 1.29 |
| 8 | Chilean Jack mackerel (*Trachurus* sp.) | 1.28 |
| 9 | Japanese Anchovy (*Engraulis japonicas*) | 1.27 |
| 10 | Yellowfin Tuna (*Thunnus albacares*) | 1.14 |
| 26* | Indian Oil Sardine | 0.397 |
| 45* | Bombay duck | 0.278 |
| 46* | Indian mackerel | 0.276 |

*Source*: SOFIA, 2012.

The year-wise world principle fish species by capture 2005-2008 suggests that inspite of the major crash sustained in eighties and nineties, at 2008 level Peruvian anchoveta (*Engraulis ringens*) stands first in order among the world's top ten fisheries by capture with the production of 7.43 MMT. Peruvian anchoveta contribute about 5.2 per cent to the total world fish production. Even though comparably to Peruvian anchoveta with very less production of 2.65 MMT the Allaskan Pollock (*Theragra chalcogramma*) occupy the second position contributing about 1.86 per cent to the total world fish capture production. Atlantic herring (*Clupea herrings*) acquired third place in the order in 2008 improving from fourth rank at 2005 - 2006 level, with the harvest of about 2.48 MMT. Skipjack tuna relegated to fourth place in 2008 from third in the production at 2005-2006 level, with the production of 2.42 MMT. Chub mackerel improved its ranking to stand at 5th place from 6th during 2005-2006 with the production of 1.88 MMT. The sixth, seventh, eighth, ninth and tenth ranks are held by Large head hairtail (was 7th at 2005-2006 level), Blue whiting (was 5th in 2005-2006), Chilean jack mackerel (was 8th at 2005-2006), Japanese Anchovy (8th in 2005 – 06) and yellowfin tuna, with the production 1.30 MMT, 1.29 MMT, 1.28 MMT, 1.27 MMT and 1.14 MMT respectively. At 2008 level the major gain in the ranking was attained by Atlantic herring, Chub mackerel and large head hairtail, while the rankings of Skipjack tuna, Blue whiting, Chilean jack mackerel and Japanese anchovy declined.

The production of top three Indian species of Indian Oil Sardine, Bombay duck and Indian Mackerel, internationally ranked at 26, 45, 46th with the production of 0.397, 0.278 and 0.276 MMT respectively.

## 2.4 SOME FACTS OF WORLD FISHERIES SCENARIO

At 2008 level with the total production of 142.29 MMT, the total marine capture production contributed to 55 per cent and the total aquaculture production accounted for 45 per cent. This production provides an apparent per capita supply of 16.7kg (live weight equivalent). The total capture production of 88-95MMT is continuing without any drastic change since the last decade. The Trend of capture fisheries in marine fishing areas show no major fluctuations with the production varying between 79 to 85 MMT. Asia contributed maximum of about 44.7 per cent of the global capture production. China was the leading producer of fish contributing about 16.48 per cent of global production, 18.6 per cent global marine capture production and 36.87 per cent of the total fish production resulting from Asia.

# Chapter 3

# WORLD OCEANS AND MAJOR SEAS

The geographical status of each ocean which is being recognized today suggests that all of them are interlinked. The functional continuity of the world ocean is maintained by continuous medium of navigable water and by oceanic currents which transport huge amount of oceanic water to the distant places within the oceanic regime. The oceanic currents in the form of horizontal and vertical deep water current continuously divert the oceanic waters from one climatic region to another.

The world oceans are known for their uniformity in the parameters. Therefore the major oceanographic parameters like temperature and salinity do not fluctuate drastically at any given place at particular time for years together. This uniformity in the oceanographic parameters and the tendency to indicate constancy makes the oceanic water as an important resource to support the life system.

However in spite of individual constancies in each ocean, there are differences in the world oceans in their climatic system, currents, oceanographic parameters, their topography and their biomass varying from one ocean to other. These dissimilarities and their different geographical status of each of world oceans compel us to identify them separately as The Pacific Ocean, The Atlantic Ocean, The Indian Ocean, The Southern Ocean and The Arctic Ocean.

## 3.1 THE PACIFIC OCEAN

- ☆ **Area:** 179.679 million $km^2$
- ☆ **Volumes:** 723.691 million $km^3$
- ☆ **Average depth:** 4026 meters
- ☆ **Deepest recorded depth:** 11034 meters (Marianas trench)

The Spanish explorer Vasco Nunez de Balboa discovered and named this ocean a Pacific, means peaceful (Bhatt 1978). Pacific Ocean is the largest, coldest and deepest of all oceans. Most of the pacific flow is very deep where the average depth exceeds 5000 m. The Pacific Ocean forms a circular shaped basin, along its periphery there are numerous, volcanoes, vaults, and trenches that form the *Ring of Fire*. Incidentally the deepest trench of Marianas is also the deepest recorded depth of World Ocean discovered under Vityaz expedition from the famous descant in 1960 by Trieste near the Challenger Deep. The Pacific Ocean occupies about one – third of total surface area of the earth. Thus it is also larger than all of the earth's combined land area. The ocean is broader in southern end and tapering towards north. The spread of Pacific Ocean is truly enormous. The Pacific Ocean has Berring Sea and the water from Antarctica marks the north and south boundaries occupying North America and Latin America in the east of pacific. In the west the Pacific Ocean lies between the continents of Asia and Australia. The maximum north to south distance of pacific is about 15000 kms, while its horizontal spread from east to west is about the 16000 kms. The circular area around the pacific has been called the Ring of Fire because of the many earthquakes that occurs there and many volcanic eruptions associated with these earthquakes. The major topographic feature of the pacific is the East Pacific Rise or Ridge, a continuation of oceanic ridge system observed also in the Atlantic Ocean (Mid Atlantic ridge). It extends northeasterly as broad rise from off New Zealand to the Gulf of California. This ridge is different from the Mid-Atlantic Ridge in having its extension across the ocean basin rather than running down the centre of the basin and also its topography is relatively smooth and shows no indication of a distinct rift valley. The crest of this rises to about 2000 to 3000 meters (about 6562 to 9843 feet) above the general level of the floor of the pacific. The East Pacific Rise is also seismically active and higher than normal heat flow. Another major feature of pacific is the presence of numerous small and big islands, combindely their number comes to about 2,500, most of which are located south of equator.

The marginal seas that drain off in Pacific Ocean are Sea of Okhotsk, The South China Sea, The East China Sea, Yellow Sea, The Japan Sea, The Sea of East Indian Archipelago, The Philippine Sea, The Sulu Sea, The Coral Sea, Sea of Celebes and The Tasman Sea etc.

The Pacific Ocean from the point of view of fish production is very significant. Even though due to its wider area the Pacific Ocean is moderately exploited than Atlantic Ocean but still it gives highest fish catch in the world, sharing about 71 per cent of the world fish catch. The Pacific has most dominant pelagic continental fishery in its Western flank than in the Eastern flank where demersal fishery is most prominent. It may be because of the fact that the continental margins of Eastern flank of pacific are very narrow while the continental shelf area of its western flank is relatively broader. Pacific abode its shore to most of the top fish producing countries in the world like China, Japan, United states, Canada, Mexico, Peru, Chile, Russia, Indonesia, Thailand, Philippines, Korea, Australia and New Zealand; many of these find places in top ten fish producing countries in the world. The most prominent fishery resource from pacific include, Peruvian Anchovita, Allaskan Pollock, Salmon, Halibut, Perch, Snappers and Grenadiers along with the supporting catch of Cod, Haddock, Whiting, Dab, Flounders, Shrimps, Oyesters, Clams and marine mammals like Pinnipids etc.

## 3.2 ATLANTIC OCEAN

- ☆ **Area:** 106.465 million km$^2$
- ☆ **Volumes:** 354.679 million km$^3$
- ☆ **Average depth:** 3352 meters
- ☆ **Deepest recorded depth:** 9000 meters (Puerto Rico Trench)

The Atlantic Ocean is the second largest ocean and probably the most explored one, for the purpose of trade, commerce and scientific expeditions.

It occupies one fifth of earth surface. The most obvious feature of the Atlantic is its shape. The ocean is narrower in equatorial belt but expands at both the extremities towards north and south of equator. It spreads between North-West European countries in the east to North American continent in west in the northern hemisphere and between West African continent in east to Latin America continent in west in the southern hemisphere. It is an elongated sinuous basin that extends more than 11000 km (over 6800 miles) in the north to south direction. The bathymetry studies of the ocean showed that it is dominated by Mid-Atlantic Ridge, a continuous ridge extending to entire length from the central part of the ocean, from Iceland in north to Cape of Good Hope extreme south of Africa, thereby dividing the ocean equally to its eastern and western flanks.

The symmetrical shape of the ocean on either side of this ridge and the outline of the adjacent continent, which would fit together like piece of jigsaw, puzzle if they were pushed together, have long fascinated scientist and support hypotheses of continental drift and more recently the discoveries pertaining to seafloor spreading. The profile of mid Atlantic ridge shows that it is part of a continuous major oceanic feature that can be traced in the form of Mid- oceanic ridge, spreading to more than 55000 kms, over 34000 miles through the Atlantic, Indian, Arctic and Pacific oceans. In the Atlantic Ocean the ridge is especially wide and occupied the middle third of the ocean; it is highly fractured consisting of numerous mountains and hills. The average height of the of Mid- Atlantic Ridge is 1160 meter and average width of 1000 kms. The most rugged topography occurs in the central part of the ridge, where a large central rift or crack occurring over the most of the ridge system.

The central rift can be as much as 2000 meters (6562 feet) below the peak of the adjacent surrounding peak. These peaks or mountains often rise to within a thousand or so meters of the sea level. In some instances the mountains protrude through the surface of the ocean, forming island such as Azores and Iceland. Studies of the central rift in the Mid- Atlantic Ridge using submersibles, showed considerable evidence of volcanic activities and faulting in the region. This type of activity is expected in the central rift region because of its sea floor spreading origin. Further evidence of sea floor spreading is seismic activity in the ridge area and the observation that most of the earthquakes are centered under the central rift area. Measurements of the rate of heat being discharged from the Mid-Atlantic Ridge show relatively high values on the crest of the ridge that may likewise be explained by the intrusion of volcanic rocks along the crest of ridge.

The marginal seas which drain off in the Atlantic are Mediterranean sea at south of Spain in the strait of Gibraltar, North sea lying between North East of United Kingdom and South of Scandinavian countries of Norway and Sweden, Baltic sea lying east of Sweden and west of Finland, Caribbean sea lying to the east of Gulf of Mexico in the region of Caribbean Island, Hudson Bay to the North–East of Canada also drain off in the Atlantic ocean. Some important rivers which drain off in Atlantic Ocean are Saint Lawrence, Mississippi in North America; Amazon, Uruguay and Palmer from Latin America and Zaire, Congo from West African and some north west flowing European rivers.

The Atlantic Ocean has some of the world's richest fishing resources especially in the water covering shelves. The major species of fish caught are Cod, Haddock, Hake, Herring, Menhaden, Mackerel, Eel, Lobsters and Whales have also been taken in great quantities. The most productive areas include The Grad Bank of Newfoundland, The shelf areas of Nona Scotia, Georges Bank of Cape Cod, The Bahama bank, the water around Iceland, the Irish Sea, The Dogger bank of North Sea and Falkland Banks. The fish production from Atlantic was highest from the world ocean in fifties but in later years it was overtaken by Pacific Ocean which now ranks to be first in order, however the fish catch per unit area is still highest from the Atlantic Ocean.

## 3.3 INDIAN OCEAN

- ☆ **Area:** 74.917 million km$^2$
- ☆ **Volumes:** 291.945 million km$^3$
- ☆ **Average depth:** 3897 meters
- ☆ **Deepest recorded depth:** 9434 meters (Java trench)

Indian Ocean is the third largest ocean and forms the share of about 20 per cent of the water on the earth surface. Historically the Indian Ocean was a well known commercial route that linked the trade centre of India, Baghdad (Iraq) and Alexandria. One contributing factor to the proliferation of sea trade among these places was the monsoon current that helped the sailors to undertake long voyages in the Indian Ocean.

The Indian Ocean is roughly triangular in shape and is enclosed by the Indian subcontinent in north, and extended to the east coast of Africa and the northern and western coast of Australia.

The continental margins of Indian Ocean are similar to those of other ocean. The major feature of the Indian Ocean is its mid oceanic ridge that appears to split at the centre of the ocean forming an inverted y (λ). One of the split limbs goes to the south of Australia into the pacific where it intersects with east pacific rise. The other split limb continues south of Africa and joins with the Mid- Atlantic ridge. The third elongated part of inverted 'λ' turns and enters into the Gulf of Aden and the Red Sea and called as Carlsberg ridge. In the Bay of Bengal there lies another oceanic ridge which coincides with 90° longitude and aptly named as 90° ridge. Like as Mid-Atlantic ridge, the Mid-Indian ridge is also rugged, seismically active and may have a continuous median rift. The Mid-Indian ridge is also situated essentially in central part of the ocean basin.

The oceans continental shelves are narrow averaging 200 km (about 125 miles) in width. An exception to this in found off Australia's Western coast where the self exceeds 1000 km (600 miles). The average depth of the ocean is about 3897 meter (12800 feet).

The peripheries of Indian Ocean include the Arabian Sea and the Bay of Bengal. India's three largest rivers in term of volume of water and the length, The Ganga, The Brahmaputra, The Indus discharge world largest amount of terrestrial sediment into in the Indian Ocean. The other eastward flowing rivers from Indian Peninsula that drain off into The Bay of Bengal are Cauvery, Krishna, Godavari and Mahanadi also contribute substantially to the adding of the sediment into the Indian Ocean. It is because of draining off sediments, the Indian Ocean is characterized by having extensive area of abyssal plain.

The extreme southern latitudes of Indian Ocean are dominated by terrigenous, sediment and Glacial out wash. The adjoining seas and water bodies to Indian Ocean include the peripheral seas like Red Sea, Persian Gulf, Gulf of Aden, Gulf of Oman, Arabian Sea, Bay of Bengal, Laccadive Sea, Mozambique Channel, Andaman Sea and Great Australian Blight.

The prominent Island includes the largest Madagascar, Sri Lanka, Maldives, Laccadive, Andaman and Nicobar, Mauritius, Seychelles etc.

In Indian Ocean fishing is confined to subsistence level. The fish and fishery resource from Indian Ocean are great and growing importance to the bordering countries for domestic consumption and export. Fishery resource point of view the Indian Ocean include some exclusive pelagic fishy resource consisting Oil Sardine, Lesser-Sardine, Anchovies, Carangid, Indian Mackerel, Seer fishes, Tunas, Bill fishes, Barracudas, Mullets, Unicorn Cod, Bombay Duck, Ribbon Fishes etc. The demersal fishery resource is supported by Lizard Fishes, Perches, Groupers, Snappers, Threadfin Bream, Elasmobranchs, Catfishes, Silver Bellies, White Fish, Rays, Eels, Sciaenids, Pomfrets, Halibut, Flounder etc. the ocean is also remarkably rich in the resource of shell fishes like Shrimps, Crabs, Lobster, Squid, Cuttle fishes, Oysters, Clam etc.

The most outstanding feature of Indian Ocean is its very rich resource of shrimps and oceanic tunas. Fishing fleets from Russia, Japan, South Korea and Taiwan also exploit the Indian Ocean mainly for shrimps and tuna.

## 3.4 SOUTHERN OCEAN

This ocean dominates the entire Southern hemisphere with no land mass interruption. The ocean extends to 40° S touching the southern tips of Africa and Australia. The Southern Ocean bordering Antarctica was intensively studied during the international Geog-physical year in 1957. Over the years U.S.A., Russia, Australia, New Zealand, Japan and India have established their base camps for conducting research on Antarctica and Southern Ocean.

The Southern ocean is fourth largest ocean covering 20327000 km$^2$. It is typically deep between 4000 and 5000 meters with only limited area of shallow water. The Antarctica continental shelf is narrow and unusually deep. Its edge lying at up to 800 meters compared to a global mean of 133 meters.

The Antarctic circumpolar current (West wind drift) move perpetually eastward chasing and joining itself and with spread of 21000 kms is the worlds longest ocean current transporting 130 million km$^3$/second of water which is hundred times more to the flow of all worlds river. The Antarctic

Icepack fluctuates from an average of 2.6 million km$^2$ in March up to about 18.6 million km$^2$ in September. The adjoining Seas surrounding to the southern ocean include Amundsen Sea, Bellingshausen Sea, Ross Sea, Co-operative Sea, Cosmonaut Sea, and Weddle Sea etc.

Illegal and unregulated fishery has been responsible for sustainability of the stock from Southern ocean. Long line fishing operation has substantially reduced the stock of tooth fish and whales. Incidences of great mortality of sea birds including the penguins from Antarctica have been recently reported. Intentionally the water and Land around Antarctica is a great attraction for the exploitation of Squids, Whales, Seals, Krill, various pelagic fin fishes, Penguins etc. The international whaling commission has prohibited the whaling form South of 40° (from around Antarctica). However Japan does not recognize this and try to carry out an annual whale-hunt which they say it for scientific research.

## 3.5 ARCTIC OCEAN

The Arctic Ocean is smallest and shallowest of world's five major oceans. It exists literally on the top of the world, almost completely surrounded by Eurasia and North America. Its basin is almost circular shape and is bordered by Russia, Scandinavia, Greenland, Canada and Alaska. The North Pole is located about 500 miles from its centre. Floating masses of ice, the polar ice pack cover most of the ocean during most of the year. The Topography of the ocean is dominated by presence of three submarine ridges. The ridges are The Alpha, The Lomonosove and a third may be the possible extension of the Mid – Atlantic Ridge, these divide the ocean into a series of basins or deeps.

The Continental shelves of the Arctic Ocean is widest in the world, it occupies between one third and one half of the Arctic floor. It is also deep which extends to a depth of 300 m or about 984 feet (of the coast of Greenland). It is because of the widest extent of continental shelf; the Arctic Ocean is also shallowest among the word ocean. The basins or deep of the Arctic Ocean are separated from the pacific and Atlantic ocean by shallow submarine ridge.

The Arctic Ocean is separated from the pacific by the Berring Strait. The ocean connects with the Atlantic through small seas on either side of the Greenland: The Green land and The Norwegian seas and the Denmark

Strait provide the connection to the East Baffin Bay, Davis Strait and the Labrador Sea to the west.

The temperature and salinity of the ocean vary seasonally as ice cover melts and freezes. Its salinity is the lowest on average of the five major oceans due to low evaporation, heavy freshwater inflow from rivers, streams, limited connection and out flow to surrounding oceanic waters with higher salinities. In summer the ice pack in the ocean shrinks to about 50 per cent.

The ocean has a fragile ecosystem, which is slow to change and slow to recover from disruptions or damage. The Arctic Ocean has relatively little plant life except for phytoplankton. Phytoplankton is crucial part of the ocean and there are massive amount of them in Arctic. Nutrients from Rivers and currents of the Atlantic and Pacific Ocean provide food for the Arctic Phytoplankton. The region also has flourished population of marine mammals, Pinnipids such as Seals, Sea lions, Walruses and also good number of Cetaceans which include major verities of Whales. The number of this exclusive population of marine mammals is rapidly reducing to the endangered level due to their massive killing in the area. The conservative measures for the protection of these marine mammals are therefore most pertinent in the Arctic Ocean.

## 3.6 MEDITERRANEAN SEA

The Roman originally named the Mediterranean Sea as Mareinternum, which in Latin means Island Sea. They later gave it its present name Mediterranean to imply "Middle of the earth". The Mediterranean Sea stretches between the Strait of Gibraltar to link it with Atlantic Ocean in the Western flank and in the South Eastern flank it connects with 163 kms (101 miles) long manmade Suez Canal. The Suez Canal further eastward connects the Mediterranean with Red Sea, Persian Gulf and Arabian Sea. The Mediterranean Sea through the strait of Gibraltar which is only about 14 kms (8.7 miles) wide, further east is almost completely enclosed by land in North by Europe and in South by North Africa. In the east it spreads between Asia in North and North Africa in South. Thus the Mediterranean Sea bounded by the coasts of South of Europe North of Africa and Asia. The Mediterranean Sea has an average depth of 1,500 meters (about 4,900 feet) and the deepest recorded point is of 5,267 metre

(17,250 feet) in the Capypso deep of the Ionian Sea. The Mediterranean Sea has several arms, The Adriatic, The Ionian and Tyrrhenian Sea surrounds much of Italy. The Aegean Sea which is another arm is located east of Greece. The arm of Black Sea extends northward between Turkey and Russia. The Mediterranean Sea is connected to Black Sea with a narrow Bosporus link. The Mediterranean sea ashore many South European, North African and few Asian countries like Turkey, Greece, France, Italy, Bosnia and Herzegovina, Spain, Slovenia, Albania, Morocco, Algeria, Cyprus, Egypt, Israel, Lebanon, Libya, Malta, Monaco, Montenegro, Northern Cyprus, State of Palestine, Syria, Tunisia etc. There are large and small islands throughout the Mediterranean which include Cyprus, Crete, Euboea, Rhodes, Lesbos, Chios, Kefallinia, Corfu, Limnos, Samos, Naxos and Andros in the Eastern Mediterranean; Sardinia, Corsica, Sicily, Cress, Kirk, Barc, Hvar, Pog, Korcula and Malta in the Central Mediterranean; and Ibiza, Majorca and Minorca in the Western Mediterranean.

Due to its unique geographical location, the Mediterranean Sea is World's major maritime route and shipping channel linking Europe, Africa, Asia and many south East Asian countries in the world, with almost a third of all international Cargo traffic passing through it. It was an important route for merchants and travelers since ancient times that allowed trade and cultural exchange between emergent people of the region.

Mediterranean sea being nearly landlocked in nature it has affected the oceanographic conditions, for instance tides are very limited as a result of its enclosed geographical status and due to lack of sufficient assess to oceanic water bodies like Atlantic in west and Indian Ocean in east. The Mediterranean is characterized and immediately recognized by its deep blue colour. Evaporation greatly exceeds the precipitation and river run off in the Mediterranean, a fact that is central to the water circulation within the basin. Evaporation is especially high in the eastern half, causing water level to decrease and salinity to increase eastward. This pressure gradient pushes relatively cool, low salinity water from the Atlantic across the basin, it warms and becomes saltier as it travel east, then sinks in the region of Levant, eastern flank of Mediterranean, nearer to Israel, Syria and also nearing to Suez Canal then circulates westward, to spill over the strait of Gibraltar.

## Ecosystem Impact and Biodiversity

### Eastern Mediterranean

The opening of the Suez Canal in 1869 created the first salt water passage between the Mediterranean and The Red Sea. The Red Sea is higher than the Eastern Mediterranean, so the canal serves as a tidal strait that pours Red Sea water into the Mediterranean. The bitter lakes which are hyper saline natural lakes that form part of the canal, earlier blocked the migration were naturally removed plant and animals from Red Sea have begun to colonize them in the Eastern Mediterranean. The Red Sea is generally saltier and more nutrient poor than the Atlantic, so the Red Sea species have advantage over Atlantic species in the salty and nutrient poor Eastern Mediterranean. Accordingly Red Sea species invade the Mediterranean biota and not vice versa it means the Atlantic species are not able to invade the Mediterranean. This phenomenon of one sided invasion or migration of Red species into the Eastern Mediterranean is known as *'Lessepsian Migration'*. The construction of Aswan high dam across the Nile River in 1960 reduced the inflow of freshwater and nutrient rich silt from the Nile into the Eastern Mediterranean making conditions there even more like the Red Sea and worsening the impact of the invasive species. The sardine production from this region is also adversely affected due to the construction of Aswan Dam and blocking of the Nile River.

*Invasive species* have become a major component of the Mediterranean ecosystem and have serious impacts on Mediterranean ecology, endangering many local and endemic Mediterranean species. A first look at some groups of exotic species show that more than 70 per cent of the non-indigenous decapods and about 63 per cent of exotic fishes occurring in the Mediterranean are of Indo-Pacific region that introduced into the Mediterranean through the Suez Canal. This makes the canal as the first pathway of arrival of "Alien species" into the Mediterranean. The impacts of Lessepian species (migrated from Suez Canal) have proven to be considerable mainly in the Levantine basin of the Mediterranean, which they are replacing native species and becoming a familiar sight. The invasive species from Eastern Mediterranean include Sharks, Rays and other Elasmobranchs, some oceanic species of Tuna, Ribbon fishes, Mackerels, decapods crustaceans, Mollusc etc.

**Western Mediterranean**

Just reversing the trend of Eastern Mediterranean where the biodiversity resembles to that of Red Sea and Indo Pacific region due to invasion of species, in the Western flank towards the link of Gibraltar, the biota resembles to that of North Atlantic. North Atlantic is considerably colder and more nutrient-rich than the Mediterranean and the marine life of the Mediterranean had to adapt to its different conditions. The Alboran Sea is a transition zone between the two seas, containing a mix of Mediterranean and Atlantic species. The Alboran Sea has the largest population of the Bottle nose Dolphins in the Western Mediterranean and is home to the last population of 'Harbor Porpoises' in the Mediterranean. It is also most important feeding ground for 'Loggerhead Sea Turtles' in Europe. The Alboran Sea also hosts important commercial fisheries, including Sardines and Swordfish. The Mediterranean Monk Seals live in Aegean Sea in Greece. In 2003, the World Wildlife Fund (WWF) raised concerns about the widespread drift net fishing endangering populations of Dolphins, Turtles and other marine mammals.

# Chapter 4

# FISHERIES OF WORLD OCEANS

The wide spread of ocean extending from continents to continents not only have supported life but also have guaranteed its dynamic growth over hundreds of millions of years of evolution, thus enabling life to exist today in countless forms, shapes, sizes, ranging from microorganism to whales. The biological wealth of the ocean is overwhelming. A drop of water may contain countless microscopic plants (phytoplankton) on which hundreds of millions of small sized zooplankton, medium sized (Nekton) and large sized animals like whales depend for their growth and existence (Banes 1973).

According to estimate the ocean contain about 40,000 species of molluscs and crustacean and some 25,000 species of fish (Chapman 1973, Cushing 1975).

It is difficult to collectively summarize fisheries of each ocean primarily because of wide spread of each of them and also due to the change in the shoreline habitat of each of them abode much diversified form of marine life. The FAO has therefore identified and classified different fishing zones of the world (Figure 4.1). In the present context the Atlantic and Pacific

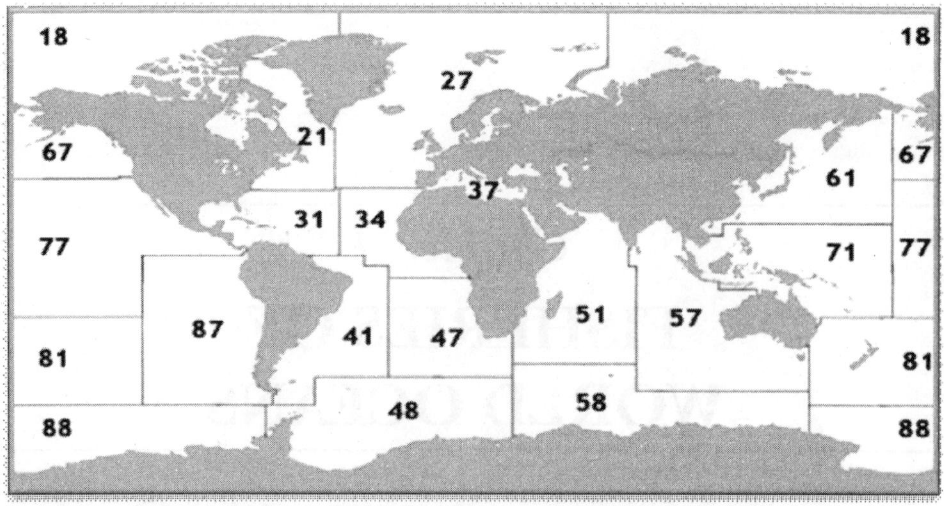


**Plate 4.1: Different Fishing Regions of the World Oceans (FAO)**

**18: Arctic Sea; 21: Atlantic, Northwest; 27: Atlantic, Northeast; 31: Atlantic, Western Central; 34: Atlantic, Eastern Central; 37: Mediterranean and Black Sea; 41: Atlantic, Southwest; 47: Atlantic, Southeast; 48: Atlantic, Antarctic; 51: Indian Ocean, Western; 57: Indian Ocean, Eastern; 58: Indian Ocean, Antarctic and Southern; 61: Pacific, Northwest; 67: Pacific, Northeast; 71: Pacific, Western Central; 77: Pacific, Eastern Central; 81: Pacific, Southwest; 87: Pacific, Southest; 88: Pacific, Antarctic.**

Ocean which have wide spread, have been therefore geographically divided into six zones to have an account of fisheries of each as North East Atlantic, Eastern Central Atlantic, South East Atlantic, North West Atlantic, Western Central Atlantic, and South West Atlantic; North East Pacific, Eastern Central Pacific, South East Pacific, North West pacific, Western Central Pacific and South West Pacific. The fisheries of Mediterian Sea and Indian Ocean are separately taken and due to non significant contribution the polar oceans are not considered here.

## 4.1 FISHERIES OF ATLANTIC OCEAN

### 4.1.1 North East Atlantic

It belongs to the world fishing zone of 27 and is bordered by Scandinavian countries of Norway, Sweden, Finland, Poland, Part of Baltic sea, Iceland, United Kingdom, Denmark, Germany (Part of North sea), France, Portugal and Spain up to the strait of Gibraltar. This region is fourth largest producer of Marine fish with the production of 9.1 M.M.T and sharing about 11 per cent of the total world fish production (FAO 2008).

This region is most prominent in the world for the demersal fishery of Cod and presently sharing about 18 per cent of the total Cod landing in the world, Cod remains depleted in North Sea and in Faeroes Island but the stock of Cod from other regions are healthier and considered fully exploited. Pelagic fishery of Herring was earlier highest in the world from this region, especially the area around North Sea. The Herring fishery sustained the set back in Eighties due to heavy exploitation. However after imposition of ban on fishing of coastal stock of Herring by the responsible countries, there has been the spectacular improvement in the landing and is highest in this part.

The other important demersal stock of significance is of Blue whiting. The catches of Blue whiting have stabilized at about 2.0 million tones/ year since 2003, and the stock is considered fully exploited. Flat fishes comprising Sole, Flounders and Plaice are also produced in large quantities. Due to strict adherence of fishing laws, the fishing mortality of Cod, Flounder and Plaice have been considerably reduced. Tuna catch in the region is represented by two species namely the Blue fin Tuna and Yellow fin Tuna. The stock of Haddock also has shown the spectacular progress with increase biomass since 2000. Earlier this region in eighties was also the highest producer of Haddock in the world. Presently there are also reports of handsome landing of Sand Eel and Capelin stocks. The harvest of Edible Oysters' among the demersal shelf fish resource is common, however fishing for Shrimp seems to have ceased in the region.

The continuous decline in the Cod catches since late 1960 earlier were counterbalanced by increase in the landing of Blue Whiting (that time considered as low valued fish) and also of Sand Eels. The catches of Blue Whiting reached the record levels of 2.0 million tonnes in 2001, declined slightly in 2002. Presently the harvest of the stock of Blue Whiting is therefore highest in the world from this region since the stock of Whiting is currently under heavy fishing; it requires more restrictive management measures. As a whole considering the information available for all stocks the region of North East Atlantic is fully exploited.

### 4.1.2 Eastern Central Atlantic

It belongs to the world fishing zone of 34. It includes the region of Atlantic lying south of Gibraltar, bordered by countries of North West Africa, *viz.*, Morocco, Mauritania, Senegal, Guinea, Cameroon, Ivory Coast, Nigeria, Gabon, Congo, Gambia, Liberia etc.

Among these Morocco, Mauritania, Ivory Coast and Senegal are intensively exploited, Nigeria is moderately exploited and rests are unexploited.

This region is dominated by fisheries of tropical waters especially in southern part of Eastern Central Atlantic represented by Sardines, few Mackerel, Tuna, Shrimps, Lobster and Cephalopods. The most important fisheries from the region are Cephalopods and Hake.

In Mauritania and Morocco the demersal stock are almost exploited and overexploited for the fishery of Cephalopods and Hake, therefore the fishing efforts should be significantly reduced, as the management measures undertaken by Morocco (FAO 1992).

The coastal stock of Sea bream, (pelagic fish) is heavily exploited in Morocco; hence the recovery of the stock is threatened from the region. In Morocco Sardine had recorded historical level of catch and improved its landing. In Mauritania and Senegal Sector the fishery has undergone major development in last 10 years. (CECAF Bulletin 2008). These countries were earlier considered as moderately exploited from the region.

Lobster harvest was slowly recovering from the effect of overfishing in late sixties but now after 2005 again is subjected to intensive fishing with pots and gill nets and need proper management measures. The large stock of Sardine, Mackerel and Horse mackerel of the region are highly valuable but their assessment is difficult. Recent trawl fishery survey in Guinea has indicated excellent coastal fishery resource inside 20 m depth which may offer handsome potential for the development of artisanal fishery.

### 4.1.3 South East Atlantic

The region belongs to world fishing zone of 47. This includes the Atlantic water from Southern region of Africa running towards the cape and in the region it confluence with the water from Indian Ocean. The countries bordering this part of Atlantic are Angola, Namibia and West of South Africa up to Cape of Good Hope.

In Angola pelagic fishery is moderately exploited, while demersal fishery is intensively exploited. In Namibia and west of South Africa pelagic fishery is moderately exploited but the demersal fishery is underexploited.

The prominent country from fisheries point of view from this region is Angola. Earlier Angola and Namibia were one of the few free fishing grounds in the world where no fishing regulations were operational, because both these countries earned their independence late. The major portions of their harvest about 43 per cent were formerly taken by distant foreign fishing fleets. Angola which became independent in 1975, in later years started emphasizing on the development of small scale coastal fishing. Now the fishery from Angola has come to the stage of reckoning with highest potential from the region. Namibia which earned its independence in 1990, requested all foreign fishing fleets to stop or seize their fishing activities from its EEZ area.

The important fishery from this region includes Hake (*Merluccius species*), South African Pilchard, African Anchovy, Cape Horse mackerel (*Trachyurs*), Cunene Horse mackerel, Round herring, White head, Sardinelis, Kings klip, Sole, Rock lobster, Squid, Perlemon Abalone etc.

There have been several changes in the status of the stock in South East Atlantic since from late nineties till last full assessment made in 2004. The important Hake resource remains fully exploited to overexploited, however there are some signs of recovery in deepwater Hake stock (*Merluccius paradoxes*) off South African coast. The status of coastal fishery remains fully exploited or depleted. A significant change concerns to the South African Pilchard stock, which was a very high biomass and estimated to be fully exploited in 2004, but is now under considerable stress and declined due to its overexploitation from the entire region. In contrast the southern African Anchovy has improved. The stock of white heads and round herring are underexploited to moderately exploited stages. The condition of horse Mackerel has deteriorated particularly off Namibia, where it is currently overexploited. The stock of Perlemon Abalone has been depleted, driven heavily by illegal fishing and is currently overfished.

### 4.1.4 North West Atlantic

The region belongs to international fishing zone of 21. It is bordered between West of Greenland to East of Canada, the New Found land Island and region of Nova Scotia up to North East of North United States of America. Also include adjoining water of Gulf of St. Lawrence, Davis Strait and Baffin Bay up to South of 78.10° N latitude.

The region is fairly rich in fish production with the potential of about 8 MMT and most of the time ranks 5th most fish productive region of the world.

The most important fishery resource which is richest in the world from this part is Atlantic Haddock. The landing of Atlantic Halibut (*Hippoglossus hippoglossus*) and Black Halibut (*Reinharditus hippoglossoides)* account for the highest landing of Halibut in the world from this region. The stock of Atlantic Herring is second highest in the world from this region.

The other prominent fishery include American Plaice *(Hypoglossoidses platessoides*), Red fish (*Sebastes marinus*), Witch Flounder *(Glyptocephalus cynoglossus)*, Yellow tail Flounder (*Pleuronectus ferruginous/Limanda ferrginea)*, Caplin *(Mallotus villous*), Pink or Deepwater Shrimp or Northern prawn (*Pandalus borealis*), Grenadiers *(Macrouridae)* and Shark *(Rajidae)*.

According to latest report of NAFO (2010), the commodity wise level of exploitation of above indicate that the stock of American plaice, Red fish, Witch Flounder and Atlantic Halibut are depleted; Black Halibut are exploited; Yellow tail Flounder, Pink or Deepwater Shrimp are fully exploited; Capelin are underexploited and the status of Grenadier is unknown. Therefore the scenario of these fisheries suggests that the future of fisheries from North West Atlantic is under great stress. There has also been great decline in the large costal and Oceanic shark population from the region, which include Hammer head, White and Thresher Shark are each estimated to have declined over 75 per cent in last fifteen years. In future strategies for the closed area models, highest priority areas for shark conservation and the need to consider effort for reallocation and site selection for marine reserves are needed to be implemented for the benefit of these threatened verities of Shark. The ground fishing around EEZ is banned except Grand Banks as a management measure to protect ground and demersal fisheries from this region.

The region was also earlier the site for heavy exploitation of Whales. Allen (1988) suggested that the average weight of whale caught in 1932 was 68 tonnes, which decreased to just 20 tonnes by 1978. The International Whaling Commission which was established in 1948 has now allocated quota for catch of different species of whales by different countries. The fishing of whale is banned from time to time according to the imposition by International Whaling Commission under Wildlife Protection Act. United States of America and Canada ceased all whaling activities for almost 20 years after agreeing to the recommendation of United Nations Conference held in Stockholm in 1972 which unanimously recommended the 10 year halt to worldwide whaling.

**Fate of Northern Cod**

The region is known in the world fisheries for the exploitation of North Atlantic Cod (*Gadus morhua*) The North Atlantic Cod was once richest stock in the world from this region but sustained set back due to heavy exploitation throughout its range, resulting in the crash of this fishery from Canada and United States during the period earlier than 1990s. The fishery of Northern Cod in Newfoundland can be traced back to 16th century. Based on reports on an average about 3 lakh tonnes of Cod landed annually until 1960s, when advance in technology enabled factory trawlers to take larger catches. By 1968, landings for the fish peaked at 8 lakh tonnes before the gradual decline set in. According to reports fishing of Cod by the fishing fleets from other countries was at peak at that time. Even the distant factory trawlers from the European countries like Spain, Norway and United Kingdom were operating for Cod in the waters around Grand Banks (New Found land). The sustained fishing load was also there from host countries of Canada and United States of America. In fact entire commercial fishing activity from Canada was dependant on Cod landing. The major fishing area of this part of Atlantic was rugged off due to the operations of trawl gear as big as the football ground. In the event of heavy fishing from Canada and United States of America, similarly inability of these countries to stop poaching into the area by foreign factory ships, the resultant effect was catastrophic. Taken as the clue of the changed age structure and size of captured specimen it was evident that during late 1960 the North Atlantic Cod stock was under great stress. These alarms about the fate of fisheries were also ignored and the fishing continued in unrestrained manner. The entire world was aghast to learn that how come the economically sound and responsible countries like Canada and United States of America were unable to avert the situation of disaster. Later after the virtual elimination in later years, the efforts were made by the responsible countries to revive the stock by imposing ban on fishing of Cod by putting restrictions on the operations of foreign fishing, disallowing the operations of factory ships to operate in the area. The effort of enforcement of conservation act was imposed by NAFO (North Atlantic Fisheries Organization). The conservations measures were followed for almost two decades. Later when the reopening of the limited cod fishery was allowed nearly 2,700 tonnes of Cod was landed in 2006. In 2007 it was estimated that the offshore Cod stock was at 1 per cent of what they were in 1977 (NAFO 2010).

### 4.1.5 Western Central Atlantic

This region of Atlantic belongs to the international fishing zone area of 31. The oceanic spread includes Central and South East United States of America up to the region of Florida, East of Atlantic of Panama, Mexico, Guatemala, Honduras, Nicaragua and Cuba, Some parts of Columbia, Venezuela, Carrabian Island, up to North of Brazil.

The maritime area of the Atlantic in this part has very narrow area of Continental shelf, indicating that the ocean acquires maximum depth in this region.

The North Western Central Atlantic has the dominance of temperate water fisheries of Menhaden which is richest in the world from this area. The notification from Atlantic State Marine Fisheries Commission (ASMFC) indicated the area is currently under heavy exploitation of Menhaden because of the high demand of fish as important source of food and similarly being used as bait for the capture of Striped Bass, Lobsters, Blue Crabs and its multifarious use as product of nutritional diet for dogs. The stock of Menhaden has been declining and is currently at lowest point in history. It is suggested that in order to recover the stock in future the harvest through fishing must be minimized to 45 per cent level.

From late seventies to late nineties the success of Menhaden fishery with high production was attributed to the implementation of best management practices. The other important fishery which finds its distribution from south of New York to Brazil including the Gulf of Mexico and the Carrabian Island is of Balao Half beak (*Hemiramphus balao*). The fishery of Lesser Bobtail Squid (*Semirossia penera*) is also undertaken at substantially high level. The fishery of Hagfish also finds prominent place in the region. The region occasionally also harvests some marine mammals especially the whales and Dolphins.

The South Western Central Atlantic is prominent for tropical fisheries, especially Mexico is intensively exploited for the fishery of Shrimps. Lobsters and tropical fin fishes like Mackerel, Tuna, Bill Fish, Snappers, Grouper, Croakers etc. According to Western Central Atlantic Fishery Commission (WECAFC) the Southern half of Western Central Atlantic brings high catch of Bivalves, Gastropods, Cephalopods Stomatopods, Shrimps, and Crabs etc. The region is also popular for the fishery of Sharks, Batoid fishery, Chimera, Bony fishes, Sea turtle etc.

In Carrabian basin the coastal reef fishery is adversely affected by the effect of draining of three large river systems namely Mississippi, Ornica and Amazon, which create El-Nino effect and cause hurricane, and heavy storms which damages and decreases coastal reef fishery but bring exclusive stock of estuarine fishes.

### 4.1.6 South West Atlantic Ocean

This zone belongs to the fishing area of 41, which exclusively include the extension of Atlantic in South or Latin America, bordering Brazil, Uruguay and Argentina coasts.

The most popular country, from fisheries point of view of which is extensively exploited is Brazil. The area of Southern Brazil is unique in characteristics due to high primary productivity influenced due to seasonal confluence of water masses from Falkland (Malvinas) and Brazil current resulting into high fish production from continental shelf. The most important fishery of the region is the demersal stock of Halibut. The wide continental shelf and rich benthic community favored the development of industrial trawling activities in the Brazilian region mostly for Shrimps and demersal stock of Halibut. Other important fisheries in the region are coastal gill net fishery and artisanal multi-gear fisheries that operate in coastal lagoon, estuaries and shallow coastal waters of Southern Brazil.

The area of Southern Brazil was productive and historically has supported important artisanal and industrial fishing activities. However during the last decade fisheries in the region have been going through a crisis, with a drastic decrease in the landing and the overexploitation of important stocks including Sharks, Croakers, Catfish, Mullets and Pink Shrimp. Other issues of concern in the region include fisheries by-catch and discard affecting commercial fish stocks of endangered fauna as for example Turtles and Dolphins. Different initiatives have been promoted to create an enabling environment for addressing the causes of unsustainability. At the local level, the Artisanal Fisheries Organization has established a co-management arrangement with the objective to promote actions and policies to recover the productive capacity of the Pates lagoon and to foster the sustainability of artisanal fisheries. Scientists and Government officials have been proposing the adoption of alternate management approaches to industrial demersal fisheries including the definition of management areas with established limits of fishing activity to avoid over exploitation of demersal stock especially of Halibut and Shrimps.

The coastal Shark species *Carcharias taurus* in South West Atlantic ranges in high numbers from Rio de Janeiro Brazil (21° S) to San Matias Gulf Argentina (41° 30′S). Although the fish is not directly fished, it does have value as a by-catch benthic trawling, gill net fisheries harvest throughout the range for commercial, artisanal and recreational purposes. Therefore this Shark species has sustained great damage not only in Brazil but also in Uruguay and Argentina.

The main fisheries of Argentina are Argentina Hake (*Merluccius hubbsi*), Southern Blue Whiting, Grenadiers, Sardinella, Mackerel, Squid, Tuna and Shrimps.

Among the countries bordering Brazil is extensively and overexploited, Argentina is moderately exploited and Uruguay is underexploited.

## 4.2 FISHERIES OF PACIFIC OCEAN

### 4.2.1 North East Pacific

This area of Pacific belongs to international fishing Zone area of 67. The area is extensive, starting from the water of Berring Strait in North down to West Coast of North America including Aleutian Archipelago, the Gulf of Alaska, near shore water of the Alexander Archipelago, the strait of Juan de Fuca and Puget Sound, extending to West Coast of Canada and United States of America, extending further South to California (San Francisco Bay), the Southern Californian Blight, Golfo de California or Sea of Cortez and Baja California.

Geographically the wide extensive maritime area of this zone is responsible for the diversified ecological conditions of polar, temperate, subtropical and tropical for its water, hence from fisheries point of view the biodiversity of this region is also extensive.

The region is fairly productive and support fishery of certain commercial commodity of fishes. The most prominent fishery of this region is of Alaska Pollock or Walleye Pollock (*Theragra chalcogramma)* which is highest in the world from this region. The region also brings high catch of Halibut.

The region indicates moderate exploitation of Jack Mackerel (*Trachurus pictaramus*). It also identifies good account of production of Pacific Salmon, Flatfishes, Ling Cod, Hake, Pacific Herring, Japanese Anchovey, Crab, Shrimp and Oysters (FAO Cooperative Document Repositry, 2010).

Landing from United States of America continue to dominate the statistics constituting nearly 90 per cent of the total landings by all countries. In the nineties the average landings from the region was 3.26 MMT with highest in 1998 of 3.8 MMT. The lowest catch of 2.97 MMT was however obtained earlier in 1991. The reduced landings in late eighties after 1985 was primarily due to the reduction in catches of North Pacific Hake, Alaskan Pollock, lower than the normal catches of flat fishes and due to enforcement of closure of ground fishing to reduce Halibut as by-catch waste.

The presence and exploitation of high numbers of marine mammals especially Pinnipids for Seal, Sea lion and Walruses are also specialty of this region mainly from the region of Pribilloff Island of Berring Sea. The Government of Canada has imposed ban on illegal fishing of marine mammals and Salmon in order to preserve, protect and prevent these diminishing stocks.

Alaskan Pollock, which is highest from this part of the world, account for slightly less than half of the total catch in the region. The burst of recruitment in the late seventies and early eighties built the Alaskan Pollock fishery to high level. The catch of Alaskan Pollock had maintained the rising trend also up to the early Nineties but a decreasing trend appeared underway later because of overexploitation of the fish after 1992 – 1993.

The countries bordering the North Pacific Ocean including North East Pacific have struck a deal to stop expansion or implement immediate cap on expansion of Bottom Trawl fishing in international waters stretching from Hawaii to Alaska to protect this 41.7 million km$^2$ area from destructive fishing techniques. The bottom trawling has damaged the marine life especially to Cold Water Corals, Deep Sea Sponges and ecosystem on the ocean floor by boat that use weighted net and other fishing gears that drag along the sea bed.

The stock of Cape Shark (*Squalus acanthias*) has been declined from Southern North East Pacific Waters but its stock appears to be stable in Alaska.

The International Pacific Halibut Commission (IPHC) established in 1924 to take care of Halibut stock, conduct research, assess stock potential and formulation of the harvesting guidelines to protect the stock of Halibut. The Halibut was the first fish to be internationally conserved through implementation of IPHC in 1924 and is still functional today. The stock of Halibut is stable, its landing decreased during late eighties but due to ban on fishing and reduction in fishing effort it has restored its good potential. The Salmon is protected and conserved in the region by the implementation of Pacific Salmon Treaty (PST) which was established in 1985 between Canada, United States of America and Japan is still functional and takes care of salmon stock.

The conditions of El-Nino, which sometimes initiate in the tropical pacific from California, brings heavy transport of water northwards in the region of Alaska and Bering Sea. This water current (Californian Current) also bring with its fish species like Californian Sardine (*Sardinops calurulea*) thereby increasing the stock of this pelagic fish which also happens to be the good food for the forage of Whales. It creates good condition for the spawners and their good growth.

### 4.2.2 Eastern Central Pacific

This area belongs to International Fishing Zone of 77. The countries bordering this part lie South of United States of America from the region of California which include the Pacific side of Mexico, Guatemala, El-Salvador, Honduras, Nicaragua, Costa Rica, Panama and part of Columbia.

The region is prominent for the production of tropical fishes like Californian Sardine, Chub Mackerel, Pilchard, Mackerel, Pacific Herring, Northern Pacific Anchoveta, Skipjack Tuna and Tuna like fishes, Sharks, Rays, Shrimps and Squids.

The fishery in this region is strongly influenced by Californian Current System and El–Nino effect. The total landing declined due to the impact of El-Nino from 1.5 million tonnes in 1991 to 1.2 million tonnes in 1993.

The major marine fisheries in this region are at the level of Maximum Sustainable Yield, Overexploited and close to Overexploitation. Therefore most of the countries form the region have oriented their fisheries towards compliance of management objectives in order to prevent collapse of their fisheries and associated negative biological, economical impacts. The real shift in the emphasis from promotion of fishing to management began in 1998 with the establishment of Code of Conduct for Responsible Fishing (CCRF) in 1995.

Since all Central American Countries except Honduras capture Tuna in their jurisdictional and international waters of the Eastern Pacific Ocean, they follow the provisions and recommendations of the Inter American Tropical Tuna Commission (IATTC).

The most noticeable change has been in the landing of North Pacific Anchovy (*Engualis mordax*) whose catches dropped sharply from 1,11,000 tonnes in 1989 to only 6000 tonnes in 1990; 21,000 tonnes in 1991; 10,000 tonnes in 1992 and just 4,700 tonnes in 1993. This was sharp decline compared to the catches well above 1,00,000 tonnes per year obtained in the early 1970, the reason for such rapid loss into the harvest of North Pacific Anchovita can be attributed to the overexploitation.

The Californian Sardine which vanished from the region of California in 1960's got rejuvenated in the region of Mexico in 1980's. In Mexico the fisheries is dominated by pelagic species in terms of volume and by Shrimp in terms of value. The region of Mexico is intensively exploited for the fishery of Shrimps.

### 4.2.3 South East Pacific

It belongs to the International Fishing Zone of 87. The region includes the pacific water, south of Columbia bordering the countries of Peru and Chile. The region is very fertile from fisheries point of view as both these countries certainly find the place among the top ten fish producing countries of the world. Due to its high productivity it is second largest producer of marine fish accounting for the total production of about 12 MMT. The region is also world's leading producer and supplier of Fish meal and Fish oil.

The region is dominated by single largest fishery in the world for Peruvian Anchoveta (*Engraulis ringens*). The efficient current system (Humboldt Current) and availability of rich nutrients through effective upwelling account for this high production of Peruvian Anchoveta.

The Anchoveta fishery had to face severe setback from its peak in sixties. It is often being referred as one of the all time crash of any fishery due to anthropogenic reasons. It is now a well known fact that the mismanagement of stock assessment, fishing and overexploitation were the prominent cause of debacle of Peruvian Anchoveta from mid sixties to seventies.

However the lessons learnt from the debacle of fishery and what followed later was proved to be blessings in disguise; to be referred as one of the classical example of recovery of mainstay fishery in the world. The immaculate management which were set in late seventies and followed in later practices with routine assessment of stock, fixing MSY levels, formulating efficient eco-friendly fishing devices, have uplifted the prospect of Peruvian Anchoveta fisheries from late eighties onward have set a very high standard of production levels.

From the time of late nineties there has been no change in the status of Anchoveta as one of the leading fish species captured in the world. The stock has been sustained and recovered from the severe El Nino event in 1997–1998 to be on the highest production scale from 2004 onwards up to 2006.

The other fisheries of repute from the region include Chilean Jack Mackerel which is richest in the world from this part. The production of South American Pilchard is also remarkably high. Jack Mackerel and

Pilchard remain in a decadal cycle of natural cycle of natural low abundance producing a fraction of the record catches observed between the mid 1980s and mid 1990s. The stock of South Pacific Hake remains underway to heavy fishing pressure with no signs of recovery. The Sword fish is also commercially heavily exploited in the region.

The other supporting fishery of significance beside Sword fish include Tuna, especially the Albacore and Skip Jack Tuna and Sardine. The high production of Anchovy, Jack Mackerel, Pilchard, Sword Fish, Tuna and Sardine has made South-East pacific to be the second highest in the world for pelagic fisheries.

Among other the Hagfishes and Cephalopods are also produced at handsome level. It was when the Peruvian Anchoveta fishery was at peril in the region, the production of Cephalopods substantially contributed to high production from the region.

### Fate of Fishery of Peruvian Anchovita

The small clupeid known as Peruvian Anchovita (*Engraulis ringens*) is a filter feeder occurring in large in large shoals, in the upwelling water mass of Humboldt Current of the West Coast of South America in Pacific, where it feeds on abundant plankton. This small fish occurred in a large number in this nutrient rich cold water before the advent of human fishing. The other major predators were various species of marine birds (Sea gulls) collectively called as Guano birds which existed in millions along these shores and produced huge, quantities of droppings or guano which were harvested for fertilizers.

The Anchovita population depends on abundant or large plankton population which in turn depends on nutrient rich upwelling water. In certain years the upwelling is blocked in this area by an influx of warn surface water known as the El Nino, when this occurs plankton disappears, the population of Anchovita drops and thus the number of birds also reduces. Hence, other than the overfishing there is natural setback for Anchovita fishery through El Nino effect.

The direct human exploitation of Anchovita began in 1950 and the fishery increased at a tremendous rate until late 1960's. The catch was 10 MMT or more than 1/6$^{th}$ of the entire world's fish catch. This huge catch was accompanied by decline in next subsequent years. The fishery dropped in number in 1965 as a result of occurrence of the El Nino effect but this temporarily setback was made up in the following years.

Fishery experts of world had estimated a maximum sustainable yield for Anchovita of 9.5 MMT. This was exceeded in 1967 when over 10 million MMT were landed but the size of the fish was decreasing and it was now apparent to experts that the fishery was in great trouble and that only few fishes were left to provide the breeding stock. As could have been forecasted the crash came in 1972, added by another El Nino and the landing dropped to 4.7 MMT. This was followed by an even worse condition in the year 1973 when only 2.3 MMT were landed. Subsequently this fishery has not recovered till late 70's, even in 1977 just 2.5 MMT were landed. However there was a moderate increase in the landing of the Anchovita after 1980 to 1985 and the catch tremendously increased to 15.3 MMT in 1989 and followed by 14 MMT in 1990. This restoration of Anchovita production was possible through very hard efforts carried out to conserve the stock with strict adherence to introduction of new fishing policies, enforcement of stringent licensing system for almost 15 years or so. The management practices were introduced right after the crash came in 1971-73 and the efforts were followed till late 80's and early 90's to conserve this valuable fish stock.

The most appreciated fishery management practices have resulted into excellent recovery of Anchovita stock which had faced total elimination earlier due to overfishing activities and has set a model example of remarkable recovery of fish stock to the world. The significant crash and decline in catch has been observed from this region yet again due to El Nino effect which hit this region in 1999, therefore this fishery was again on the threshold of threat. However there have been excellent landing of Anchovita from 2004 onwards till 2010.

### 4.2.4 North West Pacific

This part of Pacific Ocean belongs to 61 major fishing zone of the world. It covers an area spreading from western portion of Bering Sea in north to the Russian Coast of Okhotsk, extending to Kuril Island, Hokkaido to Sea of Japan between Korea and Japan, Pacific portion of Honshu island of Japan, Yellow sea up to Ryu Kyu Island, East China Sea etc.

The North West Pacific Ocean is the largest producer of marine fish in the world. The fishery potential of this oceanic region which was around 15 MMT in late seventies and early eighties, tremendously improved later with the record landing of 26.7 MMT in 1988. The production in nineties averaged around 25 MMT, when the region was responsible for sharing of 31 per cent world's marine fish catch. However the global decline in marine fish production from 2001 onwards till recent times also reflected in this region with the average production reducing between 20 – 22 MMT. The marine fish production from the region in 2008- 2009 was 21.6 MMT, contributing about 26 per cent of marine fish catch in the world. Most of the leading fish producing countries in the world ashore to this region of Pacific like Russia, Japan, China, Korea etc. The pelagic as well as demersal fisheries are intensively exploited from this part of Pacific Ocean. The region is largest producer for Salmon for the commercial fisheries of Coho and Chinook salmon. The stock of Salmon depleted in Japan during mid seventies but restored to normal level later due to enforcement of fishing under Pacific Salmon treaty with the introduction of licensing system, restricting the number of Salmon fishing vessels and strict adherence to mesh size regulation. The region is also highest producer in the world for Japanese Anchovey (*E. japonicus*) and Japanese Pilchard. Substantial harvest of stocks of Pacific Cod and Chinese Herring makes the region to be the second largest producer for these fisheries in the world after North East Atlantic. The pelagic stocks of Spanish mackerel,Horse Mackerel, Hickory Shad, Eels, Hair Tail, Yellow Tail and Mullets also forms the supporting fisheries for the region.

The stock of Pollock is sometimes highest in the world from this regi on, overtaking and challenging in this process the production resulting from North East Pacific. The harvest of Pollock was dominant in late eighties and nineties with the production of 5 million tonnes from 1986-1988, 4.8 million tonnes in 1989 and 4.2 million tonnes in 1990. The fisheries from the region is also supported by reasonably handsome production of Halibut, large and small yellow Croakers, Porgy, Silver Pomfret, Flounders etc. The region also is highest and leading producer for Molluscan fisheries, with heavy production of Edible Oysters, Mussels, Cephalopods, Clams and Pearl Oyster.

The Molluscan fishery from the region is dominant owing to high production from the natural resource as well as substantial production obtained from aquaculture practices. The high production of cephalopods is supported from Squids and Cuttle fishes. The region also brings the good production from Octopus and Abalone. It is also comparatively leading producer of Shrimps in the world overtaking the production from India. The high production of Penaeid Shrimps (*Penaeus japonicus)* is due to its production from natural capture as well as due to high prospect of aquaculture production. The production of Pendalid Shrimp is also high. The production of Crabs is also high from the region. The shore of Pacific is also responsible for high production from invertebrates with the handsome production from Sea Cucumber and Jelly fishes.

The fisheries activities in Southern part, covering sea of Japan, The Yellow Sea, Bohai Bay, East China Sea, Waters form Hokkaido are very rich and predominant having diverse fisheries with essentially multispecies production without a clear cut dominance of particular stocks.

### 4.2.5 Western Central Pacific

This region of Pacific falls in the International Fishing Zone of 71. The Central Western Pacific is shores by large area of Continental Shelf which to the West Stretches from Vietnam and Thailand down to Malaysia and Western Indonesian Islands (Sumatra, Borneo) before ending at Java Sea to the east shelf areas between eastern Indonesia, Papua, New Guinea and Australia. In north it stretches from Philippines to numerous Pacific Islands, like Marianas Islands, Marshal Islands, Caroline Islands, and Gilbert Islands etc. In south it extends in Australia at the boundary between the State of Queensland and New South Wales. Thus the area is extensive and covers tropical and subtropical regions of West Central Pacific. The region with the production of over 11.2 MMT is the third largest producer and sharing about 14 per cent of the marine fish catch in the world.

The freshwater runoff from monsoon and the big rivers from Thailand, Vietnam, Cambodia and Indonesia have immensely influenced pelagic fishery in its continental waters with substantially high production of Sardinellas, Anchovies, Carangids, Mackerels, Mullets, Scads, and Barracudas etc. The local pelagic stock of Mackerel and Round Scads are heavily exploited in the Strait of Malacca, Java, Malaysia and Indonesia while Sardines are intensively exploited in Bali Strait.

The region is most prominent for the capture of large Tuna especially from the Oceanic Islands of Pacific. The capture of Tunas and Tuna like species makes up about 24 per cent of the total fish for this fishing area. The production of demersal also contributed handsomely by Catfish (Herridae), Slip Mouth (Leognathidae), Snappers, Breams, Pony fishes, Croakers, Sharks. This region is intensively exploited and therefore is the third largest producer of shrimp (Penaeid group) in the world. In Indonesia the trawl fishing for capture of shrimp was banned since 1980 but the trammel fishing for shrimp was allowed to harvest coastal shrimp stock. The area of Northern Australia is rich producer of Banana shrimp (*Penaeus merguiensis*). The catch of squid has also shown tremendous increase. The fishing activities of the region are so much intense that the shelf area between Indonesia and Australia forms one of the extensive trawling grounds in the world.

The development of fishery in this region has began in 1960, later on with the improvisation and high production through capture it is one of the richest fishing ground in the world.

The landing of 7.3 MMT was obtained in 1990, it increased to 8.3 MMT in 1993 and in spite of the realization of globally decreasing trend of the marine fish production the region was accountable for increase in the landing up to 11.2 MMT. FAO (Sophia 2012), the production from the region has further gone up to 12 MMT in 2011. The leading fish producers of the region are still Indonesia, Philippines, Thailand and Malaysia which contribute about 65 per cent of fish landing from the region. The bulk of the landing in Indonesia and the Philippines is coming from small scale fisheries sector, where as in Thailand the Fisheries sector is relying more on a commercial scale. The region also promises high production of shrimp through coastal aquaculture. As from fisheries point of view also Vietnam and Cambodia are moderately exploited while Papua New Guinea is unexploited.

The greatest fishery potential for expansion of fishing activities appears to be around Indonesia. The tremendous rise in production form this region of Pacific is attributed primarily to the extension of mechanized fishing on to the new grounds.

The constantly high intensification of fishing from the region have already started giving its adverse impact on future of fisheries with most species assessed are either fully exploited or moderately to fully exploited. The status of species is highly uncertain. This region is highly diverse, its fisheries are mostly multispecies and detailed data for reliable assessments are usually not available for most of the stocks. Analysis of survey for some countries in the region like Malaysia, Philippines, Thailand and Vietnam has shown considerable effect of exploitation and overfishing of coastal stocks.

Few countries in this region have formulated fisheries management plans and integration but have not yet been successful to reduce the fishing pressure which may threaten these countries immediately in future through overfishing of important fish stock. Therefore these countries in order to compensate the reduction in the catch from continental shelf have entered bilateral agreement with foreign countries to explore neighboring offshore waters.

The countries like Indonesia have provided access to foreign fleets to operate 12 nautical miles off its Coasts and Archipelago primarily in South China Sea and Pacific side to fish for them.

### 4.2.6 South West Pacific

This area belongs to international fishing zone of 81. All marine waters of South West Pacific extending from 150° E meridians are occupied by this region. It include eastern coast of Australia comprising of South of Queens land, New South Wales, Victoria, Cape Howe, Tasman Sea extending up to the pacific coast of New Zealand. Many other oceanic Islands like Marcus, Society, Santa Cruz, Fiji, New Herbides, Royalty, New Caledonia, Ellice and Salmon Islands also comes under this zone. The total surface area of this zone is 27.7 million km$^2$ with only 0.4 million km$^2$ of shelf area.

This region is characterized by deep waters with many seamounts about which mesopelagic fish resource like Orange roughy (*Hoplostechus atlanticus*) is abundant and heavily exploited. Beside orange roughy the other most important and prominent fish resource from the region is Silver Hake or Blue Grenadier (*Macruronus novaezelandiae*) commonly called as Hoki especially harvested along the New Zealand coast.

The types of habitat that are exploited in this area are most varied and also support most varied types of fisheries from the coastal continental to deep water seamount fishery. As neighbors across Tasman Sea, Australia and New Zealand have had strong cooperative relationship in managing the fisheries resources in the high seas areas adjacent to the fishing zone. The south Tasman is an undersea ridge extending from Tasmania into Southern Ocean straddling both the Australian Fishing Zone and the high seas. The fishery developed in 1997 and was mainly fished by Australian and New Zealand vessels. In early 1998 Australia and New Zealand signed the Memorandum of Understanding (MOU) mainly on the management of the fishery resource of Orange roughy. The agreement which routinely got developed was still practiced in further years between 1999 and 2008. New Zealand and to a lesser extent Australia have been pioneer in developing profitable alliance and continuing deep water trawl fisheries beyond 600 meters. The captured fishery resource from the region includes mainly the four taxonomic groups which account for 78.4 per cent of the catches comprising of Gadoids (40.4 per cent), miscellaneous demersal fishes (19.2 per cent), miscellaneous pelagic fishes (8.2 per cent) and Squids, Cuttle fishes and octopus (9.6 per cent).

The fisheries resource comprise of coastal species of the Australian states of New South Wales, Northern Victoria and offshore Tasmania and of New Zealand; the pelagic resources of the South Western Pacific and Meso Pelagic species. Based on this varied fishery resource, the other prominent fisheries include pelagic resource of Pilchard (*Sardinops neopilchardus*), Blue grenadier and Golden snapper along the coast of New Zealand; Coastal and pelagic resources of Mullets, Southern Blue Whiting (*Micromesistius australis*) along the Australian coast. The demersal resources like Shrimps, Dredged oysters, the Tarakhi, Red rock lobster, Cupped Oyster are also substantially harvested from both the regions. The other pelagic resource which also forms good account of fisheries are Gem fish, Reef fish, Ocean Perch like Butterfly fish etc.

The South West Pacific has regularly been producing the smallest catches of all FAO statistical regions since 1950. Nominal catches from South West Pacific increased from less than 50,000 tonnes in 1950 to 9,17,000 tonnes in 1992 and then gradually increased to 17,40,000 tonnes. However due to efficient strategies and of rational fishery management by the cooperation between Australia and New Zealand and increased fishing effort from coastal pelagic offshore and deep sea by both the countries there has been increase into the average production of 10,00,000 tonnes between the years of 2003 to 2008. New Zealand and to a lesser extent Australia have been pioneers in developing the profitable and continuity of deep water (7600 m) trawl fisheries. The mesopelagic resource of Orange roughy (*Hoplostechus atlanticus*) and Hoki (*Macruronus novaezelandiae*) are also intensively exported from this region.

## 4.3 FISHERIES OF MEDITERRANEAN and BLACK SEA

This area belongs to FAO Fisheries statistical region of 37. The total landings from the area increased steadily reaching 1.95 million tonnes in 1982 and remained around this level until 1988 when the landing increased to 1.97 million tonnes. There was subsequent decline in production to 1.28 million tonnes in 1991. This decline can be attributed to the collapse of the Black Sea Anchovy and Sprat stocks. The other noticeable decline such as that of the Shads and Sturgeon since mid 1980s has been caused by degradation in Black sea estuarine environment. The fish landings from the region remained on an average around 1.753 million tonnes between years of 2000-2005 and increased thereafter to the landings between 1.95 million to 2.00 million tonnes up to 2008. It has been observed that the decline in the landings in nineties was primarily due to reduction in the landing from Black Sea while it continued to increase from the Mediterranean Sea.

The Mediterranean Sea is one of the few marine areas of the world oceans showing a steady increase over the time series for all major resource categories. This increase in landings is in apparent contract with a long and active tradition of fishing, large and seasonally increasing coastal populations and long standing high demand and prices for locally caught fish. The strong demand for seafood and the long history of fishing have resulted in heavy fishing intensities over most shelf areas. The high fishing intensity together with generally narrow coastal shelves and vulnerability of the resources, would have led one to expect declining catches over most shelf areas, yet this had not occurred in Mediterranean. Mediterranean Sea has successfully sustained the increasing fishing intensity or pressure out of excelled demand of seafood and has not shown yet the signs of overexploitation in its waters rather have shown steady sustained increase in the fish production.

The fish stock of Mediterranean Sea include the groups of coastal pelagic, oceanic pelagic, demersal, crustaceans and molluscs. The prominent coastal pelagic fishery includes Atlantic Mackerel (*Scomber scombrus*), Atlantic Horse Mackerel (*Trachurus trachurus*), European Anchovy (*Engraulis encrasicholus*), European pilchard/sardine (*Sardina pilchardus*) and Striped Mullet (*Mullus barbatus*). The major stock of oceanic pelagic resource include Northern Bluefin Tuna (*Thunnus thynnus*) and Sword fish (*Xiphias gladius*) and verities of Sharks like Scalloped Hammerhead Shark, White Shark, Tope Shark, Basking Shark, Dogfish, Short fin Shark, Thresher Shark, Blue Shark, Black tip Shark, Porbeagle Shark, Sand Tiger Shark etc. The demersal stock includes European Hakes (*Merluccius merluccius*), Blue Whiting (*Micromosistius poutassu*) and Common Sole (*solea vulgarisi*). The major stock of crustacean and molluscs include Norway lobster (*Nephrops narvegicus*), Red Shrimp (*Aristeus antennatus*) and common Cuttle fish (*Sepia afficianalis*).

The prominent fish resource of Black Sea includes Black Sea Shad (*Alosa kessleri*) Black Sea Anchovy (*Engraulis encrasicolus*), Black Sea Sprat (*Sprattus sprattus*), Black Sea Horse Mackerel (*Trachurus mediterraneus*), Black Sea Whiting (*Merlangius merlangus*), Black Sea Turbot (*Psetta maeotica*), Black Sea Mackerel (*Scomber scombrus*), Bonito (*Sarda sarda*), Bluefish (*Pomatomus saltator*), Golden Mullet (*Lisa aurata*), Grey Mullet (*Mugil cephalus*), Leaping gray Mullet (*Lisa* saliens), Striped Mullet (*Mullus barbatus*), Spiny Dogfish (*Squalus acanthias*), Sting ray (*Dasyatis pastinaca*), Thornback ray (*Raja clavata*) etc.

# *Chaptr 5*
# INDIAN FISHERIES SCENARIO

## 5.1 AQUATIC RESOURCES OF INDIA

The aquatic resources from India are vast and varied. India has rich marine fishery resource within an extensive coastline of 8129 kms, extending along the coastal peninsular main land itself besides rich areas of surrounding Islands like the Andaman and Nicobar Islands and the Lakshadweep archipelago. The seas that surround the Indian coast are part of the Indian Ocean, the Arabian Sea in the Western flank and the Bay of Bengal along the eastern side. The total continental shelf area of India which is among the few richest fishing grounds of the world and having pristine clear oceanic water is 0.506 million km$^2$. The continental shelf of India is more prominent along the western coast than on east coast. It is widest about 192 kms in west at about 20° N latitude and narrowing towards south until of Kanyakumari (Cape Camorin), where it is only 48 kms wide. The continental shelf area along eastern coast is as much as 160 km in the head of Bay of Bengal but narrowing down to south. Through an act of parliament India adapted in August 1976, the resolution of Exclusive Economic Zone (E.E.Z). Exclusive Economic Zone includes the extension of area of 200 nautical miles from each coast. This declaration of E.E.Z has brought India the total area of 2.02 million km$^2$, under her jurisdiction to exploit, manage and conserve the live and other natural resources. Thus the resources which were earlier dangered to be exploited by other foreign fleets have come exclusively into the domains of Indian national limits for the exploitation. The detail of the spread of aquatic and habitatwise fish biodiversity resource of India is given in Table 5.1 and 5.2 respectively.

**Table 5.1: Details of Aquatic Resource from India**

| Sl.No. | Resources | Area |
|---|---|---|
| 1. | MARINE RESOURCES | |
| | Indian Coastline | 8129 Kms |
| | Continental shelf area | 0.506 m. sq. km. |
| | Exclusive Economic Zone | 2.02 m. sq. kms |
| | Brackish water area | 1.24 million ha. |
| 2. | INLAND RESOURCES | |
| | Area under tanks and ponds | 2.35 million ha. |
| | Area available for fresh water fish culture | 5.4 million ha. |
| | Area of reservoirs | 3.15 million ha. |
| | Beels, Oxbow and Lakes | 1.3 million ha. |
| | Length of rivers and canals | 1,97024 kms. |

**Table 5.2: Habitat-wise Fish Biodiversity from India**

| Sl.No. | Habitat | No. of Species | Percentage |
|---|---|---|---|
| 1. | Marine water | 1360 | 64.21 |
| 2. | Inland water | 758 | 35.79 |
| | (a) Warm water plain | 433 | 20.44 |
| | (b) Brackish water | 171 | 8.07 |
| | (c) Cold water | 154 | 7.27 |
| | **TOTAL NO. OF FISH SPECIES** | **2118** | |

## 5.2 ASSESSMENT OF FISHERIES DEVELOPMENT FROM INDIA

There has been significant progress in terms of fish production from India, from about the modest landing of 0.839 MMT during 1955-56 at

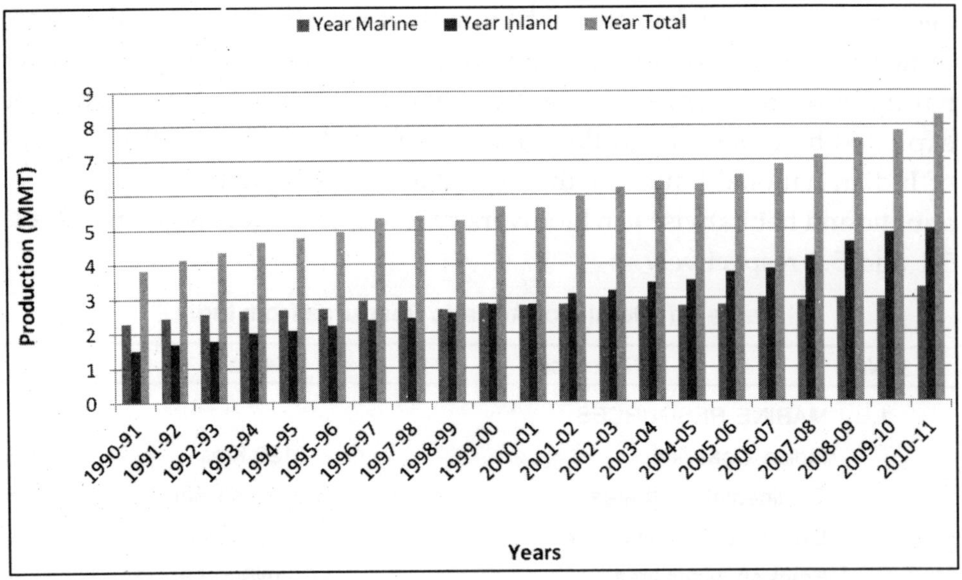


**Figure 5.1: Yearwise Total Fish Production from India (Production in MMT)**

the end of first five year plan to about 6.869 MMT in 2006-2007 at the end of 10th five year plan period. The total fish production from India in 2007-2008 was 7.120 MMT. The fish production in recent past few years has shown exemplary increase in the years after 2007 – 2008, with the production of 7.617 MMT, 7.913 MMT, 8.294 MMT respectively for the years of 2008-09, 2009-10 and 2010-11 (Department of Animal Husbandry and Fisheries, Govt. of India 2011-12). The production trend for the year 2011-12 claimed to be further increase with the production as on 09.01. 2013 stand at the all time high 8.666 MMT. This phenomenal increase of about 7 to 8 times in the landing was possible due to intensive exploration of rich coastal continental marine fishery resource and similarly intensifying efforts in exploiting vast Inland fishery resource through capture and aquaculture efforts, assuring the country the prominent second position in global fish production among top ten fish producing countries in the world. India ranks 6th in the world for marine fish production while globally it stands at prestigious 2nd position for Inland fish production. Fisheries contribute about 1.4 per cent to the total national GDP while it constitute to about 5.4 per cent to the agriculture GDP of India.

The year wise total fish production from India (Table 5.3) suggested that for almost five decades since from the time of independence to 1999-2000, the share from marine fisheries sector was greater than inland fisheries sector. However from the time of turn of the centaury till the recent time, the scenario is reversed with more shares into the total fish production from the inland sector. The aquaculture sector with an annual growth rate of over 6 per cent and likely to continue with immense promise for future in offing is responsible for elevation of inland fish production from the country.

**Table 5.3: Yearwise Total Fish Production from India**

| *Year* | *Fish Production MMT)* | | |
|---|---|---|---|
| | *Marine* | *Inland* | *Total* |
| 1990-91 | 2.300 | 1.536 | 3.836 |
| 1991-92 | 2.447 | 1.710 | 4.157 |
| 1992-93 | 2.576 | 1.789 | 4.365 |
| 1993-94 | 2.649 | 1.995 | 4.644 |
| 1994-95 | 2.692 | 2.097 | 4.789 |
| 1995-96 | 2.707 | 2.242 | 4.949 |
| 1996-97 | 2.969 | 2.381 | 5.348 |
| 1997-98 | 2.950 | 2.438 | 5.388 |
| 1998-99 | 2.696 | 2.602 | 5.298 |
| 1999-00 | 2.852 | 2.823 | 5.675 |
| 2000-01 | 2.811 | 2.845 | 5.656 |
| 2001-02 | 2.830 | 3.126 | 5.956 |
| 2002-03 | 2.990 | 3.210 | 6.200 |
| 2003-04 | 2.941 | 3.458 | 6.399 |
| 2004-05 | 2.779 | 3.526 | 6.305 |
| 2005-06 | 2.816 | 3.756 | 6.572 |
| 2006-07 | 3.024 | 3.845 | 6.869 |
| 2007-08 | 2.920 | 4.207 | 7.127 |
| 2008-09 | 2.978 | 4.639 | 7.617 |
| 2009-10 | 3.103 | 4.810 | 7.913 |
| 2010-11 | 3.313 | 4.981 | 8.294 |

*Source*: Department of Animal Husbandry and Fisheries, Govt. of India – Annual Report 2011-12.

## 5.3 STATUS OF MARINE FISH PRODUCTION

The earlier dominance of marine fisheries sector to the total fish production from India was due to increased emphasis on fishing from coastal continental waters. The need for the production of certain premium pelagic fish resource and demand for commercially important sea food commodity like shrimp intensified the fishing activity from the lesser depth of continental waters. The advancement in fishing technologies with the inception of mechanized fishing during late seventies and the use of bottom trawl gears initially and the purse seine gear improvised the fishing activity. The resultant spurt in fish production from the marine fisheries sector was therefore increased to two and half times from late sixties to 1990-91.

Even though the landing from marine fisheries sector of 2.300 MMT in 1990-91 to 2.967 MMT in 1996-97 registered increasing trend but the annual rate of increase was very marginal (22 per cent). The most catastrophic effect of stalemate into the marine fish landing was conceived from the period of 1997-98 to the end of 2007-2008 with the average production of 2.87 MMT. The marine production in some years during this period was even less than the average landing of 2.87 MMT. The all time high production 3.313 MMT, of marine fish was obtained in the year 2010-11.

The level of average fish production in the past five year period from 2006-07 to 2010-11 is stationed around 3.038 MMT. The total estimated annual production potential is of 3.9 MMT suggest, the fish resource availability of 2.21 MMT at depth below 50 meters and about 1.69 MMT from the depth beyond 50 meters.

The pattern of depth wise potential resource availability in the maritime waters of India suggests the maximum of 58 per cent from the depth of 50 m; thereafter 35 per cent from the depth of 50-200m and minimum 7 per cent from the depth of more than 200m towards the oceanic side. The maximum stress of fishing activity is therefore highest from the water of continental shelf up to 50 meters from the shore; it is also because this water from the point of view of fish bio resource is most diversified and extremely rich. The extended water of continental shelf falling beyond 50m of depth up to 200 meters is moderately exploited, for fishing. The fishing from high seas and beyond in the pelagic water of oceanic province as well as form deep sea is least explored, since the relevant technology of fishing have not yet been properly employed at commercial level in India. It seems to be most pertinent that in order to reduce the fishing from first half of continental shelf India has to diversify and shift its fishing activities in waters beyond 50 meters up to 200m depth and has to venture for fishing in oceanic province and deep sea. At present in India the fish catch is derived maximum up to the depth of 120 meters from the shore.

The reason for the dismal performance of marine fisheries sector in recent past was principally owing to the subjection of intensive fishing effort of the inshore continental waters, where fishes are being fully exploited beyond any hope of increase in production from the region. The prospect of any addition in production from the brackish water and Mari-culture side also looks gloomy, since in spite of having good potential, these activities are still not harnessed at sufficient levels in India. Therefore the marine fisheries sector calls for immediate attention to diversify its fishing in the extended water of continental shelf of increased depth, fishing from pelagic as well as deep sea from the Oceanic province and possibly from the wide spread of E.E.Z waters, to make up the loss with an opportunity of increase in production. The extension of fishing from these virgin waters would not only pave the way for reducing fishing pressure from coastal continental waters but will also bring in the harvest of all those species which are not explored as yet, to lift the fortune of Indian marine fisheries sector.

However the marine fish production recently in past few years has shown immense promise of increased landing. There has been increase into the production of marine fish from the country from 2007-08 onwards with the landing of 2.978 MMT, 2.957 MMT and 3.31 MMT for the years 2008-09, 2009-10 and 2010-11. This also reveals that the efforts to diversify and explore for the marine fish from the extended water of continental shelf, offshore pelagic and the deep sea has already been taken up from the year 2007-08 onwards. It is expected that with such judicious exploration of marine resources by diversifying and extension of fishing offshore, would not only reduce the burden of fishing but would also lead into rejuvenation of the overexploited premium fish resource from the water of continental shelf, and with the addition of new fish stock material from offshore pelagic, mid water and deep sea would certainly result into lifting the status of marine fish production from India.

## 5.4 STATUS OF INLAND FISH PRODUCTION

The Inland fish production from India has always registered the year wise increase in production, with the exception of 1982-83, since from the time of independence. There has been the over four times increase in production from the time of end of first five year plan 1955-56 with the production of just 0.243 MMT, to 4.200 MMT in 2007-08 at the end of 10$^{th}$ five year plan. The enhanced production in the sector has been registered from late nineties from the year 1999-2000 with the production of 2.823 MMT and continued to attain the high production of 4.200 MMT in 2007-2008. There has been tremendous increase into the landing of Inland fish production from India after 2007-08, with the increase of the growth rate of 10.24 per cent from the preceding year the production increased to 4.638 MMT in 2008-09. In the year 2009-10 with the increased growth rate of 5.52 per cent the yield increased to 4.894 MMT. Further in the year 2010-11 with marginal increase in the growth rate of 1.77 per cent the gain in production excelled to all time high 4.981 MMT. The prospect of inland fish production is expected to excel and attain still very high limits in coming future with the proliferation of the activity of aquaculture in the country. Unlike the marine fishery sector, the major share to the total Inland production is gained from the fish culture. Aquaculture still happens to be the largest contributor for the Inland fish production with the share of over 75 per cent. There also seems to be very high prospect of growth of Inland Aquaculture in the country and also the probability of substantially high fish production. Presently India is the second largest producer of Inland fish in the world.

The only few hindrance which realistically felt for Inland fishery sector is principally the abstraction of water from natural resources like rivers, and other wet land areas. If India can rejuvenate the condition of navigability in its river system the share from capture side can also be increased. Secondly present yield of just 0.9 Lakh tones/year from the Indian reservoirs is needed to be amply improved to at least 3.0 lakh tones, considering the high potential for increase in area of reservoirs.

Therefore for India, the loss in marine fish production has been reasonably substantiated with the increase in inland fish production. The popularity and consumable demand of freshwater fish in India is constantly increasing due to its easy availability among masses and also due to the everlasting demand of protein rich nutritious food. The increase in inland fish production has rationally contributed in excelling the per capita fish consumption of country to 9.00kg/annum. However keeping in view of the domestic requirement of fish in the country by 2020, when the estimated production level would swell to over 15 MMT, the inland fish production will have to take the pivotal role.

## 5.5 STATEWISE MARINE FISH PRODUCTION FROM INDIA

The state wise marine fish landing from India suggests that the major fish landing from India is obtained from the West Coast of India (Table 5.4). The state of Gujarat ranks first with the highest share of over 22 per cent (2006-2008) to the total marine fish landing. The coastline of Gujarat is also extensive, improvising the fishing from the extent of Gulf of Kutch to Cambay Coast.

Even though the state of Kerala attains the second place with the share in production of over 20 per cent, its harvest per unit area is still maximum in India. The marine fish diversity of Kerala is very unique and

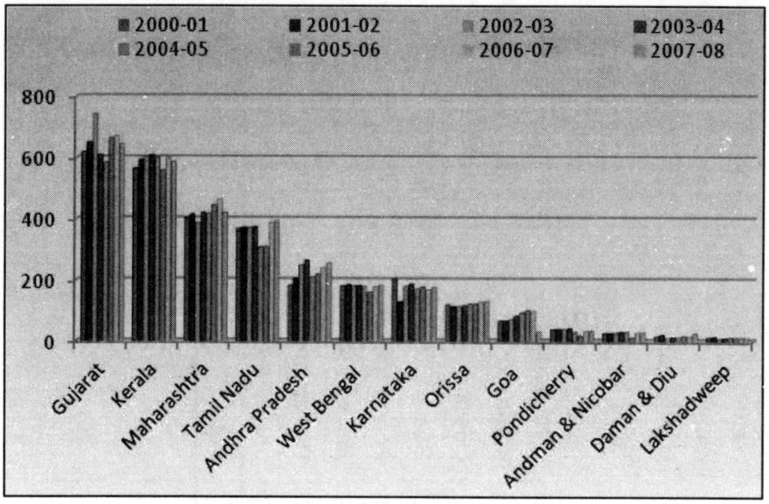


**Figure 5.2: Marine Fish Production by States from India**

**Table 5.4: Marine Fish Production by States from India**

| *Sl.No.* | *State* | *2000 -2001* | *2001-2002* | *2002 -2003* | *2003 -2004* | *2004 -2005* | *2005 -2006* | *2006 -2007* | *2007 -2008* |
|---|---|---|---|---|---|---|---|---|---|
| 1. | Gujarat | 620.47 | 650.83 | 743.64 | 609.14 | 584.78 | 663.88 | 670.51 | 644.53 |
| 2. | Kerala | 566.57 | 593.78 | 603.29 | 608.52 | 601.86 | 558.91 | 598.06 | 586.29 |
| 3. | Maharashtra | 402.84 | 414.27 | 386.86 | 420.01 | 417.77 | 445.34 | 464.09 | 419.82 |
| 4. | Tamil Nadu | 367.86 | 371.00 | 371.50 | 373.00 | 307.69 | 307.99 | 387.25 | 393.27 |
| 5. | Andhra Pradesh | 182.50 | 204.94 | 248.50 | 263.93 | 210.73 | 218.84 | 240.20 | 254.89 |
| 6. | West Bengal | 181.00 | 184.30 | 181.50 | 181.60 | 179.50 | 160.00 | 178.10 | 182.74 |
| 7. | Karnataka | 205.90 | 128.42 | 180.16 | 187.00 | 171.23 | 176.97 | 168.54 | 175.57 |
| 8. | Orissa | 121.09 | 113.89 | 115.01 | 116.88 | 121.93 | 122.21 | 128.14 | 130.77 |
| 9. | Goa | 67.33 | 66.55 | 72.29 | 83.76 | 94.81 | 100.91 | 98.97 | 32.26 |
| 10. | Pondicherry | 38.95 | 39.60 | 40.11 | 42.80 | 31.50 | 19.27 | 33.61 | 33.44 |
| 11. | Andman and Nicobar | 27.62 | 27.02 | 28.23 | 31.06 | 32.60 | 12.05 | 28.60 | 28.60 |
| 12. | Daman and Diu | 16.38 | 21.52 | 11.26 | 13.77 | 12.51 | 17.72 | 16.35 | 26.28 |
| 13. | Lakshadweep | 12.00 | 13.65 | 7.50 | 10.03 | 11.96 | 11.96 | 11.75 | 11.04 |
| | **Total** | **2811** | **2830** | **2990** | **2942** | **2779** | **2816** | **3024** | **2919** |

richly diversified. The state of Maharashtra with the share in production of over 16 per cent substantially contribute to marine fish landing, ranks third in all India marine fish landing. Among the east coast of India the marine states of Tamil Nadu, Andhra Pradesh and West Bengal ranked $4^{th}$, $5^{th}$, and $6^{th}$, in order with share in production of over 13 per cent, 8 per cent and 6 per cent respectively. Good share into marine fish landing of India is also resulted from the states of Karnataka, Orissa and Goa with the contribution of over 5 per cent, 4 per cent and 3 per cent respectively which ranked at $7^{th}$, $8^{th}$ and $9^{th}$ places. Marginal share to marine fish landing is also obtained from the small adjoining Islands of India with the contribution of 1.13 per cent from Pondicherry; 0.95 per cent from Andaman and Nicobar, 0.83 per cent from Daman and Diu and about 0.39 per cent from Lakshadweep, attaining the rank between $10^{th}$ and $13^{th}$ places.

## 5.6 STATUS OF SEA FOOD EXPORT

**Table 5.5: Annual Sea Food Export from India**

| *Year* | *Export Quantity (Tonnes)* | *Export Value (Rs. Crore)* |
|---|---|---|
| 1993 | 239918 | 2252.80 |
| 1994 | 301278 | 3565.52 |
| 1995 | 208143 | 2574.02 |
| 1996 | 353676 | 3980.02 |
| 1997 | 398977 | 4661.58 |
| 1998 | 313503 | 4709.55 |
| 1999 | 327205 | 4757.39 |
| 2000 | 421075 | 6396.57 |
| 2001 | 424320 | 5917.30 |
| 2002 | 497963 | 7011.35 |
| 2003 | 409728 | 6021.86 |
| 2004 | 450568 | 6522.39 |
| 2005 | 502597 | 7137.47 |
| 2006 | 603148 | 8299.38 |
| 2007 | 538997 | 7624.89 |
| 2008 | 595821 | 8398.26 |
| 2009 | 651692 | 9238.74 |
| 2010 | 813091 | 12901.47 |
| 2011 (p) | 810000 | 16300.00 |

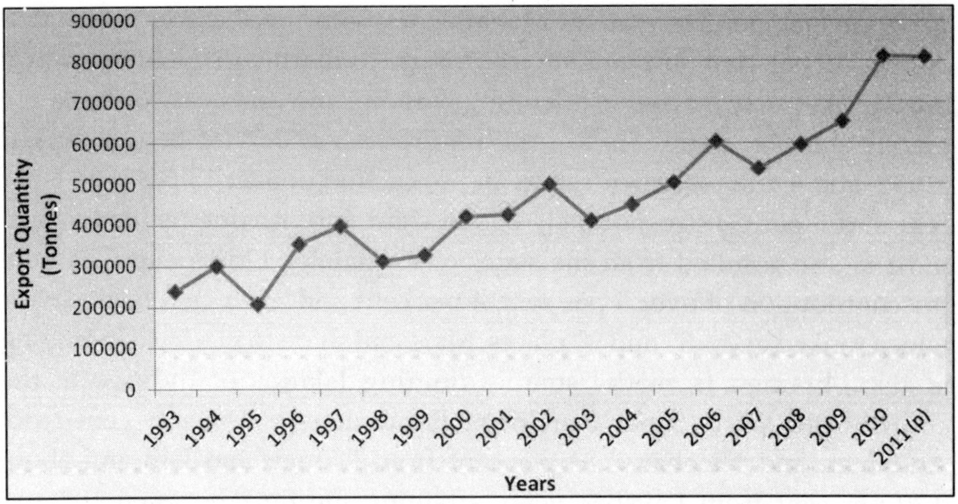


**Figure 5.3: Quantity wise Annual Seafood Export from India**

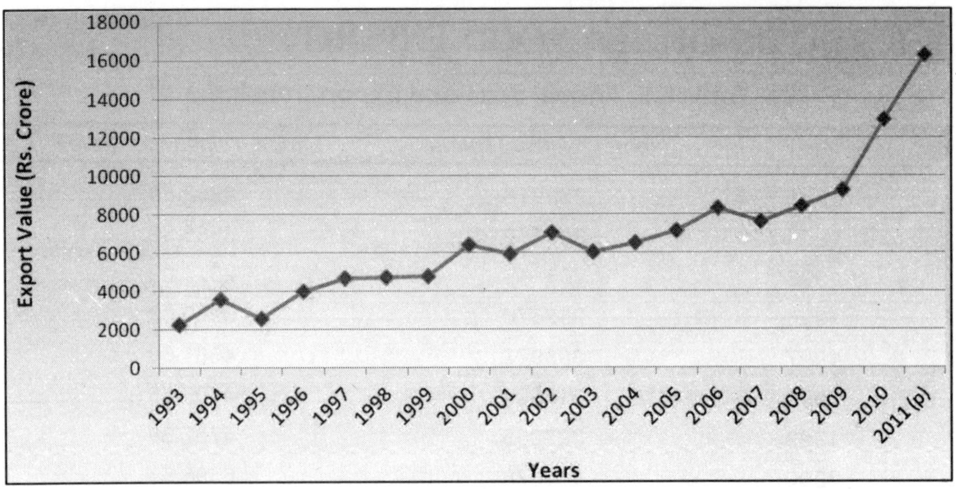


**Figure 5.4: Annual Seafood Export Earnings from India**

The most redeeming feature of Indian marine fishing industry has been the phenomenal rise in the sea food export. From the rather negligible export of 17,297 tonnes in 1961 mainly of dried and cured fish products, the quantum of export has gone up to the 6,03,148 tones, in 2006. In 2008 the total quantity of sea food export was 5,95,821 tonnes earning the total revenue of 8398.26 crore rupees to the country. There has been tremendous surge in the export of sea food and foreign exchange earnings in further years. Quantity wise this rise in export was 651692.44; 813091 and 810000

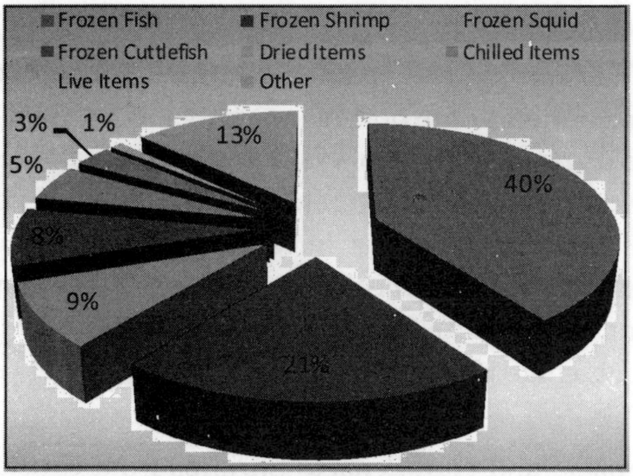


**Figure 5.5: Quantity-wise Share of Seafood Item Exported**

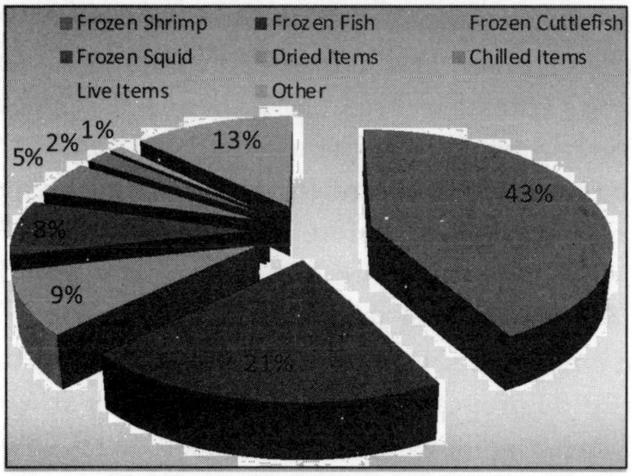


**Figure 5.6: Value-wise Share of Seafood Item Exported**

metric tonnes and the net foreign exchange earning was excelled to 9238.74, 12901.47 and 16300 crore rupees respectively for the years 2009, 2010 and 2011.

Fish sea food export has emerged as the top most among the agro-based commodities from India. India also shares about 2.45 per cent of trade in the global fish market. The annual growth rate of marine products export by quantity has shown steep increase from 9.97 per cent to 20.01 per cent from 2004 to 2006; however it has declined in 2007 to register the increase by 10.54 per cent in 2008. From the year 2008 to 2010 India witnessed the most exemplary rise in the sea food export by 26.72 per cent in quantity and 34.90 per cent by foreign exchange earnings. The foreign exchange earning has attained all time high gain of 16,300 crore rupees. The major items of export by quantity are frozen fish 40 per cent, frozen shrimp 21 per cent, frozen squid 9 per cent, frozen cuttlefish 8 per cent, dried items 5 per cent, chilled items 3 per cent, live items 1 per cent and others 13 per cent. However in terms of priced commodity frozen shrimp lead the race for export earnings of 43 per cent followed by frozen fish 21 per cent, frozen cuttlefish 9 per cent, frozen squid 8 per cent, dried items 5 per cent, chilled items 2 per cent, live items 1 per cent and others 13 per cent.

Beside Penaeid and Non Penaeid Shrimps from Crustaceans, Squids and Cuttle fishes from Molluscs, the major composition of commercial verities for export among the fishes include Pomfrets (White, Black and Chinese Pomfrets), Snappers, Croakers, Groupers, Carangids, Ribbon fishes, Reef Cod, Threadfin bream, Mackerels, Tunas etc. In 2008 the European union happened to be the top market for Indian Sea foods with the net earnings of 2857.43 crore Rs, followed by Japan with 1278.08 crore Rs, China with 1200.91 corere Rs, USA with 953.13 crore Rs and South East Asia with 831.82 crore Rs. The major buyers for the highest priced sea food commodity of shrimps in 2008 were Japan and USA with the share of about 22.1 per cent and 17.0 per cent respectively. However by quantity in 2010 European Union was the largest market for the seafood export (26.78 per cent) followed by South East Asia (16.43 per cent), China (15.41 per cent), USA (15.35 per cent), Japan (13.06 per cent) and Middle East (5.19 per cent). The USA still happens to be the biggest market of frozen shrimp for India.

## 5.7 INFRASTRUCTURE COMPONENT ON FISHERIES

According to recent census, the fishermen population of India is 3.5 million. There are about 3322 fishing villages and about 2271 fish landing centers mostly spread in the maritime areas of the country. In India the modem amenties for commercial fishing exist in 6 major commissioned harbors and in addition catering to the need of other moderate and marginal fisherman there are about 27 minor fishing harbors. There are about 2,38,772 fishing crafts, out of which there are 1,04,270 (43.66 per cent) are traditional crafts, about 75,591 (31.65 per cent) are motorized craft and about 58,911 (22.6 per cent) are mechanized fishing crafts.

## 5.8 ECONOMIC COMPONENT CONCERNING TO INDIAN FISHERIES

There has been tremendous progress made by India in the fisheries sector, since from the time of independence. The fisheries activity which was mainly pertaining in the hands of fishermen and considered mostly inferior during that time has now acquired the status of a major industry with high commercial establishment. In fact the growth rate in fisheries is considered to be higher than most of the other agricultural sectors in the country. The fisheries sector has played the pivotal role in raising the level of national economy as can be revealed from the fact that the compounded growth rate of world fisheries during the few decades was registered at 16.5 per cent level while during the same time India attained the compounded growth rate of 36.7 per cent (at Ninth –Plan level).

This significant contribution of fisheries sector to the national economy was also recognized and reflected in the policy of Indian Government in increasing the allocation of funds. The allocation of Rs 51.3 million during the first five year plan was substantially increased Rs 20700 million during the ninth plan. The 10$^{th}$ plan allocation of funds for fisheries was increased to 37154 million combindly for central out lay (central sector and centrally sponsored) and state schemes. There has been increase in the central out lay for fisheries especially after the 7$^{th}$ plan considering the remarkable progress made in the fishery sector by the country. The central out lay for fisheries sector during the ninth plan was kept at Rs 8000 million whereas during the 10$^{th}$ plan the outlay was reduced to Rs 7500 million. The fisheries sector did not derive major support during first three five year plans. However with rapid increase in production from marine capture fishery resources, the need to intensify fishing with introduction of mechanized boats for the exploration of continental marine fishery resources was felt necessary, therefore the planned budget was improvised from fourth year plan on wards. In order to sustain raising demand for mid water and deep sea fishing, the increased allocation has to be maintained for marine fisheries in the forthcoming plan budget.

The production trend was reversed during the late nineties, owing to sustained impasse in production and resultant poor growth rate from marine fishery sector and with substantiating increase in aquaculture activities, there was tremendous increase in production and growth rate of Inland fishery sector. The Inland fishery sector had then drawn the attention with the provision of increased allocation under central outlay (central sector and centrally sponsored) and state outlay from seventh five year plan on words during 8$^{th}$, 9$^{th}$ and 10$^{th}$ plan to support and boost up the Inland aquaculture activities in the country.

The other financial agencies that support activity for marine as well as inland fishery sector and have emerged to elaborate strong fisheries base in the country are MPEDA, Schemes under FFDA, and centrally sponsored schemes of ICAR, other national ministries and agencies. The major pivotal role for financing fisheries orienting schemes are also taken by National Bank for Agriculture and Rural Development Bank (NABARD), Asian Development Bank (ADB), World Bank, NACA, Rural cooperative Bank, District cooperative Bank, etc.

## 5.9 MARINE PELAGIC FISHERY OF INDIA

Pelagic fishes which occupy surface and subsurface waters are mostly migratory and venture in shoal or group. There is high abundance and rich diversity of species in this group. The most important one is the fishes belonging to the family Clupeidae which include Indian Oil Sardine, Wolf Herring, Anchovies, Hilsa and others like Bombay Duck, Half beaks, Flying Fishes, Ribbon Fishes, Carangids (Horse mackerel, scads, leather jackets), Scombroid resources like Indian mackerel, Seer fishes, Tunas, Billfishes, Barracudas, Coastal Mullets and Unicorn cod etc.

There are about 240 species of pelagic fishes in Indian waters. The fate of Indian marine fishing largely depends upon the pelagic fish resource.

The pelagic fishery resource significantly contributes with an average over 50 per cent of the total marine fish landing from India. The fishery is mainly restricted to continental waters of about 50 m depth from where over 70 per cent production of pelagic fish catch is harvested. Therefore due to constant stress of fishing in the pelagic waters most of the species either suffer from fluctuating production trend or sustain the effect overexploitation.

The major fisheries which contribute significantly to the pelagic fishery of India from 1990-2005 (Ayyappan *et al.*, 2006) are Indian Oil sardine (18.2 per cent), Indian mackerel (13.1 per cent), Carangids (11.4 per cent),

Ribbon fishes (10.4 per cent), Anchovies (9.3 per cent), Bombay duck (8.9 per cent). The other which also support to the pelagic resource are lesser sardines (7.8 per cent), other Clupeids (3.8 per cent), Tuna and Billfishes (3.7 per cent) Seer fishes (3.5 per cent), Hilsa shad (2.0 per cent), Wolf herring (1.2 per cent), Barracudas (1.1 per cent).

Coastal shallower waters of India happened to be one of the richest fishing grounds in the world in terms of the production of premium quality of pelagic fish species and also for some very valuable demersal resource like shrimps. However, since from the last one and half decade the coastal waters have been degraded and are no more amply productive. The reason behind this evident loss in production can mainly be attributed to anthropogenic effects such as; intensified exploitation by derogatory fishing practices such as fishing from purse seiners and bottom trawlers, in the limited extent of coastal waters to obtain high and high production of high quality of pelagic fishes and shrimps respectively, in addition to other disturbing problems like contamination and pollution, loss of fish breeding grounds and deterioration of natural amiable habitats from coastal waters.

## 5.10 MARINE DEMERSAL FISHERIES OF INDIA

This group includes all those fish species which are either found on sea floor from about 5 m depth and above. This group includes Sharks, Snappers, Groupers, Pomfrets, Threadfins, Catfishes, Perches, and Indian Halibut etc. which are being commercially valuable and significantly put their share to the Indian marine fisheries sector. Most of these groups include shrimp by-catch resulting from the operation of trawlers. Similarly in India where inshore fishing up to 50 meters is followed the depth wise production of marine fish harvest and their classification as pelagic and demersal does not matter much. It is because this depth is so shallow that when the trawl gear is lifted up it may include beside known demersal species some pelagic like Carangids, Mackerel, Ribbon fishes, Seer fishes etc. also in the harvest. The purse seiners operating in this depth may include not only the pelagic fin fishes but some demersal fishes also like cat fishes, perches etc. The instance of non consequence of pelagic and demersal in the harvest from operational gears can be ascertained from the fact that during 1995-2004 the average trawl landings comprised of 76 per cent demersal which included demersal fin fishes 38 per cent and demersal invertebrates like shrimp 38 per cent and rest 24 per cent comprised of pelagic fishes. Unlike pelagic, the demersal fin fishes do not get affected by temperature and other oceanographic parameters because since they occupy that depth where over the time almost uniform environment prevails. However, there is diurnal effect in the landings of most of the demersal fishes because most of them follow the diurnal and sometimes seasonal vertical migrations. The harvest from night may predominantly include Rays, Eels, Catfishes, and Flat fishes because they remain to bottom at night but venture in column waters in day light. Consequently Perches, Carangids, Squids may dominate during the day time because they pertain to sea bottom during the day time and coming up the water columns during the night time.

There has been four times increase in the average landings of demersal fishes during 2000-2004 of about 720517 tonnes to that from 1961-1965 when the average production of demersal fishes was only 174356 tonnes. This was due to intensification of trawl fishing in later years than in sixties. However, the contribution from demersal to the total marine landing which was 31.8 per cent in 1974-1988, got reduced to 28.0 per cent during 1989-2004. In 2003-2004 it further got decreased to 24.9 per cent. In 2003-2004 the region of south-east coast of India (Andhra Pradesh, Tamil Nadu and Pondicherry) recorded highest demersal fish landing of about 33.1 per cent.

There are about 21 major fish groups in the demersal resource from India which include the Elasmobranchs such as Sharks, Rays, Skates and bottom dwelling such as Eels, Catfishes, and Groupers, Reef occupying Perches, Coastal Sciaenids, Mullets and Flatheads Sole which remain under the sea bottom. Since the habitat occupied by each of them is different, therefore different types of gear are employed for their capture. The major average contribution to the landing of demersal fish resource during 2001-2004 was from coastal Sciaenids (18.4 per cent), Threadfin Bream (17.3 per cent), Catfishes (8.3 per cent), Silver Bellies (8.1 per cent), other Perches (6.5 per cent), Soles (6.3 per cent), Pomfrets (6.0 per cent), Pig face Bream (5.3 per cent) and Sharks (5.0 per cent). The other supporting resources include Lizard fishes (4.5 per cent), Rays (3.7 per cent), Groupers (3.4 per cent) and Goat fishes (1.9 per cent). The minor contributions also came from Eels, Threadfins, Snappers, Mullets, Whitefish, Halibut and

Flounders. The south east coast is characterized by the harvest of Silver bellies, Pig face breams and the south-west coast is dominated by the catch realized from Threadfin bream and other Perches. While the north-west coast region of Maharashtra and Gujarat is leading producer for Sciaenids, Cat fishes and Pomfrets.

It was observed that between the years of 1961-2004, when bottom trawlers were introduced sometime in mid sixties, the landing from three major groups of Lizard fishes (*Saurida* spp.), major Perches (Groupers, Snappers and Pigface bream) and Threadfin bream got tremendously increased, contrary to this the contribution four groups which included Elasmobranch, Catfishes, Silver bellies and White fish got decreased to the total demersal landing in the country. As evident from the composition of landing of about 44 years, the percentage contribution from Lizard fish, Major perches and Threadfin breams substantially increased from 10.3 per cent to 47.4 per cent while the contribution from Elasmobranches, Cat fishes, Silver bellies and White fishes got reduced from 47.6 per cent to 24.0 per cent. The reason which can be attributed for this pattern of landing was due to the shift in favor of trawling and resultant changes in the rate of exploitation pattern.

## 5.11 CLASSIFICATION AND FISHERY DETAILS OF MARITIME REGIONS OF INDIA

India is blessed with long extensive coastline bordering the peninsular part and demarcated as West Coast and East Coast. The west coast of India is flanked by the Arabian Sea (International Fishing Zone 51) which extends and occupies the coastal regions of Gujarat, Maharashtra, Goa, Karnataka, Kerala and part of Tamil Nadu up to Kanyakumari. The Bay of Bengal which comprise of east coast of India (International Fishing Zone 57) include the coastal regions of West Bengal, Orissa, Andhra Pradesh and Tamil Nadu states. The topography of coastal continental shelf area, deep sea floor profile and physico-chemical parameter in the spread of these maritime regions varies from place to place. Therefore each coastal region is exclusively marked with different representation of biological entity.

### 1) GULF OF KUTCH

The coastal region of north of Gujarat running parallel to Ran of Kutch is referred as Gulf of Kutch. The region is prominent for the fishery of

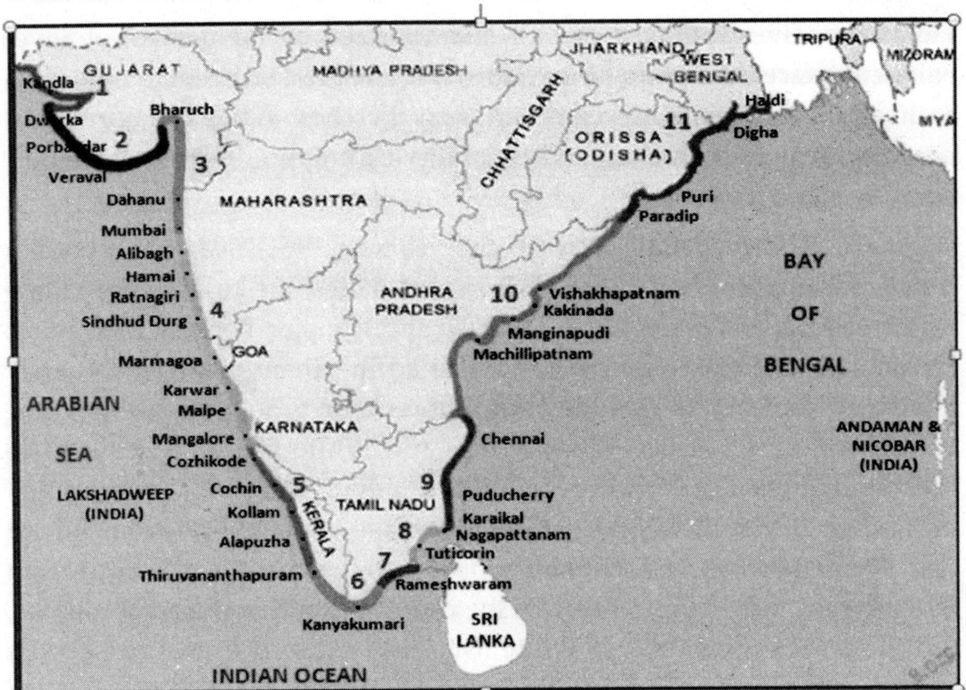


Plate 5.1: Classification of Maritime Regions of India

| | |
|---|---|
| 1. Gulf of Kutch | 2. Saurashtra Coast |
| 3. Cambay Coast or Gulf of Khambat | 4. Konkan Coast |
| 5. Malabar Coast | 6. Cape Camorin or Kanyakumari |
| 7. Gulf of Mannar | 8. Palk Strait |
| 9. Coromondal Coast | 10. A-P Coast |
| 11. Orissa, WB or Contai Coast or Sarkar Coast | |

*Polynemous tetradactylus* (Rawas); *P. indicus* (Ghol), *Pseudosciana dicanthus* (Dara), *Elutheronema tetradactylum*. The group collectively called as Indian Marine Salmon. The region also brings good catch of another species of Ghol (*Protonebea dicanthus*).

The most outstanding feature of Gulf of Kutch is the presence of extensive reef area. In fact in this gulf northern reef of Indian subcontinent occurs in the form of fringing reefs. However with the passage of time there has been great loss to the reef area with the advent of continued human interference for coral mining, dredging and pollution. The reefs were healthy some three and half decades before, but presently contain low coral diversity of 37 species under 22 genera. The most degrading effect of atmospheric threat of Gulf reefs at present is the rapidly expanding industrialization with the installation of cement, oil refineries and fertilizer industries in the coastal area of the region. Another reason for adverse effect seems to be due to deforestation of the coastal mangroves. The reefs even though enjoy legal protection as Marine National Park but better enforcement, systematic monitoring and a clear long term management strategy are urgently needed to be drawn. The present diversity of coral reefs at Gulf of Kutch which is next to only Gulf of Mannar in India, supports the rich extensive bed of pearl oyster, good account of edible oysters and coral reef associated fauna.

In the coastal wet lands of Gulf of Kutch there is marine reserve for the protection of marine mammals especially the Dolphin. The costal area include the region of North of Dwarka Port which happens to be the Southern Mouth of Kutch, and the main fishing activity is around Bedi Port, Okha, Kandla and Jamnagar.

## 2) KATHIAWAR OR SAURASHTRA COAST

The part of central Gujrat on the Arabian Sea is referred as Kathiawar or Saurashtra coast. The region is very rich form fisheries point of view. Some of the most prominent among them are Ghol, Ribbon fish, Carangids, White fish (*Lactarius lactarius*), Cai fishes, Pomfrets, Bombay duck, Threadfin, Golden spotted Anchovy (*Coilia dussumerii*), Penaeid and Non-Penaeid shrimps. Entire coastal region of Saurashtra coast is known for the extensive use of fixed bag nets or dol nets. The majority of fish harvest yield from the use of dol net. The high catch of Ghol (*Prodonibea dicanthus*) is realized from the region of Saurashtra. The harvest of one of the most important table fish Pomfret in the country is harvested from this region. There is neck to neck competition between Gujarat and Maharashtra state for the production of Pomfret. Brown Pomfret (*Parastromateus niger*) and Silver Pomfret (*Pampus argenteus*) are heavily harvested by the operation of dol net in the months of September to November and December to March respectively. Catfishes especially for *A. dussumeri* are harvested from the region of Jafrabad through the use of dol net. Dol net also happens to be the effective device for the capture of Bombay duck (*Harpadon neherus*) with the average annual production of over 25000 tonnes from the region of Nawabander, Rajpura and Jafrabad.

Fairly good amount of landing for Threadfin and Golden Anchovy (*Coilia dussumerri*) are realized during the months of March to May and

December to March respectively. Ribbon fish, Sciaenids, Elasmobranchs, Carangid and Lactarius are the basic supporting fisheries from the region. The capture of deep sea Pnaeid shrimp *Sulenovera crassicornis, Parapeneopsis stylifera, Metapenaeus brevicornis* are also prominent from the fishing area around Veraval. There are many important fishing centers from the region like Veraval, Bhavnagar, Porbandar, Nawabander, Rajpura, Jafrabad etc.

## 3) GULF OF KHAMBAT OR CAMBAY COAST

It is the inlet of Arabian Sea along west coast of India, occupying the coastal region between south of Gujarat and north of Mumbai. The gulf is known for its extreme tides, which vary greatly in height and run into it with amazing speed.

The Narmada and Tapti rivers empty into the Gulf owing to the confluence of these two major rivers, this coast is one of the most flourishing regions along the west coast for the estuarine fisheries. This coastal region happens to be excellent nursery area for growth of penaeid shrimps like *Penaeus monodon* (Tiger shrimp), *Penaeus indicus* (White shrimp), *Metapenaeus brevicornis, M. dobsoni* as well as for some of the fresh water prawn species such as *Macrobrachium rosenbergii* (Scampi/Giant fresh water prawn). There is heavy manual collection of these shrimps/prawns from this region.

The evidence of prominent estuarine fishery from this coast can also be proved by excellent landing of Wam *(Muraenosox talobon)* and Indian Shad (*Hilsa ilisha*) which is next only to West Bengal in production. The production of *Harpadon nehrus* (Bombay duck) is also highest in India from this coastal belt. This region is sometimes also the highest producer of *Protonibia dicanthus* (Ghol). Fairly good amount of catch are also realized in appreciable quantities form Cat fishes, Rays and Sharks etc. The important fishing centers from Cambay coast are Surat, Bharuch (Boarach), Dahanu, Vasai etc.

## 4) KONKAN COAST

The long stretch of coastal region from west coast extending from south of Mumbai to entire coastal belt of Maharashtra, Goa and Karnataka coast up to Mangalore is referred as Konkan Coast. There have been different postulations in literature regarding the delineation and identification of Konkan coast. In some literature the Konkan Coast is indicated to be the stretch from Gujarat to Goa coast with further subdivisions as Gulf of Kutch, Saurashtra or Kathiawar Coast, Gulf of Khambat or Cambay and then as Konkan coast. In other it is referred as the stretch from coastal region of Maharashtra up to Goa. However in present time considering the culture, livelihood of people and most importantly on the basis of language spoken Konkani among populace, the Konkan coast is considered to be the coastal region spreading from the entire stretch of Maharashtra, Goa and Karnataka states.

From the point of view of flourished fisheries, horticultural biodiversity and high prospect of tourism this coastal region is also termed as Indian Californian Coast. The fisheries wealth of the coastal region is truly remarkable with high prospect of potential for production. The Konkan coast most of the time ranks second or third in fish production among the divisions of maritime coasts of India. It stands highest for the total production of shrimps, Prawns including both Penaeid and Non Penaeid yielded from the country. The production of penaeid shrimp from Maharashtra is next only to the state of Kerala (in some years like 1977, 1978, 1987, 1988 the production of penaeid shrimp was even more than Kerala). The important varieties of Penaeid shrimp harvested from the region are *Penaeus indicus* (White shrimp), *Penaeus merguiensis* (Banana shrimp), *Metapenaeus affinis, M. monoceros, M. dobsoni* and *Parapeneopsis stylifera* (Tiny prawn or truly marine prawn). The production of *Rastralliger kanagurata* (Indian mackerel) locally called as Bangda in Konkani is also highest from this coastal region, with high share in production from the states of Karanataka, Goa and Maharashtra. Among many species of tuna or tuna like fishes, *Thunnus tonggol* (Northern Bluefin Tuna) commonly called as Gedar in Marathi is produced at highest level from this coastal region. The region is also the highest producer of wolf herring (*Chyrocentris dorab*).

The fishery of Pomfret is also highly flourishing with high production of *Pampus argenteus* (Silver Pomfret) *Pampus chinensis* (Chinese Pomfret) and *Parastromateus niger* (Black or Brown Pomfret). Pomfrets are locally called as Halwa in Konkani due to its high attributes of consumption. There is a stiff competition between the states of Maharashtra and Gujarat for the production of Pomfrets.

The conditions of high open sea of this coastal region is responsible for preferential habitat distribution for some seerfishes like King Seer (*Scomberomorus commerson*) and Streaked Seer (*S. lineolatus*) which are also produced in high quantities.

The other fishes of prominence which also support the high production are Mullets (*Mugil cephalus, Liza parsia*), Elasmobranches (Skates, Sharks and Rays), Sciaenids, Shell fishes like Edible Oysters, Clams, and Mussels.

In recent times the landscape of the Konkan region has been subjected to great changes due to anthropogenic activities like industrialization, urbanization, tourism, construction of railway and roads etc. The marine bioresource is also presently (2004 onwards) under the great stress due to over exploitation, inflow of industrial effluents and toxic metals, hot water flow which are detrimental to marine life. The fish landing from the region has sustained great loss in production in past few years as evident from the fish landing of 4.40 lakh tonnes in 2002 to only about 2.44 lakh tonnes in 2010. In order to reduce overexploitation and rejuvenate the stock of ever important fishes/shellfishes the fishermen from the region have requested the government to announce ban on fishing from purse seine and put limitation to derogatory trawling activity from its coastal waters. Not surprisingly for the coastal Konkan which till some few years before was one of the richest fishing grounds in the country, need comprehensive management policies to be implemented.

The fishing centers in Konkan coast from Mumbai are Varsova, New Ferri Warf, Sasoon dock etc. Other fishing centers from Konkan coast are Alibagh, Harnai, Jaigarh, Ratnagiri, Malwan, Vengurla, Goa, Madgaon, Sadashivgarh, Karwar, Mangalore etc.

## 5) MALABAR COAST

Malabar Coast stretches from south of Mangalore and mainly include the coastal region of Kerala state. In some of the literature it is either mentioned as the coastal region along the side of Western Ghat extending between the state of Goa to Kerala or form the state of Karnataka to Kerala. However there is no denying to the fact that since the landscape of Malabar belongs mainly to Kerala, it is the part of Kerala coast.

The Malabar Coast is front runner in fish production among all maritime coasts of India. The state of Kerala is considered to be the highest producer of marine fish. Even though in state wise Indian marine fish landing the state of Gujarat (including together Gulf of Kutch, Saurashtra or Kathiawar and Gulf of Cambay) occupies the first place but the per unit area of fish production is still highest from the state of Kerala. Therefore this coast is most fertile region of the Arabian Sea. Kerala ranks first in marine fish production contributing on an average 5 – 7.5 lakh tones sharing about 25 per cent of the total annual production of marine fish harvest in the country. The spectacular growth of marine fisheries sector are due to fisheries friendly government activities, well developed harvest with inception of improvised mechanized fishing,post harvest infrastructure and increased demand for seafood both in domestic and export markets. The state generates the foreign exchange earning of Rs. 1100 Crores from the export of seafood.

The group wise harvest of marine fish production indicates the share of 56 per cent from pelagic finfish, 22 per cent from the demersal, 17 per cent from crustacean and 5 per cent from the molluscan resources. The marine fish diversity of the Malabar coast indicate that it is highest producer of Indian Oil Sardine (*Sardinella longiceps*), Marine Cat fishes (*Arius maculatus, Arius thalassinus*), Tuna group of fishes (*Thunnus obesus, Euthynnus affinis, Auxis thazard, Thunnus albacares*), Black marlin (*Makaria indica*), Silver belly (*Leognathus species*), Carangid resource (*Caranx malabaricus*), different varieties of Trevallies represented by Cleft belly trevally (*Atropus atropus*), Largenose trevally (*Carangoides chrysophrys*), Golden trevally (*Gnathanodon speciosus*), White fish (*Lactarius lactarius*) and flat fishes represented by *Cynoglossus semifasciatus, Cynoglossus cynoglossus*. The flat fishes are captured in high quantities in shallower waters between Kadapuram in Thrissur district and Edukkad in north Kerala in the month from September to October. Due to strengthening of marine and brackish water fish culture activities the Kerala state is highest producer of Pearl Spot (*Etroplus suretensis*) also called as Karimeen which is state fish of Kerala, Bhetki (*Lates calcarifur*) and Milk fish (*Chanos chanos*).

The other prominent finfish resource from the region include Sciaenids, Groupers, Croakers and Snappers, Elasmobranchs such as Sharks, Skates and Rays, Pomfrets represented by *Pampus argenteus*, Seerfish represented by *Scomberomorus guttatus*. Through the inception of multiday trawling the harvest of Threadfin bream has also reached to the highest level.

The harvest from crustacean resource is also very high with good share in production from penaeid shrimp, spiny lobster and crabs. The state of Kerala is accountable for the highest landing of Penaeid shrimp from the country overtaking the production of the state of Maharashtra which is also the prominent producer of Penaeid shrimps. The two prominent fishing centers in the Quilon district of Kerala the Shaktikulangara and Neendakara have maximum number of shrimp trawlers and contribute about 19 per cent of Penaeid Shrimp landing. Fairly the good productions among other crustaceans are few Spiny Lobster represented by *Panulirus polyphagus* and crabs represent by mud crab *Sceylla serreta* and Christian crab *Charybdis crucita.*

The significant landings of molluscan resources are contributed by Pharoach Cuttle fish (*Sepia pharosis*) and Indian Squid *(Loligo duvaucelli)*. The prominent fishing centers from Malabar coast are Calicut (Khozikode), Cochin, Kadapuram, Edukkad, Quilon, Shakthikulangara and Neendakara etc.

## 6) KANYAKUMARI OR CAPE CAMORIN COAST

The geographical end of the Indian mainland which forms the cape at southernmost tip of India in referred as Kanya kumari or Cape Camorin coast. This part of sea shore comes under the Indian state of Tamil Nadu. At this sea shore there is confluence of three water bodies, the Arabian Sea, the Bay of Bengal and the Indian Ocean.

In his work on ancient India Ptolemy had identified Kanyakumari along with Gulf of Manner as center for pearl fishery and identified Kakai a place to the east of Kanyakumari as an emporium of pearl trade the fact has also been recorded in Travancore Census (1931).

In fact Kanyakumari along with Gulf of manner is most prominent in India for the mollusk fisheries. The Kanyakumari shore is big attraction for the tourists and due to aesthetic appeal there is great demand for shelled ornamental items like Clams, Chanks and Corals. The fishery of Clams is highest from this region represented by *Meritrix meritrix, M. casta, Katalysia opima*. The fishery of Chank and coral are also maximum from the region. Mussels represented by *Perna indica* and *Perna virdis* are also harvested in high quantities. The manual collection of pearl oyster is also popular from the region.

The other prominent shell fish resource of include fishery of Spiny Lobster, Crabs, Penaeid Shrimp (*Penaeus indicus, P. monodon*) and Squids. The region is also prominent for the production of Blood red snapper (*Lutijanus sangrines*) and Red perch snapper (*Lutijanus malbaricus*). The region also supports handsome fishery of Croakers or Rock perch (*Epinephlus dicanthus*).

The other supporting fisheries from the region are Anchovy, (*Engraulis indicus*), Sharks represented by *Scoliodon sorakowa* and *Scolidon acutus*, White fishes *Lactarius delicatulus*. The region also supports some common local fisheries for Velameen (*Mesoprion malbaricus*), Nameen (*Cybiumguttatum*), Savalaimeen (*Trichurus savala*), Vaalaimeen (Trichurus hamela), Kuthippumeen (*Clupea longiceps*) and Mulluklathi (*Triacanthus brevirostus*). The important fishing centers from this region include Kanyakumari, Cape Camorin, Kollencode, Mararikulam, Vattakottai etc.

## 7) GULF OF MANNAR

Gulf of Mannar is a large shallow bay which lies between South-Eastern tip of India and the West Coast of Sri Lanka. It occupies the South Eastern coastal area of the state of Tamil Nadu. A chain of low islands and roofs known as Adam's Bridge (Ramsethu), separates the Gulf of Mannar from Palk Bay.

### Biodiversity of Marine Commodities and their Production in Gulf of Mannar

The region harbors enormously rich biodiversity. Considering its impounding fishery wealth and rich diversity, in 1986 with the efforts of renowned scientists, a group of 21 islets lying off the Tamil Nadu coast between Thoothukudi (Tuticorin) and Dhanushkodi, declared Gulf of Mannar as 'Marine National Park'. The biodiversity of this coast is truly outstanding, the representation of approximate numbers of 3600 species in total of plants and animals of Gulf of Mannar make it biologically one of the richest coastal regions of the India. It is therefore that the Government of India and Tamil Nadu identified and declared this 10 km stretch in 1989 as 'Biosphere Reserve' to conserve the endangered coastal marine commodities such as Coral reefs, Salt marshes, Sea grass and Mangroove forest UNDP (1994).

The Gulf of Mannar is known for its pearl banks of *Pinctada rediata* and *Pinctada fucata* from many thousand years. Pilny the Elder a well known oceanographer of his time (A.D. 23-79), praised the pearl fishery of the Gulf as most productive in the world, Prasad and Nair (1973), Hornell (2009). In recent time however the catches have declined to have reduced population for pearl oysters, gorgonian coral and acron worm. Presently some of the sacred resources like Sea Turtles (Olive readily and green turtle), Sharks, Dugongs Dolphins which from old times are frequent visitors of this coastal region have also tremendously reduced in numbers to the level endangerment due to combined effect of loss of vegetation due to deforestation, overexploitation, and stress of pollution (Mulley *et al.*, 2000; Pattesson 2007; Sacratees and Karthigarani 2008.

About 510 species (23 per cent) out of the total 2,200 finfish species in Indian water are found in Gulf of Mannar. The vast diversity of marine fish include Coral associated ornamental fishes belonging to family of Chaetodontidae, Parrot fish (*Scarus species*), Clown fish (*Amphiprion species*), Squirrel fish (*Holocentrus species*), Wells (1995). Sergeant major (*Abudefuf saxatilis*), Snapper and Red perch (*Lutijanus sps.*), Rock perch or Croaker (*Epinephlus sp.*). Several species of fish inhabiting the pelagic zone contribute to the fishery in the Gulf of Mannar. Sardine with the average production of 20,249 tonnes in 2010, are represented by *Sardinella longiceps, S. gibbosa, S. albela.* The sardine fishery fluctuated widely with declining trend over the years mainly due to reduction in fishing efforts following destruction of traditional craft and gears during Tsunami in 2004. The other pelagic group of fishes includes Mackerel, Carangids, Tunas and Seer fishes, majority of them are caught by gill nets, drift gill nets, drift nets, hooks and lines. The anchovies are caught both by trawl net and shore seine (Raju, 2000). The Fishery Survey of India (1991) indicated also the great potential from demersal fishery resource in Gulf of Mannar which includes mainly Barracuda, Perches, Elasmobranches and Pomfrets. A unique endemic species of Balanoglossus (*Ptychondera fluva*), a living fossil, that link invertebrate and vertebrate is recorded only at Kurusadai, a fishing centre from this region (OSTI, July 2004).

The shell fish biodiversity resource from the region indicate 4 species each of shrimps and lobster, 106 species of crabs, 17 species of Holothurians (Sea cucumber), 5 species of Ployplacophorans, 108 species of Sponges and 100 species of the Echinoderms. The coastal reef also supports the high diversity of Molluscan resource with total number of about 466 species which include 271 species of Gastropods, 174 species of Bivalves, 16 Cephalopods and 5 Scaphalopods (UNDP, 2001). The Molluscan resource of Gulf of Mannar is highest among all maritime regions of India. As mentioned earlier, the Gulf of Mannar is validated to have one of the richest natural beds of pearl oysters, the divers who are mostly the local fisherman account for maximum collection and production of natural pearls. The attempts are also made especially with the initiative of CMFRI to culture the pearl oysters from the region. The production of edible oysters and mussels are also highest from this coastal belt, represented by *Crassostrea madrasensis, C. gryphoidis, C. cuculata* and *Perna indica, P. viridis* respectively.

The coral fauna which is unique and most flourished from Gulf of Mannar are represented by 106 species from 30 genera of Hermatype corals and 11 species from 10 genera of ahermatype corals, including13 new species, giving a total of 117 species from 14 families and 40 genus. Large areas of these reefs are in generally poor condition due to collective effect of destructive human activities like nutrient and other pollution loads, deforestation, industries of cement, coral mining and lime kilns, brick manufacturing, urbanization etc. Presently the live corals cover that is left over therefore is only about 35 per cent and the dead corals are covered by various algae. Stony coral species belonging to Poritidae and Favidae sub orders constitute the dominant reef builders in this coastal area (Venkatasawaran, 2000; Edward and Patterson *et al.,* 2007).

## 8) PALK BAY OR PALK STRAIT

This is the water body occupying the central region of Tamil Nadu lying between the East Coast of India and Mannar, the Northern Province of Island nation Sri Lanka. Thus the narrow shallower water body that separates the Indian Coastal region of Tamil Nadu from northern parts of Sri Lanka is referred as Palk Bay. The Palk Strait between India and Sri Lanka is about 75 km wide with a water depth of 9 to 13 meters except where local coral reef rises above the sea level.

Palk Strait next to Gulf of Mannar exhibit great biodiversity due to presence of reef profile in its continental shelf waters. Palk Strait and Gulf of Mannar are akin to large lagoons, undisturbed by ship traffic because of their shallow waters. Therefore they are home to wide variety of marine ecosystem. There exist a great biodiversity of flora and fauna in Palk Strait (Ramesh and Kannupandi, 1997).

The reef ecosystem exhibit great aquatic vegetation. There exist about 61 species of algae with *Halimeda opuntia* being dominant algal species. The *Caulerpa sp.* and *Sargassum sp.* are other most common plants found in the reef. The aquatic vegetation of the region happens to be the excellent forage food for Dugongs and Dolphins.

The coral commodity have large polyps and are represented by *Faviapallida; Favus; Favites virens; Goniastrea pectinata; G. retiformis; Platygyna lamellina; Hydrophora sp. Cyphasstrea sp.; Leptastrea sp.; Gonipora sp.; Pocillopora sp.; Acopora sp.* and *Montipora sp.* Among the fishery corals *Labaphylum sp.* and *Sarcophylum sp.* are most prominent.

The reef also supports a good many reef dwellers like Bryozoans Encrusting Sponges, Boring Sponges, Bivalves, other Molluscs and Echinoderms.

The Sponges are spread widely into the reef, represented by *Hercina fusca; Dysidea fragilis; Spirustrella inconstans; Calispongia diffusa.* Boring sponges which feed on corals are responsible for their massive erosion and destruction of reef system. There are about 20 species of Boring Sponges falling into 9 genera. The most conspicuous of them is *Cliona sp.*

Boring Bivalve Molluscs are represented by 17 species (Appukuttan 1973). Ramesh (1996) recorded 73 species of molluscs, 46 of them are gastropods belonging to 17 families and 27 species of bivalves belonging to 13 families. The Palk Bay is also the second largest region after Gulf of Mannar for the presence of natural pearl oyster (*Pincatada fucata)* and production of pearls. It is also promising producer of edible oysters and mussels specially the Green mussel (*Perna virdis*).

The echinoderms are identified by the presence of Sea Cucumber *Holothuria scabra* and *Holothuria arta.* The other important echinoderm includes *Penta ceraster.*

Like Gulf of Mannar this reef system also supports rich presence of ornamental fishes like Parrot fish (*Scarus sp.*), Clown fish (*Amphiporion sp.),* Squirrel fish (*Holocentrus sp.*), Red perch (*Lutijanus sp.*), Chaetedon, Surgeon fish etc. The region is known for the fishery of Dried Sea Horse

(*Hippocampus kuda*). The dried sea horse is in great demand all over the South East Asian countries for the preparation of soup and powder. The dried sea horse commands great demand due to its medicinal quality, it is considered as medicine for Whooping cough and also known to cure asthma. The powder of dried sea horse along with honey and coconut oil is spread to cure the cut wounds (Marichamy, 1993).

The region is also fascinated by the visiting turtle like Olive Readily Turtle and Green Turtles. It is also the second largest home for Dugong. Dugong exhibit seasonal migration from Gulf of Mannar to Pambam Island during south west monsoon and from Pambam to Gulf of Mannar during north east monsoon when they are unable to counter currents generated from these monsoon conditions respectively. Dolphins are also found and caught in large numbers.

The important fishing centers of Palk Bay include, Rameswaram, Mandapam, Pambam, Pudukuttai and fishing villages from Ramnad, Nagapattinum, Thanjavur and Ramnathpuram districts in Tamil Nadu.

## 9) COROMANDAL COAST

This region occupies complete coastal area of North Tamil Nadu state up to mouth of Pulicat Lake. Two major rivers from South India Krishna and Cauvery drain off in this region of Bay of Bengal.

Coromandal coast is fairly rich in its fishery resource. It is rich in pelagic as well as demersal fishery resource. The Flying fish (*Cypselurus* and *Exocoetus species*) is most important seasonal fishery bringing highest catch from Madras (Chennai) to extreme north of Coromandal coast. Fishing season for Flying fish starts towards the end of May and lasts till middle of July when it occurs in large numbers in pristine clear coastal water, when it does not rain along this part. With the onset of north easterly monsoon during early winter when the coastal water becomes muddy or turbid the shoal of Flying fish migrates to offshore deep water. The production of Seer fish is also high with the highest share from spotted seer (*Scomberomorus guttatus*) especially in the region of hypo saline (lesser saline) waters of estuaries along the Krishna and Cauvery river systems.

The fishery of Elasmobranches is also dominant with high share in landing from Sharks, Rays and Flat fishes represented by *Scoliodon sp., Carcharhinus sp., Sphyrna sp., Rhynchobatus sp., Aetobatus sp., Pristis sp.*

and *Rhinoptera sp.* respectively. The production of Elasmobranchs from this coast is sometimes highest at all India level. The Coromondel coast is also second largest producer of Marine Cat fish after the state of Kerala. The artisanal fishery of Coromondal coast is most dominant with high landing of Surgeon fish, Sting ray, Nemipterid, Coral and Sponges (Tara *et al.*, 2010). The region also supports fairly handsome landings of Sciaenids represented by *Johnius sp.*, Silver bellies represented by *Leognathus sp.* and Ribbon fish represented by *T. lepturus*.

The Coromondal coast boasts off to have maximum number of trawlers among the entire maritime belt of east coast. Therefore trawling has been the mainstay of high production of shrimps represented by *Penaeus indicus, P. semisulcatus, Parapeneopsis stylifera* and molluscs specially the Squids and Cuttle fishes. This coastal region is the third largest producer of shrimp at all India level. The important fishing centers of Coromondal coasts are Parangipattai, Port novo, Cuddallore, fishing centers from South and North Arcot Districts and Chennai etc.

## Post Tsunami Effect on Fishes

The post Tsunami effect has caused some changes in the fishery along this coast. A rare fish *Plataxteria sp.* which is found mainly in the Andaman Sea has been found in the Coromondal coast as its new native ground. There has been regular migration of this species along this coast from Andaman in the years that followed after Tsunami hit this region. Tsunami is also considered as reason for the flourished stock of Puffer fish, Red crab and some ornamental fishes like Parrot fish, Angel fish, Clown fish and Butterfly fish along the shallower seabed of the coast. Consequently the number of Seer fish, Pomfret, Murrel, Flat fish and Flying fish have decreased may be due to changes in aquatic life after Tsunami in the coastal areas of Tamil Nadu.

## Trawling Boats, Emerging Markets Spell Trouble for Coromondal Region

Presently the Coromondal coast is facing a severe crisis of resource depletion caused by mix of over exploitation and destructive fishing practices. The document pertaining to the trends of fish catch and the dynamics in associated markets over the last thirty years indicated that with the inception of trawling in late 1970's the catch/unit effort and the rewarded income increased in initial early period but subsequently decreased with the passage of time. The effect of trawling proved derogatory to the extent of steep decline to its lowest level of production over most recent years till present. The trawling was employed mainly to harvest high priced commodity of Shrimps and Cephalopods. The production of Shrimps and Cephalopods increased in the initial years due to fishing from relatively virgin waters, that time used exclusively for artisanal fisheries. However in later years especially in recent time the production of Shrimp and Cephalopods decreased to its lowest level with high proportion of trash fish in the yield which is referred as by catch waste.

The increase in number of units of trawler over the years was responsible for rapid setting of overexploitation of stock; it also reduced the income of trawl owner from Shrimps and Squids. It seems unfortunately that now the trawl operator fish for not obtaining the priced stock of Shrimps and Squids but for obtaining the by catch waste of trash fish. There is great demand of by catch waste of trash fish in the region for its reduction into protein enriched chicken meal due to highly flourished installation of poultry units for fish meal and manure. (Tara and Bhalla 2010; Tara *et al.*, 2008; Lobo *et al.*, 2010).

## 10) ANDHRA PRADESH COAST

The coastal area of Bay of Bengal extending from North of Pulicat lake up to the boarder of Orissa coast and represents the entire coastal area of the state of Andhra Pradesh. It is one of the long maritime coastal area occupying about 980 kms of area of Bay of Bengal. The coastal Andhra include the Districts of Srikakulam, Vizianagram, Visakhapatnum, East Godavari, West Godavari, Krishna, Guntur, Prakasan and Nellore (Murthy 2012).

The fishery wealth of the Andhra coast indicates that although it is rich in fishery potential but has not been exploited extensively. The reason may be due to the fact that Andhra and Orissa states experience routinely the El Nino effect, as a result the fishery habitat and fishing activities of the region are severely hampered. In some areas the mechanization of fishing is not evenly being undertaken. The areas of Srikakulam, Visakhapatnum and Kakinada are the hub of high fishing activity due to improvisation of mechanization but in other areas, especially in North Andhra Pradesh coast the fishery activities are still at artisanal level. The fishing for Lesser Sardines (Kawalla in Telugu) represented by *Sardinella fimbriata, S. albela, S. gibbosa, S. dayi* and *S. clupeoides* are high with the employment of traditional gears in the coastal region of North Andhra Pradesh (Luther, 2001). In fact the Andhra Pradesh coast is the highest producer of Lesser Sardine in India.

Along Andhra Pradesh coast the pelagic fishery is also dominated by Wolf Herring (*Chyrocentris dorab*), Indian Shad (*Hilsa ilsha*), Anchovies, White bait, other Clupeoides, Ribbon fish, Carangid and Seer fish. The demersal fishery of the region is dominated by Eels, Catfishes, Perches, Polynemids, Sciaenid's, Silver bellies, Pomfrets and Shrimps etc. The production from pelagic fishery is more than the demersal fish stock (Rao, 1986).

The supporting fishery of prominence from the region include Yellowfin Tuna (*Thunnus albacares*), traditionally through hook and lines and through mechanized long lines and trolling (Rohit Pratibha and Ram Mohan, 2009); Elasmobranchs (P. James, 1973), Sciaenids (Rao, 1975) and Nemipterid (Vinci, 2011). Mechanized fishing is undertaken in full sway with high production of Shrimps from the coastal region of Kakinada, Srikakulam and Visakhapatnum (Rao, 1979), while the artisanal fishery of prawns is undertaken in the region of Uppeda (Lalitha Devi, 1985). Recently the fishery of Cephalopods also dominates in the region. The region is therefore high producer of fin fishes, crustaceans and cephalopods. It is found that majority of them have prolonged spawning and about 41 species of them spawn during January. Mohanraj *et al*. (2000) suggested that in order to safeguard the high production of these at sustainable level and considering the spawning intensity and catch rate of them, the trawl operations may be banned in April and during November and December.

Krishna Delta, located about 90 km south east of Vijayawada near Machillipatnam is ecologically important area of coastal Andhra Pradesh. The region supports for excellent larval fishery resource of many molluscs including 23 species belonging to 20 genera mainly of Univalve, Bivalve and Gastropods; 18 species and 8 genera of Prawns belonging to Penaeid and Non-Penaeid; 11 species belonging to 10 genera of Zoea crabs and the larval fin fishes 106 species belonging to 78 genera, represented by

Mullets, Croakers, Indian shad, Cat fishes, Grunteres, Perches, Pomfrets, Goat fishes and Eels etc.

There are also reports for the mass mortality of Olive Readily Turtle (*Lepidochelys olivacea*) at Srikakulam due to high trawling activity, using trawl gears without TED devices (Murthy and Ramamurthy, 2011). These turtle regularly visit Andhra coast on their way to Orissa coast for nesting, hence their protection and conservation is highly necessary.

According to some reports (Keya Acharya, 2009) there is growing danger of coastal crisis that leaves fishermen from pockets marooned. The traditionally poor fisherman from fishing villages nearer to Visakhapatnum were dependant for their livelihood on coastal fisheries are presently under extreme financial crisis due to the consequence of changing times. The depleting fish catch is due to reckless pollution from the coastal industrial installations of Steel plants. Thermal power, Petrochemicals, Fertilizers etc have deprived them of harvest of quality fishes they were harvesting in yester years. It is presumed that due to pollution fishes like Sharks, Hilsa, Polsa and large Snappers are disappeared from coastal waters to about 40 kms away. The non availability of funds like loans from banks or from government support, forced them to borrow loan from money lenders, which they are unable to pay off due to high rate of interest. The plight of fishermen became pathetic also due to displacement of fishing villages because of rapid industrialization at Vishakhapatnum Steel plant and Bhaba Atomic Centre Gangavaran. Even though these installations have given jobs to some hundred of fishermen but made jobless over some thousands of fishermen.

The important fishing centers form Andhra coast are Machalipatnum, Srikakulam, Fishing villages from Nellore and Bapatla districts, Vishakhapatnum, Kakinada, East and West Godavari districts etc.

The region of Nellore south of Andhra Pradesh is recognized as Aquaculture capital of India. The culture of Penaeid Shrimps was scientifically taken up during late eighties. The coastal swampy area around Nellore was chosen and excavated for the brackish water culture of Shrimps with the support of Government of India and Andhra Pradesh. The region was developed as the major centre of activity of culture of shrimps. Many private agencies established their units for shrimp culture.

Through the intensive aquaculture farming the high production of shrimp was attained for almost a period of a decade. It also proved to be highly profitable enterprise for the Shrimp farm owners. However due to outbreak of White spot disease the production of Shrimp got severe setback and collapsed to the level of closure. Most of the shrimp farming units were closed due to loss they sustained from outbreak of the disease. The attempts are presently undertaken to rejuvenate the Shrimp farming from this aquaculture sites.

## 11) ORISSA COAST

This coastal area is part of of Bay of Bengal spreading between north of Andhra Pradesh coast and occupying the coastal region of the state of Orissa. It is about 480 kms long. The coastal area of Orissa is famous for ashoring to one of the largest lagoon of salt water in Asia, the Chilka Lake which is abode for vast biodiversity resource. The effort of State government is also laudable for the establishment of India's first natural marine sanctuary park at Gahirmatha (spread for about 120 kms comprising of six districts) for the conservation of nesting Olive Readily turtle, a rare endangered species from North Pacific, flocking the area every year in very high numbers for laying eggs on beaches. The sanctuary is also a safe pristine place for the conservation of other marine flora and fauna. Environmentally the Orissa coast is a disturbed area, since it experiences routinely the effect of El Nino, which causes severe loss to coastal installations, fishery resource due to wide spread effect of cyclone and flooding.

In spite of having good potential of resource for marine fisheries it is not substantiated with sufficient production. The principle reasons for poor production may be due to restricted and prohibition of fishing due to turtle related conservation measures around 120 kms of Gahirmatha. Besides a substantial area of it has also been declared as prohibited area for about 7 months from November to May each year. The occurrence of cyclone also unfortunately intercepts with the fishing season. The result of prohibition of fishing has affected the livelihood of around three lakhs of fishermen (Venkatesh 2006; Hemant 2010). The present indication is that the inshore fisheries of the region have been reached to maximum production level and the offshore waters are not explored as yet due to inadequate policy support or suitable fishing practices. There has been reduction in production of marine fish from 1, 56,081 tons in 1997-98 to 1,16,880 tones by 2003-2004 with the alarming 25 per cent decline in production during the span of these 6 years (Directorate of Fisheries, Orissa). The Indian shad *Hilsa ilisha* is most sought for at commercial level along the Orissa coast. The region is second highest producer of Hilsa after the state of West Bengal (Pati 2011). *Rhizopriondon oligolinx* is an important component of the shark fishery of Orissa coast (Talwar, 2011). The fishery of Bombay Duck have recurrence of fish stock along the east coast in the region of Orissa and West Bengal, amply proves also the fact that Bombay Duck fishery is recognized for its discontinuous distribution. The fishery of Nemipterids is also high from the regions (Vinci, 2011). It has been observed since from past that the substantial portion of trawl catch along the Orissa coast comprise of Crockers (Sciaenid). The catch analysis during the period of 1984-1995 showed that about 12.28 per cent of total catch landing from trawl in the state was contributed by the Sciaenid (Anna, 1997). The major fish stocks which are available for exploitation are Elasmobranchs, Cat fish, Sciaenid, Silver belly, Perches, Promfrets, Horse mackerel and Lesser Sardines. The main component of trawl catch beside Shrimp along the east coasts are Perches and Rays (John and Sundarsen, 1998; FSY, 2008). The important fishing centers from the Orissa coast are Balasore, Bhadrak, Puri, Ganjam, Kendrapara, Jagat Singh port etc.

## Chilka Lake and its Fisheries

Chilka Lake is a brackish water lagoon, spread over the Puri, Khurda and Gunjam districts of Orissa on the east coast of India. It is situated at the mouth of the Daya River, flowing into the Bay of Bengal. It is separated from Bay of Bengal by a 60 km long narrow strip of marshy island and sand flats. Chilka is the largest coastal lagoon in India and the second largest lagoon in the world. About two lakhs fishermen are depending for their livelihood on the lake fisheries of Chilka.

The lake ecosystem support great variety of aquatic life which include about 37 different fish, 28 varieties of shrimps/prawns and 35 species of brachysoma crabs and two varieties of Spiny Lobster. About 65 species breed in the lake, 27 species in fresh water and remaining species migrate to the sea to breed. The great variety of fin fish includes about 21 species of Herring and Sardines of the family of Clupidae. The other stock includes

Milk fish, Indo Pacific Tarpan, Ten Pounder, Bream, Hilsa, Mullets etc. The shrimps mainly *Penaeus indicus, Metapenaeus monoceros, M. affinis, M. dobsoni* (Kadal shrimp). Rare and endangered marine mammals like Irrawady Dolphins and Dugongs. Irrawady Dolfhin *Corcaella brevirostris* is the flagship species of Puri. Chilka is one of the two lagoons in the world that are home to this species. The dolphin is classified as critically endangered in five of the six other places it is known to live. In addition to this, small population of Bottle Nose dolphin also migrates in the lagoon from the sea (Department of Forest and Environment, Orissa 2011). In early to late nineties the total production of fish and shellfish was just average about 1500 – 1700 tones mainly due to siltation and pollution in the lagoon. However due to the efforts towards the improvement of lagoon ecosystem and measure for upgrading the hydro biological intervention for restoration of lake with the opening of a new mouth in 2000 resulted in high significant recovery of the lake fisheries. The average of fish landing between 2001 and 2010 increased to 11,676 tones. The all time highest fish production 14,228 tones was obtained in the year 2011 – 12 (Patnaik, 2012).

The year wise fish production from Chilka lake from 1999-2000 to 2008-2009 indicate that the production increased to more than double than in the year 1999-2000 with opening of the new passage in 2000-2001 (Table 5.6). The total fish production recorded high levels from the year 2000-2001 onwards.

**Table 5.6: Year wise Fish Production from Chilka Lake**

| Year | Fish | Shrimp/Prawn | Crab | Total |
|---|---|---|---|---|
| 1999-2000 | 1556.32 | 180.40 | 9.03 | 1725.75 |
| 2000-2001 | 3817.81 | 1071.38 | 93.60 | 4982.79 |
| 2001-2002 | 9530.03 | 2347.78 | 111.07 | 11988.88 |
| 2002-2003 | 8265.16 | 2478.82 | 149.81 | 10893.79 |
| 2003-2004 | 10286.34 | 3611.37 | 155.51 | 14053.22 |
| 2004-2005 | 8097.77 | 5000.71 | 161.89 | 13260.37 |
| 2005-2006 | 7774.81 | 4296.02 | 154.08 | 12224.91 |
| 2006-2007 | 6463.92 | 3368.97 | 122.94 | 9955.83 |
| 2007-2008 | 6610.23 | 3298.08 | 139.12 | 10047.43 |
| 2008-2009 | 6534.85 | 3929.68 | 237.50 | 10702.03 |

The breakup of the fish harvest indicated that the production of fish even though increased from the year 2000-2001 it fluctuated in between the years up to 2008-2009. This was because the share of Shrimp production to the total landings substantially increased from the year 1999-2000 onwards with the highest production of 5000 tonnes obtained in the year 2004-2005. The production of crabs also indicated the similar trend in production with the highest production of 237.50 tonnes in 2008-2009 (Orissa Fisheries, 2010). The lake ecosystem also support high prospects of production of cultured Shrimp from the raising of weirs and cages in the shallower water of lagoon.

## 12) WEST BENGAL COAST

The state of West Bengal has the coast line of 210 kms spread over the districts of Midnapur and 24 Parganas lying on either side of the mouth of river Hooghly. In some literature the coastal area of Bay of Bengal has been included together along with Orissa coast to be referred as Contai or Sarkar Coast.

The aquatic wetland regime of West Bengal exhibits truly diversified form of ecosystem which include the great inland water resource drained by Gangetic channels and tributaries, semi saline due to Hooghly and Matlah estuaries, marine water along coastal region of Midnapur and 24 Paraganas and from the point of view great biodiversity the wetland of Sundarbans. The mangrove forest and mud flats of Sundarban provide vital breeding and nursery ground for large proportion of finfish, crustaceans and molluscs.

The state of West Bengal is the leading producer of fish in India however with high production in share from inland sector than the marine sector. Among 120 species of fish, nearly 26 commercial species of fish and shell fish account for an annual yield of 22,225 tones from the estuarine waters and from the marine waters the fish yield is about 20,000 tons per year.

The state of West Bengal also is the leading supplier and distributor in India for seeds of Inland fishes and Prawns. The seed collection and supply has acquired the status high commercial trade, about 75 per cent of fish culturist in India depends on the supply of fish seeds from West Bengal.

The presence and confinement of about 85 per cent of area of India mangrove in West Bengal indicate the ecological importance of the state. About 0.405 million hectare area of mangrove have been reclaimed for the fish culture. The fish and prawn culture is practiced in about 30,000 hectare area giving average yield of 500 kg/hectare.

The Pawn/Shrimp fishery in the state is threatened by the increasing capture of post larval and early juvenile of prawns together with its growing trade for supply. The construction of Farakka bridge on the Ganges and flushing of Hooghly with bypassed freshwater from Ganges has significantly reduced not only the salinity of the estuary but also the tributary. The one time gradient zone in respect of salinity is now virtually a freshwater zone. This has posed a serious threat to the estuarine fisheries providing livelihood for many fishermen.

The marine fishery sector is at low key level since there are only few marine fishing villages along the coast of West Bengal. The bulk of the catch along the coast come through mechanized sector, but lack of breathing and mooring facilities stand in the way of expansion of fishing fleets. Marine fishing sector in West Bengal also lack basic amenities like good trading, marketing, clod storages and processing facilities. Trawlers based at Visakhapatnum regularly fish in this coast (Das, 1985). The trend of fish catch along the costal districts from 2005-2008 indicated more proportion of marine fish than inland fish in Midnapur while in South 24 Parganas the share from marine and inland fish production was nearly equal (Pandey and Sinha, 2011). Digha is the largest fish landing centre of West Bengal with fairly high proportion of landing of Elasmobranchs comprising of Rays, Skates and Catfishes (Chatterjee *et. al* 2010). The exploratory surveys conducted by Fisheries Survey of India since from eighties have indicated rich shrimp fishing ground in the sand heads of West Bengal. It also has indicated high potential of production in the shelf area extending between 100-400 meter for deep sea Shrimps, Perches, Nempterids, Piracanthids, Drift fish and Black ruff. Pomfrets are also known to occur in high numbers along the coast (Khan, 2011). The state of West Bengal is the highest producer of Hilsa (*Tenualosa ilisha*). The Government of West Bengal declared Hilsa as State Fish vide G. No 659-fish/C-VI/4M-2/2007 dated 27-03-2007. Hilsa is also the ultimate cuisine in Bengalis due to its delicate taste.

**Fate of Hilsa Fisheries**

In past few years, the population of Hilsa has been steadily declining, all due to the human being upsetting the natural balance through overfishing of the stock. Hilsa is an anadromous fish which mean it lives in ocean but travel to rivers to spawn and after spawning it travels back to sea. There are many literatures citing the example of occurring and production of Hilsa upstream the Ganges as far up to Allahabad and Kanpur. In sixties record production of Hilsa was obtained from Buxar (Bihar). However due to construction of Farakka dam the fish is not able to reach to the stretches of Gangetic system to breed. Even the opening of some passage of Farakka dam could not restore the migratory pattern of the fish in Ganges. The closing of the migratory route for the fish to the potent fishing ground of Ganges has resulted into finding their passage for breeding within the state into nearby inland water areas or their migration to the river stretches in Bangladesh.

Presently in West Bengal the fish is under heavy exploitation as adults when they travel from sea to river, similarly as juveniles on their way back to the sea. As being basically oceanic species and similarly due to complexities involved in the understanding of its breeding, biology, physiology and migration behavior, the culturing or rearing of Hilsa is difficult. It therefore requires some urgent management measure like imposing the blanket ban jointly by India and Bangaladesh on commercial fishing of Hilsa during the time of breeding which may help in their conservation. India also could learn from Bangladesh in limiting harvesting of Hilsa by implementing judiciously the minimal size of harvesting. There are similar regulations as issued by West Bengal Government too but the implementation and adherence to these by coastal fishermen is not worthy to be mentioned. In future people participation, consumers motivation to conserve this species, strict enforcement and vigilance at the fishing site and marketing places may help in conserving this valuable fish stock (IANS, 2012).

The important fishing centers of West Bengal are Shankarpur in Midnapur district, Freserganj in South 24 Parganas, Barge Jetty at Namkhau, Digha, Diamond harbor etc.

## 5.12 COMPARATIVE DIFFERENCE BETWEEN THE FISH PRODUCTIVITY OF WEST COAST AND EAST COAST OF INDIA

There is the marked difference between the west coast and east coast of India as regards to the fish production. Based on the statistics of year wise fish landing on an average the West Coast shares about $3/4^{th}$ while the east coast contributes about $1/4^{th}$ of total marine fish landing from India. Apparently the west coast shares about 56 per cent and the east coast shares about 44 per cent of the total harvest of marine fish in the country. The major share into the landing of west coast is realized from premium quality of pelagic fin fishes and shrimps from the demersal commodities.

### Reasons for the Better Fish Productivity of West Coast than East Coast of India

1. The west coast bordered by the Arabian Sea is blessed with stable oceanographic parameters than the east coast. The efficient physicochemical conditions which are relatively stable and uniform (without much fluctuations) are responsible for creating effective current system and improving the upwelling and mixing processes. The process of upwelling results in bringing of important nutrients to surface waters form deeper waters for the flourished growth of plankton which happens to be the main food for pelagic fishes.

   In contrary, the physicochemical conditions, in Bay of Bengal bordering east coast of India are rough. The east coast is more prone from disturbances out of cyclonic conditions owing to creation of low pressure and El Nino effect. The occurrence of cyclone routinely along the east coast not only damages the coastal installations, fishing villages, boats and appliances but also hamper the biological productivity of this maritime region. There is also net reduction in number of fishing days since fishing is abandoned during the rough and hostile weather conditions.

2. The occurrence of south west monsoon along the west coast is strong and most accurately timed, which create conducive conditions for most of the pelagic fish to spawn with high intensity.

It is therefore that the recruitment of new stock of pelagic fish in high numbers is guaranteed every year to increase their production along the west coast.

The lower half of east coast receives the rainfall mainly in winter through north east monsoon. This monsoon is of low intensity since it gets developed due to dry continental winds drawn towards Bay of Bengal and therefore does not carry moisture laden clouds. This monsoon does not help to induce spawning among pelagic fishes.

3. The average salinity value of the water from Arabian Sea bordering the west coast is more. Therefore marine fish fauna derives the advantage of enhanced growth in such hyper saline conditions of water.

   The salinity of water along the east coast is on lower side due to draining of more rivers, fresh water lagoons and streams into the Bay of Bengal. It is therefore along the east coast the conditions help more for estuarine fisheries than the marine fisheries.

4. Mud banks which make their appearance in shallower coastal water during the post monsoon months along the west coast mainly the coastal areas of Kerala, Karnataka, Goa and Maharashtra draw large numbers of early fish spawners, juvenile shrimps which attains faster growth in nutrient rich hypo saline water. The mud banks proves to be the excellent nursery ground for newly spawned marine pelagic fin fishes and juvenile shrimps. The occurrences of mud banks are rare along the east coast.

5. The fishing ground of west coast is broader and extensive than the east coast due to wider area of continental shelf. It is therefore the continental water of west coast of India is one of the richest fishing grounds in the world.

6. The existence of fishing amenities, like mechanization of fishing crafts, on shore facilities like provision of fishing harbors, jetty for imparting porting facilities for fishing vessels, chartering facilities for fish harvest like means of transport, cold storage and post harvest processing avenues are much strongly established at the fishing centers of west coast than the east coast.

In short the fishing related activities including the marketing and trade are efficiently organized at most of the fishing centers along west coast, in contrary the fishing is still basically at the artisanal level with most of the landing centers along the east coast lacking some basic amenities of fishing.

# Chapter 6
# PROMINENT MARINE FISHERIES OF INDIA

## 6.1 INDIAN MACKERAL

### Scientific Classification

| | | |
|---|---|---|
| *Class* | : | Teleostomi |
| *Sub-Class* | : | Actinopterygii |
| *Order* | : | Perciformes |
| *Family* | : | Scombridae |
| *Genus* | : | Rastrelliger |
| *Species* | : | 1. *R. kanagurta* |
| | | 2. *R. brachysoma* |
| | | 3. *R. Faughmi* |

### STATUS

The past statistics indicates that the mackerel contributes about 2 – 20 per cent with average of 6 per cent to all Indian marine fish landing; however the average contribution increased to over 13 per cent between the years of 1990 – 2005. Recent trend suggest that it shares about 7.8 per cent to the annual marine fish landing of India. The mackcrel is commercially very important pelagic fish resource. It has high local and marginally uprising export demand especially when the production of herring sustain loss in production from the European waters.

## DISTRIBUTION

Internationally the fish is widely distributed between 30° north to 30° south and longitudinally between 30° east to 160° west. Mainly it is the fishery of South-East Asian countries up to North and West of Australia, spreading from Persian Gulf, Red Sea, Pakistan, India, Sri Lanka, Myanmar, Thailand, Indonesian Islands, Malaysia, Singapore, China, Taiwan, Philippines, Papua New Guinea, Solomon Island and North East of Australia. In India, the fishery of Mackerel predominates along west coast than the east coast, about 77 per cent of the annual catch of fish comes from west coast and about 23 per cent comes from east coast. The distribution in west coast is spread from Quilone in Kerala up to Ratnagiri in Maharashtra. Highest concentration of fish occurs along South West coast of India.

## DIAGNOSTIC FEATURES

The body is slightly deep and the head of the fish is longer than the body. The golden thin dark longitudinal bands on the upper part of the body of fish are clearly visible on fresh specimens. These fishes also have a black spot near the lower margin of the pectoral fin. Dorsal fins of fish are yellowish with black tips, the caudal and pectoral fins are yellowish and the remaining fins are grayish. The extreme ramification of gill rackers acts like sieve as a filtering device suggests that the Indian mackerel is plankton feeder.

## FOOD AND FEEDING

The fish is predominantly the phytoplankton feeder and abundantly distributed in the nutrient rich water of continental self area where plankton distribution is abundant. The important food items of fish include diatoms (Biddulphia, Astreonella, Coscinodiscus, Chaetoceros, Fragilleria); dinoflagellates (Ceratium, Dinophysis) and zooplankton (Copepods like Acartia, Centropages, Eucalanus, Cladocera, Mysids; Decapod crustaceans like Lucifer and prawn larvae; Polycheata, Molluscan larva etc.).

## GROWTH, DEVELOPMENT AND SPAWNING

The fish attains length of 10 cm, 18 cm and 20–30 cm in I$^{st}$, II$^{nd}$ and III$^{rd}$ year of age respectively. Based on habitat generally two strains of mackerel are recognized in India *i.e.* West coast and East coast strains. The first maturity for the west coast strain is attained at 19 – 20 cm length when the fish is in late III$^{rd}$ or IV$^{th}$ year of age while the east coast strain it is attained between 20 cm - 25 cm length when fish is in its IV$^{th}$ year of age.

**Table 6.1.1: Spawning and Spawning Periodicity of Mackerel**

| *Phase of Spawning* | *West Coast Strain* | *East Coast Strain* |
|---|---|---|
| Commencement of spawning | February to March | Early September |
| Intensive spawning period | June to August | October to January |
| Termination of spawning | September to October | June onwards |

The spawning is commenced for the west coast strain from February to March with the intensive spawning period during June to August and it terminates anytime between September and October months. In the east coast strain the spawning begins in early September, the intensive spawning period spans from October to January and the termination of spawning occurs from June onwards. The spawning periodicity suggests that the monsoon conditions are necessary for breeding and spawning of fish. It can be observed that for the west coast strain the intensive spawning period of the fish coincides with the South-West monsoon during the months of June to August while for the east coast strain the intensive spawning period occurs during the North–East monsoon between September and October months. Further when there is no spawning activity along the west coast it happens to be the intensive spawning period for the east coast or Andaman strain, similarly when the spawning terminate for mackerel along the east coast the timing coincides with intensive spawning season for the west coast strain. It is therefore the rational fishing time for the mackerel is from October onwards for the west coast strain and the June onwards for the east coast strain so that the most part of the harvest would include only the adult fishes which have already undergone the activity of the spawning and the next batch of generation of juvenile mackerel is recruited and sustained for the growth and production for the future.

## MIGRATION AND SHOALING BEHAVIOUR

Mackerel is a shoaling migratory fish showing typical migratory pattern along south west coast of India. The migratory trend and production details of fish stocks are studied by performing tagging experiments in relation to the fishing season. The shoaling fish moving with speed of 8 to 10 miles per hour in the surface water of continental shelf and the shoal can be spotted as dark brown patch with ripples of waves at surface in day time. In night it produces light when fish group passes through planktonic ostracads and amphipods.

**Table 6.1.2: Migratory pattern and Fishing Season along the South West Coast of India.**

| *Zone* | *Nature of Concentration of Fish* | *Fishing Season* |
|---|---|---|
| Southernmost zone from Cape Camorin to Ponnani and Quilone | Highest concentration in August and ceases after February | August to February |
| Ponnani to Mangalore | High concentration in September and catch reduces in April | September to April |
| Mangalore to Ratnagiri | High concentration in October and catch declines in March | October to March |

The typical migratory pattern of mackerel in relation to different fishing season at the different places along the west coast is divided into three zones. The fishing of mackerel starts in the first zone the southernmost area from Cape Camorin to Ponnani and Quilone with high concentration of mackerel from August and fishing ends in February. The stock of the fish which escape the harvest from the first zone, starts arriving in second zone from Ponnani to Mangalore, the fishing season in this second zone extends from September to April. Likewise the final lot of mackerel shoal arrives in the third zone from Mangalore to Ratnagiri and the fishing season in this third zone lasts from October to March. This fixed pattern of the movement of mackerel shoal indicates that the migration and fishing season initiates first from Kerela, extending northwards and ending at Ratnagiri. The commercial fishery of mackerel is non-existent north of Ratnagiri. The evidence of the migratory pattern of mackerel shoal along the west coast over the years can further be proved by having the maximum and minimum catchment of mackerel from the second and third zone respectively.

## CAUSE OF MIGRATION

It was mooted earlier that the fixed pattern of Mackerel migration along the west coast was possibly due to availability of choicest plankton material as food; however this suggestion lacks conclusive evidence since various biological studies have indicated that the plankton biomass along the west coast of India is hardly varying. It has been found that the mackerel migrates in large shoal in inshore water of continental shelf all around the west coast at regular time specificity with the occurrence of north easterly and easterly winds. This striking discovery also revealed that during such condition the salinity and temperature values of the sea water are below than normal probably giving the mackerel shoal, a needed stimulation to perform migration into the inshore waters. Occurrence of easterly winds towards the shore is a regular phenomenon all along the south west coast of India. Thus it can be suggested that the hydro biological conditions are the chief cause for migration of mackerel in a fixed pattern along the south west coast of India.

## CRAFTS AND GEARS USED FOR FISHING

The fishing of mackerel is traditionally held from the coastal inshore waters of continental shelf by using country made traditional crafts such as Catamaran, Plank built boats, Outrigger boats using various traditionally known fishing gears and devices like Cast nets, Boat Seine, Shore seine, Gill nets, Hook and Lines etc. However in the recent times the commercial fishery of mackerel is accomplished by the employment of mechanized Purse seine operation especially from the state of Karnataka and Goa.

**Table 6.1.3: Craft and Gear Employed for the Fishing of Mackerel**

| *Sl.No.* | *Craft* | *Gears* |
|---|---|---|
| 1 | Outrigger boat | Cast net, boat seine |
| 2 | Dugout canoe | Gill net |
| 3 | Catamaran | Shore seine |
| 4 | Plank-built boat | Hooks and line |
| 5 | Mechanised craft | Purse seine at 50 metre, Nylon drift, gill netting at surface with current. |

However the most important fishing device for the capture of mackerel is Rampani, a kind of a shore seine gear which is best suited for fishing of mackerel from the continental waters up to 30 metres where due to shallowness and rough bottom topography mechanized fishing cannot be held, similarly the other traditional gears cannot be used on account of having smaller size and cannot bring the commercial landing of fish catch in large number. Rampani is a large replica of Mahajal but comes under the category of shore seine gear because this very large gear is operated manually from sea shore. This gear has proved to be the excellent catching device when large shoal of mackerel is sighted in inshore or coastal waters. Therefore in Indian conditions Rampani is the most important gear for commercial fishing of mackerel from inshore waters.

## ANNUAL CATCH TREND

The fish catch statistics of last three to five decades suggests that earlier the highest catch of mackerel was recorded in 1971 with the production of 2,04,575 tonnes sharing about 17.6 per cent to total marine fish landing from the country, this highest production was emulated later in 1989 with production of 2,09,000 tonnes and all time high production of 2,09,733 tonnes in 1999. The lowest catch was recorded in 1968 with the production of just about 21,703 tonnes sharing only 2.3 per cent to the total marine landing. Years of 1970, 1971, 1972 and 1974 were extremely productive years when mackerel yielded more than 1 lakh tonnes of fish, while the years 1962, 1964, 1966, 1967 and 1968 were extremely poor when mackerel production was just 2.35 per cent.

**Table 6.1.4: Year-wise Mackerel Landing**

| *Year* | *Production (tonnes)* | *Year* | *Production (tonnes)* |
|---|---|---|---|
| **1971** | 204575 | **1999** | 209733 |
| **1989** | 209000 | **2000** | 134556 |
| **1990** | 150256 | **2001** | 90134 |
| **1991** | 102749 | **2002** | 49447 |
| **1992** | 87256 | **2003** | 47920 |
| **1993** | 155778 | **2004** | 57573 |
| **1994** | 201554 | **2005** | 125000 |
| **1995** | 169246 | **2006** | 108952 |
| **1996** | 190785 | **2007** | 128613 |
| **1997** | 127962 | **2008** | 114269 |
| **1998** | 108175 | **2009** | 120822 |

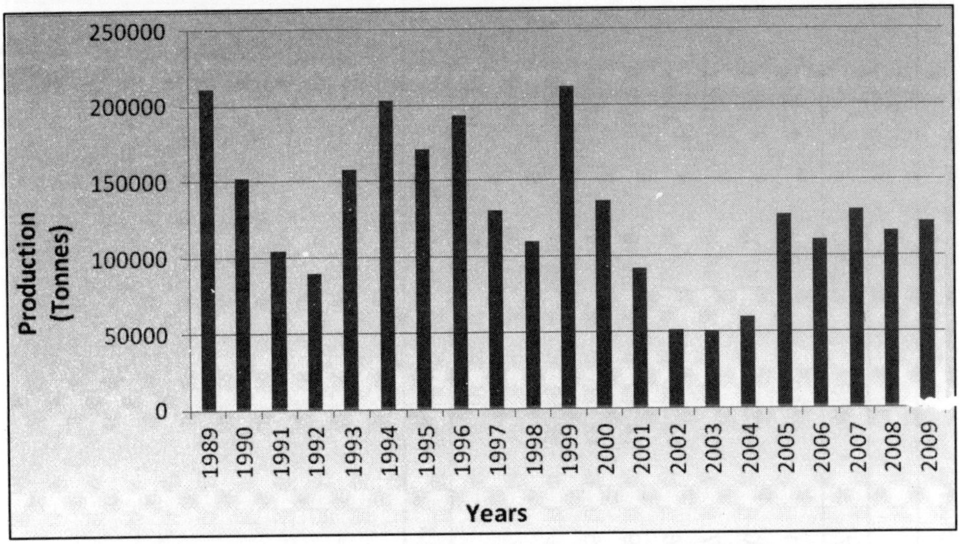


**Figure 6.1.1: Year-wise Landing of Indian Mackerel (1989-2009)**

Further the annual landing records suggest that in the years 1980 to 1985 the fish production was poor. The years of 1986 to 1991 were extremely productive. With the exception of 1992 the high trend of mackerel production continued from 1993 to 2001. The years of 2002, 2003 and 2004 were poor productive years. The production was fairly good from 2005 to 2009. This particular trend of fish production of mackerel suggests that the fishery follows fluctuating trend of cyclical pattern of poor and good productive years. This means that that the years of low production is subsequently followed by extremely productive years for mackerel production. The productive years of mackerel production invariably yielded over one lakh tonnes of fish.

## STATE WISE CATCH TRENDS

In earlier times the major production of mackerel was obtained from the West Coast of India with the share of 38 per cent from Karnataka, 34 per cent from Kerela together contributed about 72 per cent of the total mackerel landing from the country, from the west coast the production from the states of Goa and Maharashtra was also fairly high and the state of Tamil Nadu was leading producer of mackerel from the east coast with the share of 5.7 per cent.

**Table 6.1.5: State-wise Production of Mackerel**

| Years / States | Production (tonnes) | | | | | | | Avarage (2006-2009) |
|---|---|---|---|---|---|---|---|---|
| | 2003 | 2004 | 2005 | 2006 | 2007 | 2008 | 2009 | |
| **Kerala** | – | – | – | 46884 | 45601 | 45459 | 45335 | **45820** |
| **Maharashtra** | 14118 | 21041 | 17877 | 11591 | 29530 | 12667 | 14503 | **17073** |
| **Tamil Nadu** | – | – | – | 21013 | 12527 | 11193 | 11641 | **14093** |
| **Andhra** | 1180 | 8627 | 6263 | 11912 | 10528 | 10859 | 15115 | **12103** |
| **West Bengal** | 4885 | 8815 | 8551 | 7470 | 11429 | 14262 | 9949 | **10777** |
| **Karnataka** | 7610 | 8931 | 8921 | 4541 | 15245 | 13120 | — | **8226** |
| **Orissa** | 3092 | 3889 | 4567 | 5241 | 3335 | 6319 | 8417 | **5828** |
| **Goa** | 16589 | 5779 | 12006 | 0 | 0 | 0 | 15169 | **3792** |
| **Daman and Diu** | 446 | 491 | 429 | 300 | 418 | 390 | 392 | **375** |
| **Total Catch** | **47920** | **57573** | **58614** | **108952** | **128613** | **114269** | **120522** | |

There has been a major shift in state wise production of mackerel from India, as can be seen from Table 6.1.5 for the years between 2006 and 2009. In recent times Kerala ranks first with the average production of 45,820 tonnes followed by Maharashtra with the average production of 17,073 tonnes. There has been substantial reduction in the production of the state of Karnataka which was ranking first in earlier years, with the average production of just 8,226 tonnes it ranks at sixth place next to Tamil Nadu, Andhra Pradesh and West Bengal which are ranked at third, fourth and fifth places with the average production of 14,093; 12,103 and 10,777 tonnes respectively between 2006 to 2009. The recent production figures also reveals that unlike the production of previous years there has been tremendous gain into the landing of Indian mackerel from the east coast with high share in production from the states of Tamil Nadu, Andhra Predesh, West Bengal and Orissa.

## RECOMMENDATION FOR INDIAN MACKEREL FISHERY

The harvest pattern of Indian Mackerel as evident from the production from the last 3 decades suggests that the production trend is highly fluctuated. It means that the fishery performs good production for few years to be alternately followed by poor production. As evident from percentage contribution of Indian mackerel to all Indian marine fish landing, from 2002 to 2007 with average 6 per cent, suggest that the fishery has followed unsteady trend over the years. It is therefore highly essential to follow certain guidelines to ensure sustainably high production level. The placement of Indian mackerel fishery over unit Ryder Scale indicates that potential resource of 220 as against the estimated yield of 190 units clearly indicate that the fishery can be under threat in near future owing to the constantly increasing fishing efforts especially from the coastal waters. The fishery in future may concern with the threat of over exploitation. The Indian mackerel fishery at present has yet not reached to the danger mark of over exploitation only because of the effort of fishing for harvest is centered around coastal water mainly with eco-friendly device of gear called Rampani. The employment of mechanized fishing method like purse seining from open water may be highly devastating. This is because the purse seine captures the fish in bulk, if the method of fishing follows at indiscriminate level only few fish would escape the harvest and further recruitment of mackerel stock will be greatly declined in the absence of natural brooders.

The age and growth studies and the age at the first maturity which is quite prolonged indicate that the maturity age of fish is over 3 years and that once the fishery comes to danger level; it would take much longer time to recover. It has been seen that sometimes the mackerel does not follow the set pattern of breeding or spawning, instead in some years mackerel breeds throughout the year and liberates the egg in batches; however the prolonged spawning periodicity and liberation of eggs in batches inflict adverse effect on success of fishery because the breeding fish does not attain good growth and recruitment of stock of mackerel in large number provides the danger of also harvesting of small juvenile stock. Similarly if the fisherman wait for capturing only the post spawners (mature adult fish), much of the valuable time of fishing is lost. Therefore the management measures to be undertaken for obtaining the sustainable high production of mackerel, which are as follows:

- ☆ Avoid devastating fishing method like purse seining and nylon drift gill netting.
- ☆ Encouragement must be given for the use of eco-friendly Rampani gear as it is happening from age old times.
- ☆ Improvement of the recruitment of young mackerel stock is necessary through successful spawning strategy. Therefore no juvenile stock of mackerel is to be harvested.
- ☆ The age of capture must be prolonged to ensure that each fish finds the chance to undertake the breeding process.
- ☆ When sorting goes on immediately after hauling the gear the live young mackerel should be thrown back immediately in water ensuring discard of young juvenile stock from harvest.

## 6.2 INDIAN OIL SARDINE

### Scientific Classification

| | | |
|---|---|---|
| *Class* | : | Teleostomi |
| *Sub-class* | : | Actinopterygii |
| *Order* | : | Clupeiformes |
| *Family* | : | Clupeidae |
| *Genus* | : | Sardinella |
| *Species* | : | *Sardinella longiceps* |

## STATUS

The Indian oil sardine is neretic, pelagic, clupeid fish. This is the most important clupeid resource from India. A single species, *Sardinella longiceps* commercially contributes about 15 to 20 per cent to all India marine fish landing. The fishery is characterized by its remarkable and wide fluctuation both seasonal and annual, on the basis of catch statistics. The fluctuation in the yield have been recorded as one of the fishery which is worst affected by over exploitation.

## DISTRIBUTION

Indian oil sardine is internationally distributed mainly in tropical areas from Gulf of Oman, along the Makharan coast of Pakistan, all along the west coast of India and around Sri Lanka. It is interesting to note that very large shoals of *Sardinella longiceps* occur across Somali coast.

Nationally the fish is generally restricted to the west coast of India but is also found along the east coast, particularly in Andhra Pradesh in the inshore water up to narrow coastal belt of 3 to 20 km. The fish has commercial importance because of its food value and industrial use.

## DIAGNOSTIC FEATURES

The body of Indian oil sardine is elongated; belly is slightly rounded and has 8 rays on their pelvic fin. The fish have very large number of gill rackers suggesting the fish to be a plankton feeder. It contains a faint golden spot behind the gill opening, a faint golden mid lateral line and a black spot on the hind border of the gill cover.

## FOOD AND FEEDING

This fish feeds predominantly on phytoplankton and zooplankton. Its food is mainly composed of diatoms like *Fragellaria oceanica*. Besides some copepods and dianoflagellates, the gut content analysis of fish contains larvae of prawn, fish eggs, and blue green algae along with detritus. Juvenile oil sardine are mainly carnivorous while adults feed mostly on phytoplankton. *Fragellaria oceanica* is the choicest food item of fish. During unfavourable conditions when planktonic bloom reduces in surface water due to lack of nutrient, the fish descends down or migrates to deeper water and feeds on detritus matter and zooplankton.

## GROWTH DEVELOPMENT AND REPRODUCTIVE BEHAVIOR

*Sardinella longiceps* attains sexual maturity at the length of 150 mm to 160 mm and at around one year of age. The life span of this fish is approximately 2.5 years. Sexes are separate as distinguished by muscular papilla as copulatory organ in males and membranous genital opening in the females. Spawning season along west coast extends from June to October with maximum activity during June to August and along east coast it extends from December to February. According to Nayar (1959), the period of intense activity in August to September depends on early or late monsoon. The fish is believed to spawn once in a lifetime and is a prolific breeder. It spawns in night hours and fecundity is around 38,000 to 80,000 eggs per fish per season depending on size, age and condition of the fish.

## MIGRATION AND SHOALING BEHAVIOUR

The shoaling and migratory pattern of the fish has been studied in detail by Balan (1962), the shoaling behavior of fish is as follows:

### Surface Shoals

a) **Flipping:** More common in morning hours characterized by jerky movement and splashy noise.

b) **Pattering:** More common in bright day. Mixed sound in succession but without the jerking movement.

c) **Leaping:** More common in bright day, the shoal is recognized by leaping of complete group of fish outside the water in succession for some time.

d) **Rippling:** Common during night time making small ripples of waves on surface water.

e) **Coloured Shoal:** Recognized by bluish and pinkish discoloration in surface water during daytime.

f) **Luminescent Shoal:** During night time, recognized by emission of light produced.

### Bottom Shoals

a) **Bubbling:** Releasing series of bubbles which come out from below and bursting at surface in the form of froth when shoal feeds on zooplankton and muddy detritus at the bottom.

b) **Odoriferous Shoal:** Secretes mucous and emits strong fishy odour, if remain submerged in high concentration of shoals.

Leaping and luminescent shoals are common for identification of Indian oil sardine. They move in shoals with large number of fishes of similar size and age groups moving at almost the same speed *i.e.* 5 km per hour. The shoal of oil sardine is 2 to 25 meter in length and 1 to 25 meter in breadth.

## CRAFTS AND GEARS USED FOR FISHING

The fishing of Indian oil sardine is mostly traditionally held with intense fishing activity along the Kerala coast. The traditional crafts are maneuvered in the inshore waters any where up to three to five kilometers from shore and operate many boat seines, gill nets, cast net etc.

Different country made traditional crafts used for fishing of Indian oil sardine is as follows.

- ☆ **Odum:** Odum is 9 to 12 meter fishing craft in length having displacement capacity of 3 to 5 tonnes.
- ☆ **Vanchi:** It is a smaller craft with 8 to 9 meter length displacement capacity of 1 to 2 tonnes.
- ☆ **Outrigger boats**: Plank built Outriggers boats are used mainly along the Karnataka coast.

The important gears used for the fishing of Indian oil sardine are as follows.

- ☆ **Boat Seine:** Some important boat seine gear used for the fishing of Indian oil sardine are Karavala, Peddavala, Nethalvala, Nonavala, Odamvala, Thanguvala, Kollivala, Pattenkollivala, Paithuvala, Arakollivala etc. These gears are generally used from Odum boat.
- ☆ **Gill Net:** The gill nets used are Mathichalavala/Chalavalai
- ☆ **Cast net:** The important cast net used is Veechuvala. It is used from Vanchi.
- ☆ **Bag net:** Edovalai is the bag net used for fishing of Indian oil sardine.

In recent times however the commercial fishing of Indian oil sardine is performed from mechanized crafts operating Purse seine gear. In Tamil Nadu paired trawlers are operated at 12 to 60 meters of depth in Rameshwaram area while the Ring seines are operated in Palk Bay.

## FISHING SEASON AND CATCH TREND

Fishing starts soon after monsoon from June and continues up to March. The fish is highly produced throughout the Kerala except March to May. In Karnataka-Goa belt the season starts during September-October with peak from October-January. In south east coast it is from April to December.

## ANNUAL CATCH TREND

During last 50 years all India production of oil sardine range from 14,000 tonnes in 1952 to all time high of 3.77 lakh tone in 2003 contributing 0.1 per cent to 31.9 per cent respectively to total marine fish landing of India. This indicates aptly the fluctuating trend in the production of fish over the years.

**Table 6.2.1: Annual Catch Trend of Indian Oil Sardine**

| *Year* | *Production (tonnes)* | *Year* | *Production (tonnes)* |
|---|---|---|---|
| **2003** | 377158 | **2004** | 273272 |
| **2005** | 262652 | **2006** | 224819 |
| **2007** | 222188 | **2008** | 244423 |
| **2009** | 221502 | | |

The production was quite low during 1950 to 1956 with an average of 27,000 tonnes. During 1975 to 1979 realized the handsome landing of the fish with strong support from traditional and artisanal sectors. The oil sardine catch was increased from 78,000 tonnes in 1986 to 2,79,000 tonnes in 1989 but declined to 47,000 tonnes in 1994. The resuscitation of Indian oil sardine stock after an ever low landing in 1994, manifested from heavy recruitment that followed which culminated in a highest production of 3.77 lakh tonnes in 2003.

The average annual landing from 1999 to 2003 along the west coast was 1,47,989 tonnes (73 per cent) and while it was 53,984 tonnes (27 per cent) from east coast. The production from 2004 to 2009 have resulted

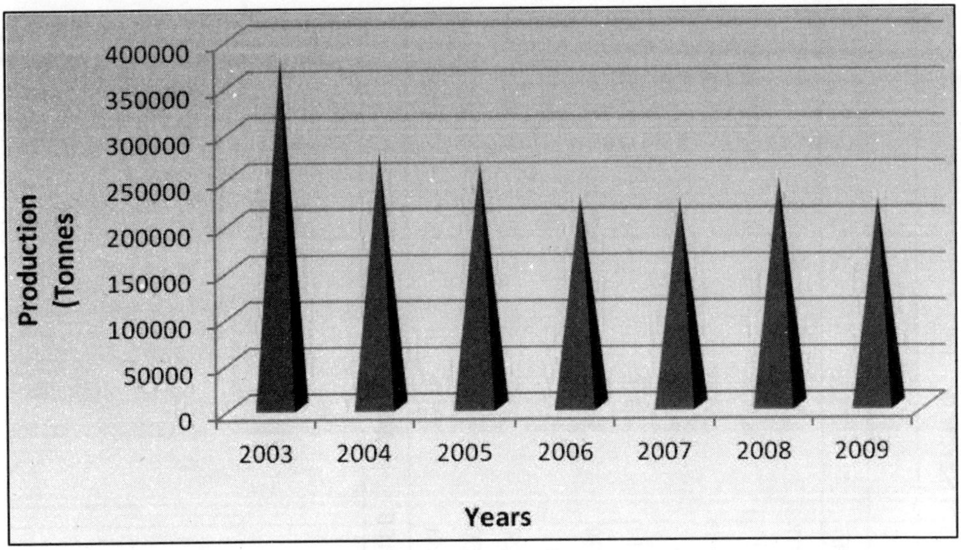


**Figure 6.2.1: Year-wise Production of Indian Oil Sardine (2003-2009)**

into fairly handsome landing yielding over 2 lakh tonnes each year with the average production of 2,41,476 tonnes in between these years.

### Inverse Relationship between Indian Oil Sardine and Indian Mackerel

According to Chidambaran and Nayer (1959) there exist a strong inverse relationship in production between Indian mackerel and Indian oil sardine in the country possibly because of high competition between these two species for space, food and breeding.

## STATEWISE CATCH TREND

Kerala is the highest contributing state for the production of Indian oil sardine with the average production of 1,57,264 tonnes. The Indian oil sardine in the state of Kerala is regarded as producer of the family because the economic condition of the fisherman from the state largely depends on the success of the fishery of Indian oil sardine. The state of Karnataka ranks second, followed by the state of Maharashtra at the third place. The production figures also suggest that the share of west coast is substantially more to the production of Indian oil sardine than the east coast of India. Among the east coast the states of Andhra Pradesh, Orissa and West Bengal are the leading producers.

**Table 6.2.2: State-wise Production of Indian Oil Sardine**

| Years | Production (tonnes) | | | | | | | Avarage (2006-2009) |
|---|---|---|---|---|---|---|---|---|
| States | 2003 | 2004 | 2005 | 2006 | 2007 | 2008 | 2009 | |
| | 2003 | 2004 | 2005 | 2006 | 2007 | 2008 | 2009 | |
| **Kerala** | 175508 | 171847 | 149375 | 162376 | 156120 | 156314 | 154247 | **157264** |
| **Karnataka** | 31652 | 24119 | 30215 | 45637 | 38291 | 41728 | – | **31414** |
| **Maharashtra** | 27902 | 22638 | 28014 | 0 | 0 | 24236 | 20818 | **11264** |
| **Andhra Pradesh** | 1015 | 12976 | 11911 | 13488 | 7514 | 7910 | 9442 | **9588** |
| **Orissa** | 9164 | 3847 | 4910 | 5322 | 5939 | 6774 | 6707 | **6185** |
| **Goa** | 18195 | 29397 | 28246 | 0 | 0 | 0 | 21946 | **5486** |
| **West Bengal** | 5996 | 6462 | 8452 | 8505 | 8824 | 743 | 1228 | **4825** |
| **Tamil Nadu** | 0 | 0 | 0 | 1541 | 3756 | 4982 | 5310 | **3897** |
| **Ponddicherry** | 1726 | 1986 | 1529 | 1777 | 1744 | 1736 | 1804 | **1765** |
| **Total Catch** | **377158** | **273272** | **262652** | **224819** | **222188** | **244423** | **221502** | |

## FACTORS AFFECTING THE FISHERY OF INDIAN OIL SARDINE

1. Blooms of *Fragellaria oceanica, Pleurosigma* due to the upwelling of coastal waters with the right time onset of South West Monsoon.
2. Minimum average rainfall of 30 mm daily for successful spawning.
3. Water temperature should not exceed 27° to 28° C for shoaling which happen to be the optimum temperature and the optimum salinity is 22.8 – 33.5 ppt.
4. Variation in the pattern of coastal currents and drift. It is quite possible that the pelagic fishery of Indian west coast is related to these coastal drift.

## UTILIZATION OF CATCH

1. Fresh consumption.
2. Canning and freezing.
3. Sun dried or salt cured oil sardine are exported to Sri Lanka.
4. Oil extraction from body muscle and is used in painting boats, dressing of leather and tampering of metals.
5. As fertilizer, Press cake or guano fish meal which is a rich source of calcium and phosphorus.

## 6.3 LESSER SARDINES

### Scientific Classification

| | | |
|---|---|---|
| *Class* | : | Teleostomi |
| *Sub-class* | : | Actinopterygii |
| *Order* | : | Clupeiformes |
| *Family* | : | Clupeidae |
| *Genus* | : | *Sardinella* |
| *Species* | : | 1. *Sardinella fimbriata* |
| | | 2. *S. gibbesa* |
| | | 3. *S. albella* |
| | | 4. *S. dayi* |

5. *S. melanura*
6. *S. sirm*
7. *S. clupeoides*
8. *S. jonesi*
9. *S. sindensis*

## STATUS

This group comprise of sardines other than *Sardinella longiceps*. In the Indian water the group is constituted by *Sardinella fimbriata, S. gibbesa, S. albella, S. dayi, S. melanura, S. sirm, S. clupeoides, S. jonesi* and *S. sindensis*. The group contributes about 5-8 per cent of share to the total marine fish landing from the country.

## DISTRIBUTION

They are distributed throughout the Indian coasts but contrary to Indian Oil Sardine (*Sardinella longiceps*), they occur in high numbers in the east coast with high concentration along the south-east cost of India, they also occur in substantial quantity in south-west coast of India.

## FOOD AND FEEDING

Lesser sardines mainly feed on phytoplankton, zooplankton, copepods and crustaceans which include mainly lucifer, larvae of prawns, mysis, acetes, fish larvae, crabs larvae and molluscan larvae.

## GROWTH DEVELOPMENT AND REPRODUCTIVE BEHAVIOR

Most of them are small sized with the exception of *S. jonesi, S. sirm, S. clupeoides*. The smaller one attains the sexual maturity by first year of its age but the larger ones belong to 1 to 2 year class of fishery.

## CRAFTS AND GEARS USED FOR FISHING

The fishery is mostly artisanal type. The commercial landing is obtained by the use of gill nets of small mesh sizes and shore seines along the south east coast. The plank built boats and canoes having the facility of out board engines operate boat seines and ring seines along the shallower waters of south-west coast for the capture of fish. The fish is also known to capture mechanically from deeper water by the employment of purse seine and pelagic trawling.

## ANNUAL CATCH TREND

**Table 6.3.1: Annual catch trend of Lesser Sardine.**

| *Year* | *Production (in thousand tonnes)* | *Year* | *Production (in thousand tonnes)* |
|---|---|---|---|
| **2006** | 192263 | **2007** | 183967 |
| **2008** | 156751 | **2009** | 118654 |

The production of lesser sardines fluctuated between low of 68,267 tonnes in 1986 and high of 1,28021 tonnes in 1995, during the 15 year period of 1986-2000. The east coast of India was major contributor with the average landing of 67,172 tonnes and share of 65 per cent while the west coast with the average landing of 35.449 tonnes contributed about 35 per cent of total production of lesser sardine in the country. The production of lesser sardines was all time highest in 2006, with fairly very rich average landing of 1,62908 tonnes between the years of 2006 to 2009.

## STATEWISE CATCH TREND

The state wise catch trend of Lesser Sardine shows that the Kerala is the leading producer of the fish with the average production of 70966 tonnes. Tamil Nadu is the second highest producer of Lesser Sardine with the production of 34966 tonnes followed by Goa with the average production of 24037 tonnes. In contrary to earlier reports the average share of the total lesser sardine landing from west coast was more than east coast during 2006–2009.

**Table 6.3.2: Statewise catch trend of Lesser Sardine**

| *States* | *Years/Production* | | | | *Avarage (2006-2009)* |
|---|---|---|---|---|---|
| | *2006* | *2007* | *2008* | *2009* | |
| **Kerala** | 74464 | 70115 | 70654 | 68633 | **70966** |
| **Tamil Nadu** | 43980 | 33357 | 30601 | 31925.37 | **34966** |
| **Goa** | 31282 | 28800 | 34517 | 1550 | **24037** |
| **Maharashtra** | 28233 | 37205 | 95 | 0 | **16383** |
| **Andhra Pradesh** | 7421 | 7488 | 8072 | 6915 | **7474** |
| **Andaman and Nicobar** | 2078 | 2289 | 3655 | 3635 | **2914** |
| **Orissa** | 2265 | 3086 | 2001 | 3269 | **2655** |
| **Pondicherry** | 1446 | 1604 | 2600 | 2707 | **2089** |
| **Karnataka** | 1092 | 0 | 4531 | 0 | **1406** |
| **Daman and Diu** | 2 | 23 | 25 | 20 | **17** |
| **Total Catch** | **192263** | **183967** | **156751** | **118654.4** | |

## UTILIZATION OF CATCH

Lesser sardines are great source of protein. At the places of landing it is consumed in fresh condition or ice stored and transported to the distant market of demand from the landing centers. They are also sundried, salted and sold as dry fish in distant markets of India. The dried and pulverized powder of sardines used for protein supplementation of feeds for poultry, cattle and shrimp.

## RECOMMENDATION

The potential of Lesser sardine in Indian waters is reckoned at about 2,80,000 tonnes while the maximum sustainable yield (MSY) is estimated around 40,000. The average annual production of Lesser sardine of 1,22,243 tonnes during 1996-2000 is well below MSY. Therefore there is further scope of increasing the production of lesser sardine from Indian waters.

# 6.4 TUNAS

### Scientific Classification

| | | |
|---|---|---|
| *Class* | : | Teleostomi |
| *Sub-class* | : | Actinopterygii |
| *Order* | : | Perciformes |
| *Family* | : | Scombridae |
| *Sub Family* | : | Thunninae |
| *Genus/Species* | : | *Auxis thazard* (Short corsellated frigate mackerel) |
| | | *A. Thynnoides* (Long corsellated frigate mackerel) |
| | | *Sarda orientalis* (Oriental Bonito) |
| | | *Gymnosarda unicolor* (Dogtooth tuna) |
| | | *Euthynnus affinis* (Little tunny) |
| | | *Euthynnus alletteratus* (Atlantic Little Tuna) |
| | | *Thunnus orientalis* (Oriental bluefin tuna) |

**Figure 1: INDIAN MACKERAL (*Rastrelliger kanagurta*)**

**Figure 2: INDIAN OIL SARDINE (*Sardinella longiceps*)**

**Figure 3: LESSER SARDINE (*Sardinella fimbriata*)**

**Figure 4: TUNA (*Thunnus orientalis*)**

**Figure 5: TUNA (*Auxis thazard*)**

**Figure 6: SEER FISH (*Scomberomorus commerson*)**

**Figure 7: POMFRET (*Pampus argentius*)**

**Figure 8: ANCHOVY (*Stolephorus indicus*)**

**Figure 9: ANCHOVY (*Coilia dussumieri*)**

**Figure 10: CARANGIDS (*Decapterus russeli*)**

**Figure 11: CARANGIDS (*Selar crumenophthalmus*)**

**Figure 12: BOMBAY DUCK (*Harpadon nehereus*)**

**Figure 13: RIBBON FISH (*Trachiurus lepturus*)**

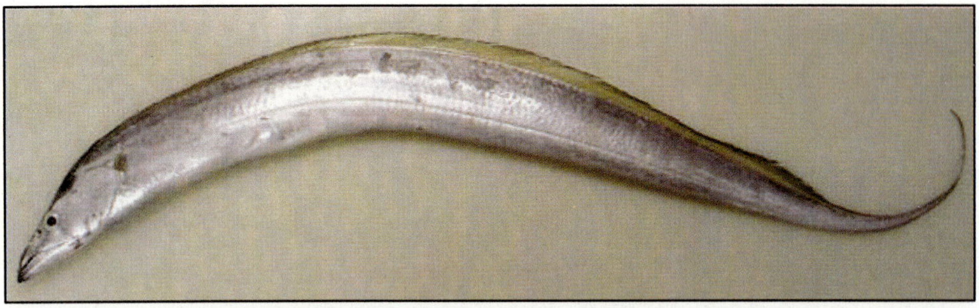

**Figure 14: RIBBON FISH (*Lepturacanthus savala*)**

**Figure 15: HILSA (*Hilsa ilisha*)**

**Figure 16: BARRACUDA (*Sphyraena barracuda*)**

Figure 17: BARRACUDA

Figure 18: SKATES (*Rhinobatus obtusus*)

Figure 19: GROUPER (*Epinephelus lanceolatus*)

**Figure 20: SNAPPERS**
**(*Lutjanus campechanus*)**

**Figure 21: SNAPPERS (*Lutjanus malbaricus*)**

**Figure 22: PERCHES (*Lethrinus. Sp.*)**

Figure 23: SCIAENIDS (*Johnius dussumieri*)

Figure 24: SCIAENIDS (*Protonibea diacanthus*)

Figure 25: SILVER BELLIES (*Gazza minuta*)

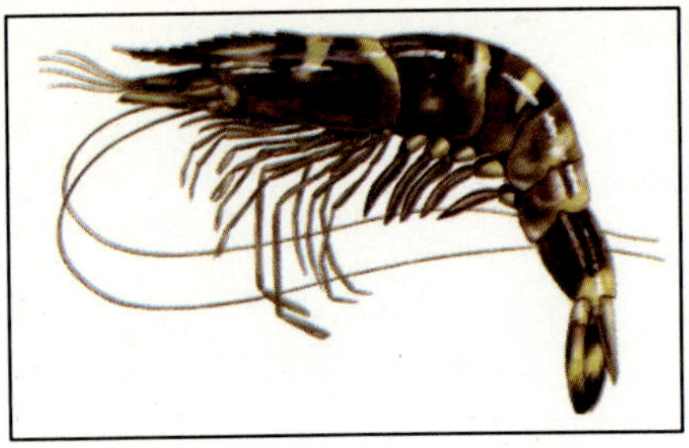

**Figure 26: GIANT TIGER SHRIMP (*Penaeus monodon*)**

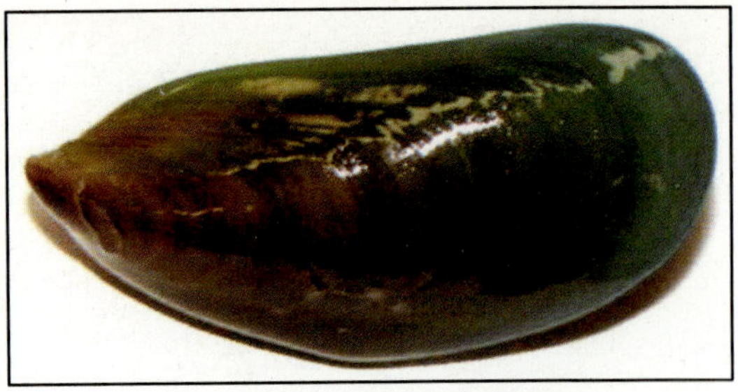

**Figure 27: GREEN MUSSEL (*Perna viridis*)**

**Figure 28: INDIAN WHITE SHRIMP (*Fenneropenaeus indicus*)**

**Figure 29: INDIAN SQUID (*Loligo duvauceli*)**

**Figure 30: YELLOW CLAM (*Meritrix meritrix*)**

# PROCESSED AND POPULAR FISH PRODUCTS

**Figure 31: Fried Pomfret**

**Figure 32: Frozen Pomfret**

**Figure 33: Roasted Pomfret**

**Figure 34: Smoked Carangids**

**Figure 35: Drying of Bombay duck on bamboo scaffolds**

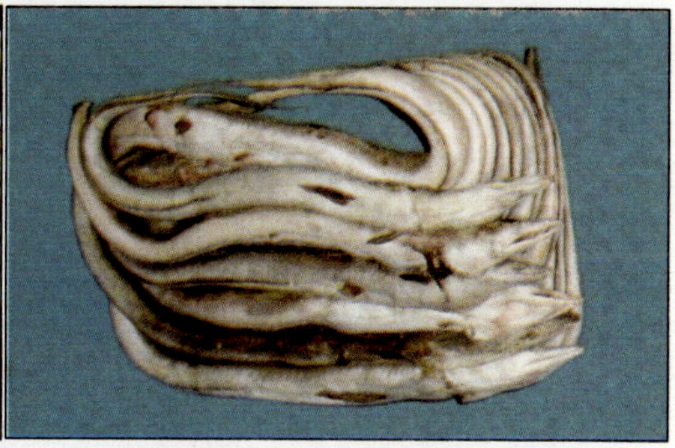

**Figure 36: Frozen Ribbon fish**

**Figure 37: Head-on Cooked Shrimp**

Figure 38: Frozen Shrimp

Figure 39: Frozen Spiny Lobster Tails

Figure 40: Frozen Cuttle Fish

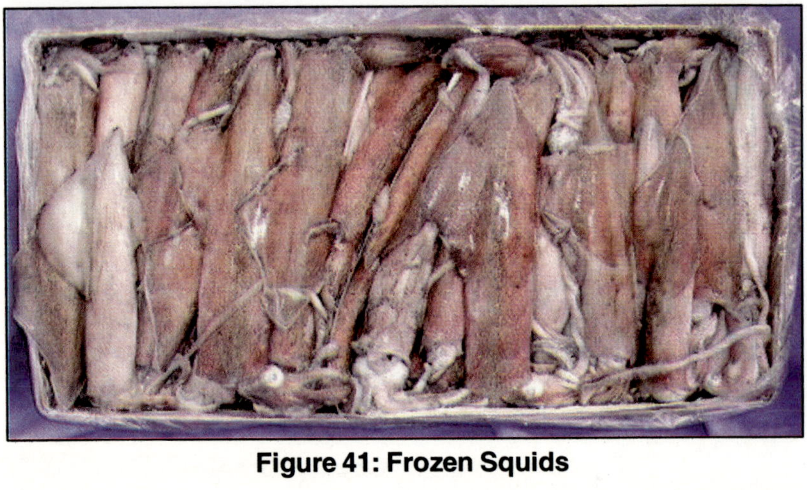

Figure 41: Frozen Squids

*Thunnus obesus* (Bigeye tuna)

*Thunnus alalunga* (Albacore tuna)

*Thunnus albacares* (Yellowfin tuna)

*Thunnus tonggol* (Northen bluefin tuna)

*Katsuwonus pelamis* (Skipjack tuna)

The term tuna derives from Latin word Thunnu. There are about fifty different species of tuna belongs to the family Scombridae existing in international waters. However there are about 12 species over listed which form the commercial fisheries of Tuna in India.

## INDIAN EEZ IN RELATION TO TUNA FIHERIES

As a part of National policy for the judicious exploitation of living resources within the E. E. Z. of India, greater emphasis has to be given for tuna fisheries both in artisanal sector and in high seas. Even though the tuna production of last two decades suggests the increase of augmentation of coastal indigenous tuna species, through live bait fishing and multiday gill netting, Tuna still remains one of the least exploited scombroid resource of Indian seas accounting for just about 3- 5 per cent.

Tunas are large sized extremely active and agile free to roam from coastal to high sea waters. Therefore their capture demands highly skillful fishing techniques. Another problem with Indian tuna fishery resource especially from high sea offshore waters is the effect of poaching by fishing fleets of other nations. The available information indicates that the tuna resource immediately after the adoption of EEZ by India in 1976 had been exploited by the long liners of Japan, Taiwan and the Republic of Korea. Between 1975 – 77 there had been major input of tuna from Japan and Taiwan where tuna does not exist in large numbers this evidently proves the gain in tuna landing by these countries, this was possible due to fishing from Indian and adjoining waters. The average long line catch suggests that during that time about 42 per cent of yellow fin tuna, 24 per cent of Big Eye Tuna and 19 per cent of Stripped Marlin were lifted form Indian waters. It is therefore felt that there is dire need to protect high potential of valuable tuna fish stock from Indian waters. The round the clock surveillance of maritime waters by naval coast guard in later years however has reduced the illegal fishing by foreign fishing fleets in our waters. The fish which does not know such barriers of international boundaries are free to roam around from coast to EEZ to International waters. It is thus highly essential that India should adopt the bold and advent strategy of fishing to take advantage of this valuable fishery resource. There is great need to evolve fishing strategy through employment of multiday gill netting, pole and line, live bait fishery in surface water of continental shelf beyond 50 m zone and long lining and trolling in offshore and international waters.

## DISTRIBUTION

Tuna is internationally distributed in tropical and sub tropical parts of world oceans because it is temperature specific in its distribution owing to the requirement of maintaining high body temperature to generate high speed. In the Indian Ocean they are dominant in Indian peninsula and Indo-pacific Archipelago. Tuna also occur in sub-tropical and semi-temperate oceans, especially in offshore mid Atlantic waters. There are certain species of tuna like Skipjack tuna, Yellow fin tuna and Albacore tuna are most widely distributed in international waters. Thus Skipjack tuna and Yellow fin tuna are regarded as international fish species and find prominent places in the List of Top Ten Production of Principle Fish Species by Capture.

In India even though the fish is found to be distributed all along the west coast and east coast, it exhibits species specific distribution like oceanic skipjack tuna (*K. Pelamis)* is found to occur in high numbers in Lakshadweep waters. *Thunnes tonggol* occur in high concentration and outnumber other species throughout the Konkan coastal belt comprising of Maharashtra, Goa and Karnataka etc. *A. thazard, S. orientalis, E. affinis, T. albacares, T. alalunga* form the commercial fishery of Malabar or Kerala coast and Coromondal or Tamil Nadu coast.

## DIAGNOSTIC FEATURES

Tunas are large sized extremely active fish. The size range of small *E. affinis* is 10–78 cm, *A. thazard* 16–52 cms. Larger, T. *tonggol* 30–100 cms, *T. albacare* 50–150 cms and *K. pelamis* from 35–80 cms. Unlike other fish, which have white flesh, the muscle tissue of tuna is pink to red; the red coloration of tuna is due to high content of mayoglobin.

## FOOD AND FEEDING

Almost all the species of tuna are pelagic but are plankton feeder only during early juvenile stages. Adults are however highly voracious and carnivorous in their diet. The choicest food items for tuna include Anchovies, Flying fish and *Leognathus* species, larva and adult of shrimps, lobster and crabs etc.

## REPRODUCTIVE BEHAVIOR

Most of the tuna species which are large and fast growing collectively attain the first maturity at an average size of 400 mm. Tuna is prolific breeder, breeding throughout the year with high intensity of spawning in winter months from October to November. *E. affinis* spawns during pre monsoon months of April and May. Most breed in post monsoon months from September to October and for skipjack tuna the spawning peak is from January to April.

## CRAFTS AND GEARS USED FOR FISHING

The crafts and gears mainly employed for the fishing of tuna from coastal areas are generally the traditional types. Dugout canoe, Outrigger boats and Catamarans are some crafts whereas Gill nets, Boat seine, Hand lines, Cast net and traps are some gears used for fishing. Mechanized Pablo boats, Mechanized Launches are advanced fishing crafts used for fishing from offshore waters, operating the important gears for the fishing in offshore water are multi day Nylon drift gill nets, Purse seine, Multiple troll lines, and Tuna long lines.

## LIVE BAIT FISHERY OF TUNA

The live bait fishery for capture of Oceanic Skipjack is one of the most important commercial fishing methods employed specially in Minicoy Island of Lakshadweep. The tuna fishing boats are sturdily built and fishing is accomplished in early morning hours. The fisherman stand in alert position ready with fishing rod lines along the starboard side of the boat. The fishing boat has the provision of a fish hold where bait fishes are held in bulk in live condition. Upon going some distance and visualizing the opportunity for tuna shoal, the live baits are casted in water. The live baits which mostly comprise of anchovy, flying fishes and *Leognathus* species which are all shadow loving fishes. These fishes preferably occupy the area of shadow casted by the moving fishing vessel, instead of venturing freely away from the vessel. The tuna as being highly carnivorous are therefore lured towards the vessel to feed on baits. Fishermen then rapidly operate the fishing lines which end into unbarbed unbaited hooks. The hooks are unbarbed because the release of fish while jerking from the fishing rod is easy. These fishermen are highly skilled persons who rapidly use the lines to capture fish. Along with the oceanic skipjack tuna, yellow fin and other tunas are also captured in large numbers.

## FISHING SEASON AND CATCH TREND

Fishing starts from March to May before the commencement of monsoon. The important fishing centers from Kerala are Cochin, Calicut, Vizhingam and Neendakara. *Euthynnus affinis* (Little tunny) and *Auxis thazard* (Short corsellated frigate mackerel) are two important species of Tuna from Kerala. The important fishing centers from Tamil Nadu are Tuticorin, Rameshwaram and Chennai and the important fish species are *T. albacores, E. affinis, A. thazard and T. tonggol.*

### ANNUAL CATCH TREND

The production of tuna fluctuated between 30,285 tonnes in 1987 and 54,007 tonnes in 2000 with an annual average of 41,443 tonnes forming 3.6 per cent of the total pelagic fish. Among the 8 major species of Tuna occurring along Indian coasts 5 are coastal and 3 are oceanic and

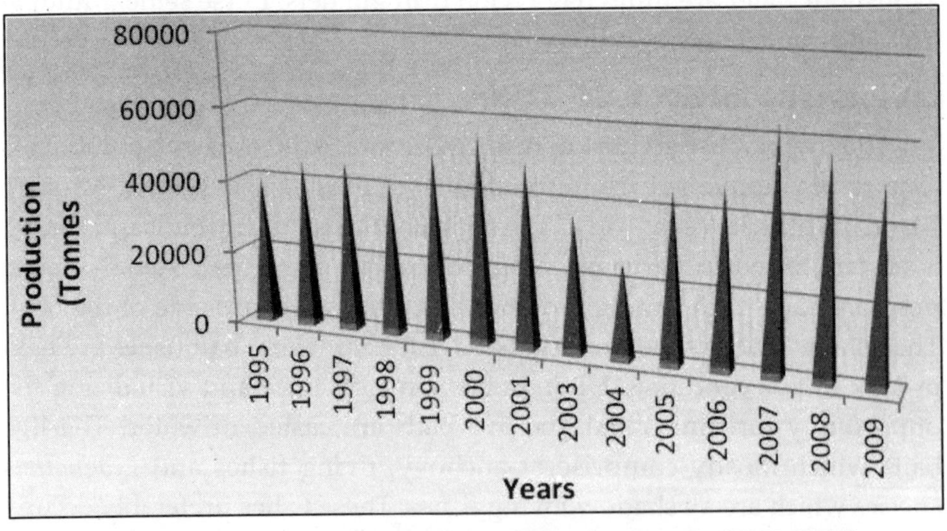


**Figure 6.4.1: Annual Production of Tuna from India (1995-2009)**

migratory. The fishery of tuna in India is limited to small scale level with negligible inputs form the industrial sector. The small scale coastal fisheries are *Euthynnus affinis, Auxis thazard, A. rochei* (Bullet tuna), *Sarda orientalis* and *Thunnus tonggol*. The oceanic species are *Katsuwonus pelamis, T. albacares* and *T. alalunga*. The major species found along both coasts are *E. affinis, A. thazard* while *T. tonggol* and *T. albacares* are found along the North West coast.

In India the tuna fisheries is mainly artisanal activity, excepting for brief phase of chartering and joint venture for tuna fishing by long liners in 1990s. However the tuna catches substantially improved by nearly 58 per cent in 1990–2002, compared to earlier times, mainly due to motorization of traditional crafts, distant water multiday gill net fishing, targeting oceanic tunas and adoption of progressive and innovative fishing techniques by mainland fisherman.

The tuna landing form India from 2003 to 2009 exhibited fluctuating trend varied between minimum of 23633 tonnes in the year 2004 with all time maximum yield of 61368 tonnes in 2007. The average production of tuna for the five year period (after minimum production in 2004) from 2005 to 2009 was fairly high of 51224 tonnes which was possibly the highest average production of five years ever and also indicate the rising trend and good future for tuna fisheries in the country.

**Table 6.4.1: Yearwise tuna landings**

| *Year* | *Production (tonnes)* | *Year* | *Production (tonnes)* |
|---|---|---|---|
| **1995** | 37789 | **2003** | 34791 |
| **1996** | 43321 | **2004** | 23633 |
| **1997** | 43941 | **2005** | 43421 |
| **1998** | 39830 | **2006** | 45744 |
| **1999** | 48525 | **2007** | 61368 |
| **2000** | 54007 | **2008** | 56227 |
| **2001** | 47912 | **2009** | 48852 |

## STATEWISE CATCH TREND

The state wise average catch trend between 2006 to 2009 indicate that the state of Kerala ranks first with the production of 12351 tonnes followed by the state of Gujarat at second place with the production of

9893 tonnes, the Island of Lakshadweep proudly at the third place with the production of 9185 tonnes and the states of Andhra Pradesh and Maharashtra ranking at fourth and fifth places with the production of 5709 tonnes and 4212 tonnes respectively. Even though the west coast shares more production of Tuna in the country, the share from east coast is also promising. This evidently proves the fact that the Tuna fisheries in India are represented by both the coast.

## UTILIZATION OF CATCH

The fish internationally commands a very high demand as can be ascertained from the fact that a fish weighing 162 kg was sold in Tokyo in the year 1992 at an auctioned price for about an amount equivalent to Rs. 20,00,000 *i.e.* a price at Rs. 12,780/Kg.

Tuna is a very valuable fish having not only the local but also high international demand therefore the fish demands judicious post harvest management measures to utilize the harvest in more efficient manner. Tuna is considered to be a high delicacy for the demand of red meat therefore much preferred to be consumed in fresh condition locally, however the fresh sale may not be profitable since there is high demand for tuna internationally. Considering the high importance of international demand, the attempts have been made to freeze head on tuna, to be exported to international market of Japan, Singapore, USA, France, Spain etc. The cured tuna is also exported.

On an average about 74 per cent of the total tuna landed are Iced and marketed for fresh consumption, about 10 per cent of the landing are utilized for Masmin production, 9 per cent are frozen, chilled and exported to Gulf countries and Europe. 4 per cent utilized for canning and 3 per cent are salt cured for interior market.

### Masmin

A special product out of tuna is produced in Minicoy Island of Lakshadweep. Oceanic skipjack tuna (*K. pelamis*) fish is cut into big slices wrapped in palm strips then boiled in brine water and then smoked repeatedly to harden resulting into a golden coloured special product called Masmin. It fetches very high price locally in India and also exported to South East Asian countries like Sri Lanka, Singapore, Thailand and Malaysia.

**Table 6.4.2: State-wise Production of Tuna**

| *Years* | *Production (tonnes)* | | | | | | | *Avarage (2006-2009)* |
|---|---|---|---|---|---|---|---|---|
| *States* | *2003* | *2004* | *2005* | *2006* | *2007* | *2008* | *2009* | |
| **Kerala** | 13717 | 1141 | 11881 | 12702 | 12254 | 12263 | 12183 | **12351** |
| **Gujarat** | 0 | 0 | 0 | 8236 | 14830 | 10365 | 6141 | **9893** |
| **Lakshadweep** | 6656 | 6656 | 8828 | 8661 | 8874 | 9228 | 9978 | **9185** |
| **Andhra** | 1221 | 2680 | 4109 | 1975 | 6977 | 7114 | 6769 | **5709** |
| **Maharashtra** | 4563 | 2303 | 4116 | 4598 | 5336 | 4180 | 2733 | **4212** |
| **Tamil Nadu** | 4599 | 4599 | 4599 | 2550 | 4667 | 4685 | 4880 | **4196** |
| **Andaman and Nicobar** | 0 | 0 | 38 | 2068 | 2359 | 2036 | 1984 | **2112** |
| **Ponddicherry** | 0 | 0 | 0 | 1044 | 1352 | 1470 | 1811 | **1419** |
| **Goa** | 911 | 1308 | 3313 | 589 | 1916 | 2095 | 1044 | **1411** |
| **Daman and Diu** | 395 | 456 | 797 | 1246 | 1139 | 611 | 943 | **985** |
| **Karnataka** | 2125 | 3968 | 5225 | 1175 | 959 | 1465 | — | **900** |
| **Orissa** | 604 | 522 | 515 | 675 | 619 | 711 | 359 | **591** |
| **West Bengal** | 0 | 0 | 0 | 225 | 86 | 4 | 27 | **86** |
| **Total Catch** | **34791** | **23633** | **43421** | **45744** | **61368** | **56227** | **48852** | |

## RECOMMENDATIONS FOR IMPROVEMENTS OF TUNA FISHERIES

Many exploratory surveys conducted in and around India have indicated immense stock of coastal and oceanic tuna. The production of tuna therefore can be increased by manifolds through the judicious exploitation of tuna not only from the coastal continental waters but efforts must be directed towards harvesting off-shore oceanic tuna stock. The prime steps in the high sea tuna fishery in India requires to utilize the technological capacity of the vessels, equipments and the expertise of the developed nations through joint venture and chartering arrangements.

The demonstration of Pelagic Purse Seining and Deep Sea Long Lining must be held for its adoption by the fishermen. The intensified efforts must be made around Lakshadweep and Andaman Sea which hold high potential for surface species of tuna. Along with the increase in the tuna landing it is also highly essential to update the post harvest and processing strategies especially for tuna for its efficient utilization. Intensified programmers for tuna are also necessary along the south west and south east coast of India with the employment of vessels having quick chilling and storing facilities and greater operational range for fishing.

In India stock of tuna in the oceanic water is in plenty while in spite of such a large potential only negligible harvest of oceanic tuna has been possible. Therefore one of the major requirements in the planning of tuna fisheries development is the need to maintain and improve the production targets with appropriate management measures. In this regard since 1983 the Fishery Survey of India has undertaken long lining survey and studied the distribution and abundance of these highly migratory species in Indian E.E.Z. They found that the Big Eye Tuna is dominant in equatorial waters, while Skipjack Tuna is abundant in Northeastern region. Extension of fishing to offshore and oceanic waters, through multiday gill netting, pole and lining, purse seining, long lining and intensification of troll lining may help to augment tuna production from Indian waters.

## 6.5 SEER FISHES

### Scientific Classification

| | | |
|---|---|---|
| *Class* | : | Teleostomi |
| *Sub-class* | : | Actinopterygii |

| | | |
|---|---|---|
| *Order* | : | Perciformes |
| *Family* | : | Scombridae |
| *Species* | | 1. *Scomberomorus commerson* (King Seer) |
| | | 2. *S. guttatus* (Spotted Seer) |
| | | 3. *S. lineolatus* (Streaked Seer) |
| | | 4. *S. koreanus* (Korean Seer) |
| | | 5. *Acanthocybium solandri* (Wahoo) |

## STATUS

Seer fishes are closely allied to Mackerel but are large in size and also known as 'Spanish Mackerel'. The seer fish catch of 50,376 tonnes in 2000 was just 1.85 per cent to total marine fish production but was valued at 4.03 billion rupees. This justifies the high unit value and economic returns from Seer fish. Seer fish support greatly to artisanal fisheries and are a major income for gill net, hook and line fisheries. Seer fish due to their high delicacy is considered to be high grade table fish. Commercially very high in demand at national markets and at international level it has great prospect and future for export.

## DISTRIBUTION

The seer fishes are inshore pelagic fish distributed in the tropical waters mainly in the areas within 60 meters depth. Seer fish are caught all along the coast of India often along with sardine and anchovies on which they prey. The fishes are distributed from the west and east coast of India with bulk of catch obtained from Tamil Nadu and Andhra Pradesh on East coast and Kerala, Maharashtra and Gujarat from the west coast.

## SPECIES WISE AND STATEWISE DISTRIBUTION

- ☆ **King Seer:** It occurs in high numbers from Cape Camorin to Cochin and all along the west coast in Maharashtra.
- ☆ **Spotted Seer:** It is found in Andhra Pradesh, Kerala and Tamil Nadu. Fish is dominant in Kerala coast from south of Cochin up to Visakhapatnam in Andhra Pradesh.
- ☆ **Streaked Seer:** It is most common along the west coast of India from Karnataka, Goa, Maharashtra and Gujarat.

## PREFERENTIAL HABITAT DISTRIBUTION OF SPECIES OF SEER FISH

The most characteristic feature of seer fish is that it exhibits peculiar preferential habitat distribution.

- **KING SEER:** In crystal clear water of high salinity in the surface water and in the region of perfect buffer system of oceanic water where thermo-mixing of water having different salinities and different thermal gradients is more common. The major distribution of fish occur along the west coast from Cape Camorin to Maharashtra where the oceanic water is pristine clear and greater upwelling results in the perfect buffer conditions of oceanic water due to efficient mixing of water of different salinities and different thermal gradients.
- **SPOTTED SEER:** It is found most dominant in areas where surface salinity conditions are low due to discharge of fresh water streams, rivers and other water run offs. It may due to that the fish occur in high concentration from Kerala (south of Cochin) where fresh water streams and lakes are abundantly draining in sea and from Tamil Nadu to Andhra Pradesh where majority of East flowing rivers terminate in the region of Bay of Bengal lowering the salinity of shallow coastal sea water.
- **STREAKED SEER:** Streaked seer is dominant in the region where there is open ocean and no backwater area, having high salinity. The species therefore occur in high numbers along the West Coast, North of Karnataka, Goa, Maharashtra and Gujarat where open ocean beaches are in plenty having higher salinity of shallower coastal waters and only few backwater areas exist in the coastal zone.

## DIAGNOSTIC FEATURES

The body of Seer fishes is similar to Mackerel but is larger in size. Lateral line has many fine auxiliary branches extending dorsally and ventrally. First dorsal fin contains 15 to 18 spines, usually 16 or more and second dorsal with 18 to 24 rays.

## FOOD AND FEEDING

The fish is a surface feeder, found to be plankton feeder in early stages of life but is carnivorous in adult stage. Large King seer feeds mainly on teleosts, Spotted seer feeds on teleosts, squids and prawns while Streaked seer feed exclusively on fish such as sardine, anchovies and silver bellies.

## GROWTH, DEVELOPMENT AND REPRODUCTIVE BEHAVIOR

Large seer fishes mainly king seer spawners disappear from fishing grounds and coming into strictly inshore bays for spawning. The length at first maturity for King Seer is 75 cm and the spawning is extensive extending from January to September. The weak brood is released in January – February, a strong brood during April – May and another weak brood in July – August. Spawning season for spotted seer extends from January – August and for Streaked seer is from January – May.

## MIGRATION AND SHOALING BEHAVIOUR

The uniformly high abundance of especially the Streaked and King seer along the entire west coast during the winter months (during late fourth and half of first quarter) and instances of harvested fish stock from the minimum of Cape Camorin to the maximum for the Gujarat coast, indicate that the stock originates from Cape Camorin and spread from there to northwards up to Gujarat, along the west coast. Low surface salinities arising from North East monsoon and run off during the fourth and initial months of first quarter along the east coast (early to late winter months) and South West monsoon along the West Coast in second and third quarter (early to late summer months) are favourable for the occurrence of Spotted seer. King seer is abundant in the first and second quarter (early winter to summer month) of relatively higher surface salinities along the South West and South East coast of India.

It is therefore can be concluded that seer fish are highly sensitive to environmental changes and exhibit seasonal variation in their distribution.

## CRAFTS AND GEARS USED FOR FISHING

In India the seer fish formed the maximum mainstay and represented as major input from artisanal sector especially during the early four decades after the independence due to their traditional fishing from inshore coastal waters with the use of gill net, hook and lines etc. However in later years to present time their fishing has been improvised also through the mechanized fishing.

Gill nets are most popular along the east and west coast. Gill nets with larger mesh size of 120 mm to 170 mm have been found very efficient for seer fish exploitation. Gill nets have contributed to 65 per cent of total seer fish catch in the country. Hooks and line are also found efficient for the selective fishing of Seer fishes.

Trawling also has been attempted lately for the exploitation of smaller seer fishes, Nylon Drift gill nets having smaller mesh size of 64 mm to 80 mm are employed for the spotted seer and one year old King seer. The larger fishes especially King seer of more than two year old are caught by gear having larger mesh size. Purse seining has also been employed for the capture of Seer fishes from shallow waters of continental shelf.

CIFT has demonstrated and devised a very successful method of fishing of Seer fish on commercial scale by employing the Multiple Trolling to be operated from sail or mechanized boats using artificial jigs to lure the fish for capture.

Fishing starts in summer months (March to September) with high landings in the month of March. The catches are poor during the winter months (October to February), reaching the lowest in February.

## ANNUAL CARCH TREND

The annual seer fish catch from 1985 – 2003 showed an increasing trend. During the last 5 decades fluctuations ranging from minimum of 4505 tonnes in 1953 to an all time peak of 115684 tonnes in 2005. The years between, 2003 to 2005 were extremely productive years for Seer fish landing, the production crossing over one lakh tonnes during these years. The production however sustained decline from the years between 2006 and 2009. The average production of Seer fish between the years of 2006 and 2009 was 54721 tonnes. Even though the production of seer fish was prominent from both the coasts over the years but its increase along the west coast was remarkable. Considering the great demand there has been remarkable progress in the production of seer fish especially after late nineties due to greater efforts made for their exploitation and improvising the fishing from both the artisanal to mechanized sectors.

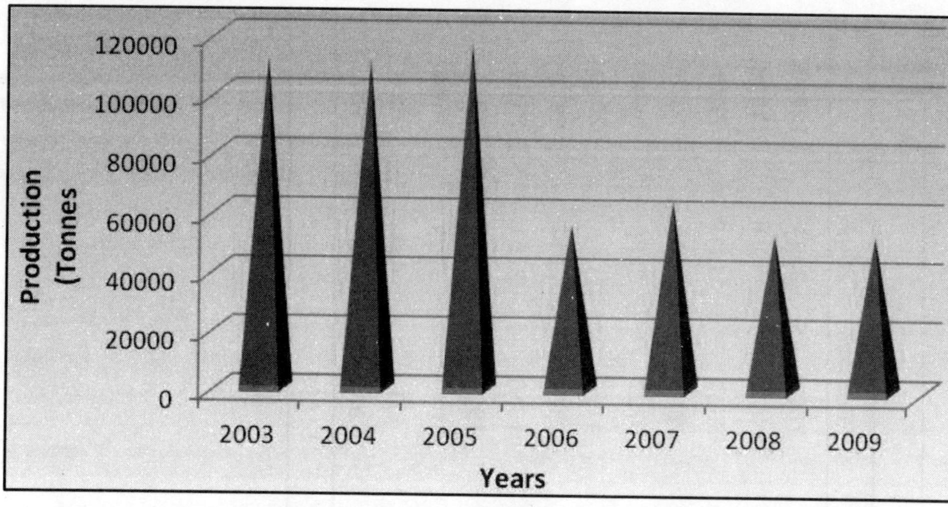


**Figure 6.5.1: Year-wise Landing of Seer Fishes from India (2003-2009)**

**Table 6.5.1: Year-wise Seer Fish Landing**

| *Year* | *Production (tonnes)* | *Year* | *Production (tonnes)* |
|---|---|---|---|
| **1953** | 4505 | **2000** | 50376 |
| **2003** | 110175 | **2004** | 109873 |
| **2005** | 115684 | **2006** | 54202 |
| **2007** | 62543 | **2008** | 51093 |
| **2009** | 51048 | | |

## STATEWISE CTCH TREND

As Seer fishes are landed form both the west and east coast of India. In earlier times between 2003 and 2005 the states of Kerala, Tamil Nadu and Maharashtra were the leading producers of Seer fish. The production pattern from 2006 to 2009 suggested that the state of Maharashtra is the leading producer followed by the state of Gujarat at the second and Andhra Pradesh at the third place. The average production during this time for the state of Maharashtra was highest at 12733 tonnes followed by the state of Gujarat with 11998 tonnes and Andhra Pradesh with 7718 tonnes. This also suggest that the state of Maharashtra has maintained its high production trend, also there was major gain in the production by the state of Gujarat and Andhra Pradesh while there has been severe decline from the states of Kerala and Tamil Nadu in landing of Seer fish in the recent times.

**Table 6.5.2: State-wise Production of Seer Fish**

| *Years* | *Production (tonnes)* | | | | | | | *Avarage (2006-2009)* |
|---|---|---|---|---|---|---|---|---|
| *States* | *2003* | *2004* | *2005* | *2006* | *2007* | *2008* | *2009* | |
| **Maharashtra** | 11044 | 11194 | 7496 | 16768 | 18162 | 7607 | 8394 | **12733** |
| **Gujarat** | 7202 | 7293 | 9258 | 11403 | 14460 | 11071 | 11058 | **11998** |
| **Andhra Pradesh** | 2504 | 10474 | 9653 | 2739 | 8158 | 8559 | 11418 | **7718** |
| **Tamil Nadu** | 23538 | 23538 | 23538 | 7758 | 6027 | 7895 | 9001 | **7670** |
| **Goa** | 1398 | 2274 | 9556 | 3522 | 4407 | 3777 | 2285 | **3498** |
| **Karnataka** | 3341 | 5124 | 6415 | 3511 | 2847 | 4199 | – | **2639** |
| **Kerala** | 56657 | 45194 | 46559 | 2648 | 2556 | 2560 | 2517 | **2570** |
| **Orissa** | 1872 | 2171 | 2167 | 2155 | 2052 | 1816 | 2751 | **2193** |
| **Pondicherry** | 0 | 0 | 0 | 1648 | 1910 | 1922 | 2018 | **1874** |
| **Andaman and Nicobar** | 1842 | 1842 | 374 | 1150 | 1204 | 1019 | 1029 | **1100** |
| **Daman and Diu** | 586 | 578 | 548 | 778 | 665 | 572 | 483 | **624** |
| **Lakshadweep** | 191 | 191 | 120 | 122 | 95 | 96 | 93 | **101** |
| Total Catch | 110175 | 109873 | 115684 | 54202 | 62543 | 51093 | 51048 | |

## UTILIZATION

The seer fish particularly the larger king seer are one of the high grade table fishes in great demand all over the country, therefore are much preferred to be consumed in fresh condition.

In recent times the distribution and marketing of Seer fishes have shown great promise. Even Delhi and other North Indian towns receive the Seer fish from the coastal areas which are supplied for marketing. The fish are frozen and are either air lifted or transported in cold chain for distribution. The future holds rising promise for the export of frozen Seer fish.

# 6.6 POMFRETS

## Scientific Classification

| | | |
|---|---|---|
| *Class* | : | Teleostomi |
| *Sub-class* | : | Actinopterygii |
| *Order* | : | Perciformes |
| *Family* | : | Stromateidae |
| *Species* | | 1. *Pampus argentius* (Sliver Pomfret) |
| | | 2. *Pampus chinensis* (Chinese Pomfret) |
| | | 3. *Parastromateus niger* (Black Pomfret) |

## STATUS

Pomfrets contribute to one of the major table fish in India, very popular due to very less spines and appropriately called as Halwa in Maharashtra. It is a pelagic fish generally found near the bottom during the day, rising to near the surface at night.

## DISTRIBUTION

Internationally found to occur in tropical Indian Ocean, Indo-Pacific Archipelago. It is found nationally all along the West and East coast of India, however it occurs in high numbers in Gujarat and Maharashtra states along the West Coast and Orissa and West Bengal states in the East Coast. There has been major input for fishery of Pomfrets from Andhra Pradesh in some recent years. Contrary to the earlier times, during 2006 to 2009 the production of Pomfrets is more from the east coast of India than west coast of India.

## DIAGNOSTIC FEATURES

Body of Pomfrets is deep and compressed laterally having convex dorsal and ventral profiles. Average length is 30 cm. Mouth is terminal with a single row of small conical teeth. Dorsal fin with 4-5 short spines and anal fin contains 2 spines.

## FOOD AND FEEDING

The Pomfrets feed on macro-zooplankton. The juvenile feed mainly on small crustaceans *i.e.* Acetes, Mysids, Lucifer etc. Pomfrets appears to be mid water species, which leads the bottom life of inshore waters during the early immature stages and the change of habitat may be one of the reason for the change in food habit.

## GROWTH, DEVELOPMENT AND REPRODUCTIVE BEHAVIOR

Silver Pomfrets attains first maturity at the size of 27 to 30 cm, the maximum size being 35 cm. Spawning in west coast is from October – December and fecundity from 65,700 to 1,72,000 eggs in fish ranging from 20 – 32 cm length. *P. niger* attains first maturity at the length of 30 – 60 cm maximum size being 76 cm. The spawning is from July – October with peak season in August – September.

## MIGRATION AND SHOALING BEHAVIOUR

The Pomfrets do not shoal like sardine and mackerel but move in large numbers. They are generally found from the surface to lower column waters.

## CRAFT AND GEARS USED FOR THE FISHING

Principle gear for capture is driftnet of 148 – 155 mm mesh size while dol net is also employed for its capture along the North West coast. Nylone drift gill netting is emerging to be the main device of capture, similarly they can also be captured by Mid- water trawl gear. In India fairly handsome landing of Pomfrets is also obtained from trawl gear.

## OVEREXPLOITATION

The fishery of Pomfrets had collapsed in the North West coast during the 1990, restriction of dol net operation to minimize recruitment overfishing and regulation of gill nets to minimize growth overfishing have been prescribed as best management measures.

Many young small and immature Pomfrets especially Silver Pomfrets come as by-catch from inshore operating shrimp trawler. It is therefore needed that the shrimp trawlers should extend the area of fishing not to operate in inshore water to avoid young Pomfrets being captured.

Along the Bombay coast, the fishing season for Pomfrets is from September – January and the peak season is October-December. On the Gujrat coast also the fishery starts in September but continue up to May, the peak period being March-May. In general the fishing season for Silver Pomfrets is from January to June with peak from March to April. *P.niger* is harvested from November to May with peak season extending from December to March. The main fishing centers from west coast are Veraval, Porbandar, Gangoli, Badagara, Versova, Alibagh, Satpati, Ratnagiri etc, while along the east coast the Pomfrets are caught in high numbers from Nellore, Visakhapattanum, Puri, Ganjam, Ballasore, Midnapoore,

## ANNUAL CATCH TREND

**Table 6.6.1: Year-wise Pomfret Landing**

| *Year* | *Production (tonnes)* | *Year* | *Production (tonnes)* |
|---|---|---|---|
| **1998** | 57359 | **1999** | 34478 |
| **2000** | 40956 | **2001** | 39415 |
| **2002** | 83696 | **2006** | 83903 |
| **2007** | 72946 | **2008** | 68288 |
| **2009** | 81759 | | |

In most of the time during eighties to nineties the annual average catch of 38,000 tonnes of Pomfrets constituted about 2 per cent of all India marine fish landings. With the exception of 1999 the reasonably high annual production of Pomfrets started from 1998 onwards. The production from 1998 to 2002 which indicated the fluctuating trend with the production of 57,359 tonnes in 1998 followed by 34,478 tonnes in 1999, 40,956 tonnes in 2000, 39,415 tonnes in 2001 and the highly inspiring production of 83,696 tonnes in 2002.

However the average landing of Pomfrets between1998 to 2002 indicated comparatively very high production of 51,180 tonnes to be much higher than the average production of 38,000 tonnes obtained during eighties and early nineties. The highest production of Pomfrets for all the

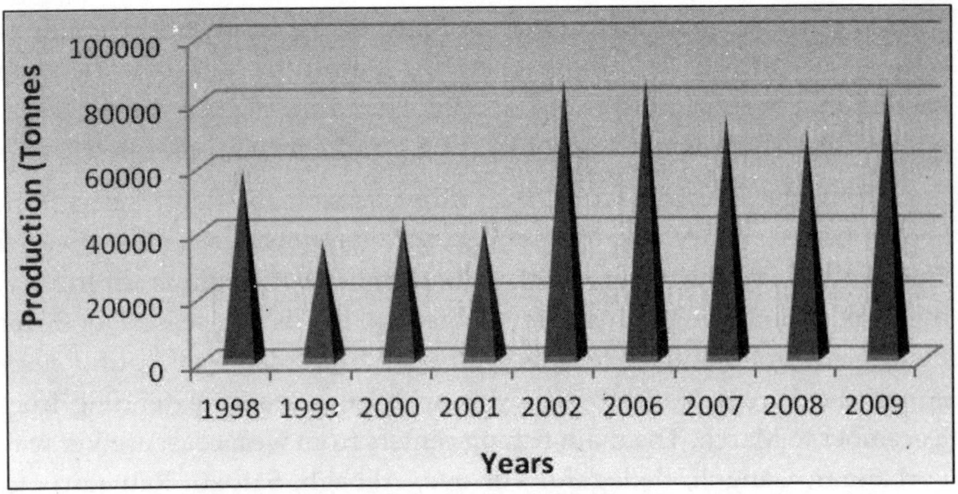


**Figure 6.6.1: Annual Landing of Pomfrets from India (1998-2009)**

species was obtained in 2006, with the landing of 83,903 tonnes. The average yield for Pomfrets still reached further at the record levels of 76,724 tonnes between 2006 and 2009. This aptly indicate that in the recent times due to rousing national and international demand the major emphasis to the extent of targeted fishing is now given for the capture of Pomfrets in India.

## STATE WISE CATCH TRENDS

The table indicates that Gujarat is the highest contributing state for the production of Pomfrets with the average production of 21,869 tonnes. Andhra Pradesh and Maharashtra are in 2nd and 3rd position in the production of Pomfrets with the average production of 17,049 tonnes and 10,979 tonnes respectively. In earlier times, the state of Maharashtra was the second largest producer of Pomfrets in the country. The state of West Bengal ranks fourth with fairly handsome average landing of 11,701 tonnes. The state of Orissa with the average production of 8,151 tonnes ranks fifth. The average production figures between 2006 and 2009 also reveal the complete reversal trend for Pomfrets landing of previous years, when the west coast constituted more share in production than the east coast of India. The recent trend (2006 to 2009) suggests that the contribution of 52.43 per cent from the east coast is more than the west coast which shares about 47.56 per cent to the total Pomfrets capture in the country.

**Table 6.6.2: State-wise Production of Pomfret**

| States | Years/Production | | | | Avarage (2006-2009) |
|---|---|---|---|---|---|
| | 2006 | 2007 | 2008 | 2009 | |
| **Gujarat** | 27624 | 20288 | 22654 | 16910 | **21869** |
| **Andhra** | 21190 | 13067 | 13372 | 20570 | **17049** |
| **Maharashtra** | 10321 | 15475 | 6190 | 11932 | **10979** |
| **West Bengal** | 8694 | 8623 | 9799 | 19688 | **11701** |
| **Orissa** | 8004 | 8067 | 8356 | 8177 | **8151** |
| **Tamil Nadu** | 2443 | 1980 | 1985 | 2080 | **2122** |
| **Kerala** | 1549 | 1534 | 1523 | 0 | **1151** |
| **Karnataka** | 1572 | 967 | 1760 | – | **1074** |
| **Daman and Diu** | 861 | 1258 | 849 | 880 | **962** |
| **Pondicherry** | 890 | 814 | 838 | 808 | **837** |
| **Goa** | 446 | 559 | 534 | 284 | **455** |
| **Andaman and Nicobar** | 309 | 314 | 428 | 430 | **370** |
| **Total Catch** | **83903** | **72946** | **68288** | **81759** | |

## UTILIZATION

The Pomfrets are high grade as well as high valued table fish in India. They command extremely encouraging national and international demand. The freshly harvested Pomfrets are instantly iced, chilled and frozen and through rapid transport are supplied to the affluent hotels and restaurants of metro cities in India. They are also frozen and cold stored for meeting with high export demand in Middle-East, Singapore, Malaysia, European countries and the other foreign markets.

# 6.7 ANCHOVIES

## Scientific Classification

| | | |
|---|---|---|
| *Class* | : | Teleostomi |
| *Sub-class* | : | Actinopterygii |
| *Order* | : | Clupeiformes |
| *Family* | : | Engraulidae |
| *Genus* | : | *Stolephorus, Encrasicholina* (Whitebaits), *Colia, Setipinna, Thryssa, Thryssinna.* |

*Species* : *Stolephorus Commersoni*

*S. baganesis, S. andhraensis, S. indicus, S. dubiosus, S. waitei, S. insularis*

*Encrasicholina devisi, E. heterolobus, E. punctifer, Coilia dussumieri, Coilia ramcarati* (Golden Anchovy)

## STATUS

Anchovies are widely distributed in Indian waters, mostly comprising of 6 genera represented by *Coilia, Setipinna, Stolephorus, Thryssa* and *Thryssinna*. The fisheries of these are intensively held from the maritime states of Maharashtra, Karnataka, Kerala, Tamil Nadu and Andhra Pradesh.

## DISTRIBUTION

Genus *Stolephorus* is commonly referred as Whitebaits. The whitebaits form prominent fisheries of south west and south east coast of India, extending from the state of Karnataka, Kerala, Tamil Nadu and Andhra Pradesh. The other Anchovy group is represented by genus *Coila*, which include golden anchovy and other small anchovies. The golden anchovy indicate the patchy discontinuous distribution, mostly concentrated along the north west coast of India from Maharashtra and Gujarat and then constituting the fisheries along the north east coast of India along the coastal areas of West Bengal and Orissa.

The production trend of total anchovies suggests that it constitute 11.2 per cent to the total pelagic landings of India with an average annual catch of 1.31 lakh tonnes between the years of 1985 to 2003. The annual landing increased from late eighties to the nineties from 1.05 lakh tonnes in 1987 to 1.66 lakh tonnes in 1991. The statistical analysis of total landings between 1985 -2003 suggested that the major share to the total production of anchovies is realized from the whitebaits with the share of 48 per cent, followed by *Thryssa* 26 per cent, Golden or Grenadier anchovy (*Coilia dussumieri*) 24 per cent and *Settipina* 2 per cent. The whitebaits dominate the south west to south east coast of India with the share of over 60 per cent while the Golden or Grenadier anchovy dominated anchovy fishery from north west and north east coast of India with an average landing of 32,040 tonnes during 1985-2003.

## DIAGNOSTIC FEATURE

Anchovies are small or moderate in size usually 10 to 20 cm in length. The fishes have pig-like snout projecting beyond the tip of the lower jaw. The lower jaw is long, slender and its articulation is well behind the eye. The dorsal fin is short and usually near the midpoint of the body. The pectoral fins are low on the body. The back of the fish is blue-green; the sides are silver and the fins are faint yellow.

## WHITEBAITS

The Whitebaits forms the prominent fisheries from the south west to south east coast of India representing by ten species belonging to genus *Stolephorus* and *Encrasicholina*. They are *Encrasicholina devisi, E. heterolobus, E. punctifer, Stolephorus commersoni, S. baganesis, S. andhraensis, S. indicus, S. dubiosus, S.wati and S.insularis*. Among these species *E.devisi, E. punctifer, S. commersoni, S. indicus* and *S. waiti* are the major supporter of anchovy fishery.

## BIOLOGY

Whitebaits are small pelagic fishes and found in shoals in the areas of high density of zooplankton in the coastal continental waters. Most of them are short lived with the mean age of 0.5 years and belong to '0' year class. They spawn very early and are proliferic breeder with multiple spawning. The spawning season extends from November and last till July.

## CRAFTS AND GEARS USED FOR FISHING

The major gears employed for the capture of whitebaits are Boat seines, Shore seines, Bag nets and Gill nets operated from catamarans and other small traditional plank built boats and boats fitted with out board engines. The purse seine, ring seines and trawl nets are also effectively utilized for their capture. The boat seines with stretchable cod-end mesh size of 10 mm, shore seine with stretchable cod-end of mesh size of 20 mm are operated for their capture along the south east and south west coast of India. Along the south west coast a special gill net called Netholivala is employed for their capture. Instances of their capture by purse seine since 1970 and ring seines from plank built boats operated by out board engines since mid 80's are common along the coastal areas of Karnataka and Kerala.

The fishing season of whitebaits varies from place to place; it is between October to March in Karnataka, July to December in Kerala, April to December in Tamil Nadu and October to March in Andhra Pradesh. The whitebaits are also reported to undertake seasonal migration along west coast moving southwards in April – May and reaching in Gulf of Mannar during August to September.

The overall production trend of Whitebaits (1991-2003) suggested that they contribute about an average landing of 64,000 tonnes forming about 1.7- 5.8 per cent of total marine fish landing from India.

## GOLDEN ANCHOVY

The Golden anchovy also called as Grenadier anchovy (*Coilia dussumieri*) forms the prominent fishery of north west and north east coast of India. It is represented by another species of *Coilia ramcarati* especially along the north east coast of India.

### FISHERY ASPECT

In earlier times the entire landing of golden anchovy was most prominent as Dol net fishery. However after the inception of trawl for the fishing the landing of golden anchovy was tremendously increased during early nineties. The contribution of trawl to Dol net production of golden anchovy indicated the contribution of 38 per cent and 60 per cent during 1986 – 1990, while during 1996 – 2000, the contribution by trawl gear increased to 70 per cent of the total catch.

The production of Golden Anchovy ranged from 19,048 tonnes in 1987 to 46,268 tonnes in 1998 with an average production of 32,050 tonnes. The time series analysis of the data on the landings of Golden Anchovy during last 15 years together with co-existing species like Bombay duck and non penaeid prawns indicated that decline in landings of Bombay duck coincided with that of Golden Anchovy (*C. dussumieri*), while the landing of non penaeid prawn showed the increase during the same period.

## ANNUAL CATCH TREND FOR ANCHOVIES

The production of anchovies from 2003 to 2005 indicated unsteady trend however it significantly increased during 2006 to 2009 which are presumed to be the most productive years for anchovies with the average landing of 1,06,197 tonnes. The annual production for the anchovies in these years was 1,05,362, 1,08,465, 1,04,370 and 1,06,589 tonnes respectively for the years of 2006, 2007, 2008 and 2009.

**Table 6.7.1: Annual Catch Trend of Anchovies**

| *Year* | *Production (tonnes)* | *Year* | *Production (tonnes)* |
|---|---|---|---|
| **2003** | 93091 | **2004** | 87617 |
| **2005** | 77715 | **2006** | 105362 |
| **2007** | 108465 | **2008** | 104370 |
| **2009** | 106589 | | |

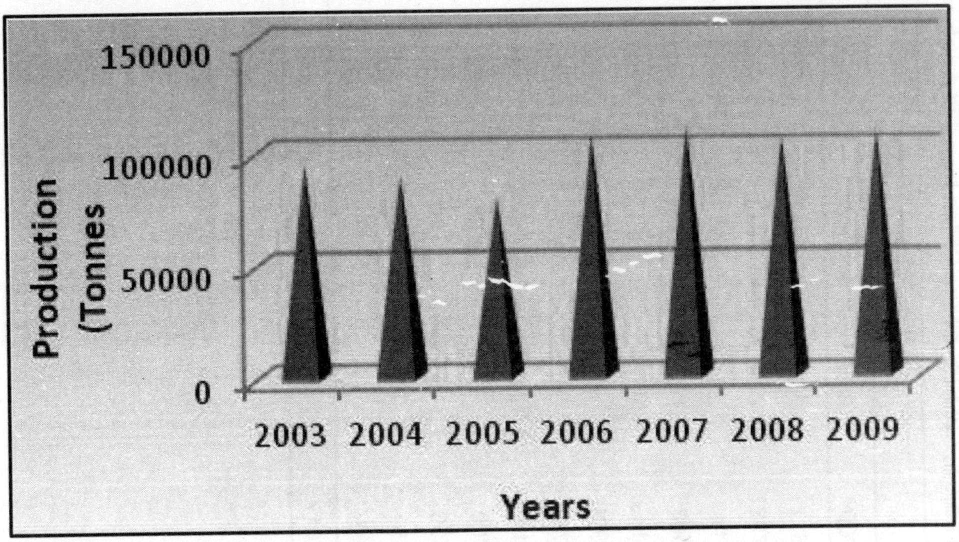


**Figure 6.7.1: Annual Production of Anchovies from India (2003-2009)**

## STATEWISE CATCH TREND

The production trend between 2006 and 2009 suggested that Kerala is the leading producer of Anchovies with the average production of 36249 tonnes followed by Maharashtra at second place with the average landing of 21143 tonnes and the state of Tamil Nadu at the third rank with the average production of 18935 tonnes. The production trend also suggested that in the state of Kerala and Tamil Nadu the production of Whitebaits dominated the landing where as in the state of Maharashtra and Gujarat the production of Golden Anchovy and others contributed intensively to

**Table 6.7.2: Stat-ewise Catch trend of Anchovies**

| *Years* | *Production (tonnes)* | | | | | | | *Avarage (2006-2009)* |
|---|---|---|---|---|---|---|---|---|
| *States* | *2003* | *2004* | *2005* | *2006* | *2007* | *2008* | *2009* | |
| **Kerala** | 41282 | 35177 | 30084 | 36876 | 36228 | 36293 | 35600 | **36249** |
| **Maharashtra** | 19248 | 17987 | 22104 | 21602 | 23742 | 20687 | 18543 | **21143** |
| **Tamil Nadu** | 3147 | 3147 | 3147 | 19054 | 18808 | 18809 | 19069 | **18935** |
| **Gujarat** | 13529 | 10665 | 10922 | 8257 | 10426 | 9550 | 10627 | **9715** |
| **Andhra Pradesh** | 800 | 6149 | 4523 | 8671 | 7207 | 7454 | 11798 | **8782** |
| **West Bengal** | 6800 | 6900 | 579 | 539 | 1208 | 2567 | 4619 | **2233** |
| **Orissa** | 2217 | 1722 | 3133 | 3756 | 4257 | 2987 | 3626 | **3656** |
| **Karnataka** | 3658 | 4140 | 2408 | 2366 | 1461 | 1809 | 0 | **1409** |
| **Andaman and Nicobar** | 760 | 760 | 0 | 2308 | 2981 | 3010 | 1684 | **2495** |
| **Pondicherry** | 446 | 550 | 112 | 1037 | 1193 | 1147 | 628 | **1001** |
| **Daman and Diu** | 132 | 357 | 686 | 866 | 951 | 0 | 0 | **454** |
| **Goa** | 1072 | 63 | 17 | 30 | 3 | 57 | 395 | **121** |
| **Total** | **93091** | **87617** | **77715** | **105362** | **108465** | **104370** | **106589** | |

the production. The annual catch trend during this time also suggested that for the total production of Anchovies the contribution from the west coast was more than the east coast of India.

## UTILIZATION OF CATCH

The whitebaits are known to be used as baits for the fishery of hook and lines and even as live bait for capture of coastal species of tuna. It is mostly consumed fresh; the surplus amount is dried and cured for the internal market. The other products include its freezing for the introduction of artificial dryers and canning in tomato sauce which are some modern and commercial ways of utilizing whitebait for future times.

# 6.8 CARANGIDS

## Scientific Classification

| | | |
|---|---|---|
| *Class* | : | Teleostomi |
| *Sub-class* | : | Actinopterygii |
| *Order* | : | Perciiformes |
| *Family* | : | Carangidae |
| *Species* | : | *Decapterus dayi; D. russeli, D. macrosoma, Selar crumenophthalmus, Megalaspis cordyla, Caranx para, C. carangus, C. malabaricus, C. ignobins Selaroidei leptolepsis* |

## STATUS

Carangids occupy a dominant position with an an average production of 1.33 lakh tonnes, constituting about 4.1 per cent of the total marine fish production. About 46 species occur in Indian waters but fisheries mainly comprise of Horse mackerel, Round scads, Selar scads, Queen Fishes, Trevallies, Leatherjackets and Pompanos. They are mostly occupying shallow coastal waters up to the depth of 80 meters. The fishery has emerged as one of the important pelagic fish groups especially in mechanized sector.

The species comprise of scads such as *Decapterus dayi; D. russeli, D. macrosoma,* Selar scad include *Selar crumenophthalmus, Megalaspis cordyla,* Travelly such as *Caranx para, C. carangus, Selaroidei leptolepsis.*

## DISTRIBUTION

Carangids are distributed throughout the tropical and subtropical regions of the oceans. Internationally it occupies the pacific, Indian, and Atlantic Oceans. In India they occur in the coastal region of east coast, north west coast and south west coast, inhabiting the continental shelf including reefs, bays, lagoons and even estuaries.

## DIAGNOSTIC FEATURES

Carangids are small to large-sized fish with deep, compressed body characterized by a prominent gill racker and strong jaws. The dorsal portion is convex and tapering. The dorsal fin is in two parts, the first consisting of spines and the second of spines followed by a numbers of rays. The anal fin has detached spines. The caudal fin is large and forked and the pectoral fin is large, usually longer than the head.

## FOOD AND FEEDING

The carangids are carnivores, feeding predominantly on fishes and crustaceans. *Megalaspis cordyla* feeds mainly on clupeids and crustaceans. The young ones measuring about 8 cm in length feed on post larval fish, juvenile prawns and other crustaceans. *Decapterus russelli* feeds on clupeids, diatoms, copepods and other crustaceans, its juvenile of 4 cm to 12 cm size feed on Acetes, Copepods and other Crustaceans.

## GROWTH, DEVELOPMENT AND REPRODUCTIVE BEHAVIOR

In *M. cordyla* the size at first maturity is 250 mm. its spawning is prolonged and recruited almost round the year. In the east coast, peak spawning occurs during March to May, followed by peak recruitment in April to May. In north west and south west coasts, recruitment takes place in two different peaks. In north west there is a minor recruitment in October and a major one in January, while in south west coast, the minor recruitment occurs in April and the major one in July. The spawning peak is found around July in north west coast while along south west coast the spawning peak is in January.

## CRAFTS AND GEARS USED FOR FISHING

Carangids are extensively exploited by many or a multitude of gears like trawls, drift gill nets, bottom set gill net, hooks and line, shore seine, ring seines, purse seine etc. The catamarans, plank-built boats and trawlers are major fishing crafts exploiting carangids. The non-selective trawls exploit scads such as *Decapterus dayi, D. macrosoma* and *D. ruselli. Selar crumenophthalmus, Megalaspis cordyla* and Travellies.

The peak fishing season for scads along Kerala coast is August to October, corresponding with monsoon and post monsoon months.

## ANNUAL CATCH TREND

The landings increased from meager 24,560 tonnes in 1969 to a phenomenal 1.97 lakh tonnes in 1995, but decreased to 1.11 lakh tonnes in 2000. The average annual production of Carangids in 1985 to 2003 was 1.33 lakh tonnes of which scads alone constitute 39 per cent, followed by Horse mackerel 14 per cent. The annual catch trend production from 2006 to 2009 indicated minor fluctuations, with about 1,22,095 tonnes in 2006, increasing to 1,34,884 tonnes and 1,35,437 tonnes in 2007 and 2008 respectively, then declining to 1,14,044 tonnes in 2009. The average landing of the carangid from 2006 to 2008 was 1,26,615 tonnes.

**Table 6.8.1: Annual Catch Trend of Carangids**

| *Year* | *Production (tonnes)* | *Year* | *Production (tonnes)* |
|---|---|---|---|
| **2006** | 1,22,095 | **2007** | 1,34,884 |
| **2008** | 1,35,437 | **2009** | 1,14,044 |

## STATEWISE CATCH TREND

Kerala is the highest contributing state for the production of Carangids with the average production of 51010 tonnes during 2006 to 2009. The catch trend of Carangids indicates that in Kerala the production of fish is in decreasing order from 2006 to 2009. Tamil Nadu and Goa are in 2nd and 3rd rank in the production. Fairly good landing of the Carangids is also reported from Maharashtra and Andhra Pradesh states.

## UTILIZATION OF CATCH

The carangids are high quality table fish in great demand and marketed mostly to the high places of metro cities and other consuming centers. During the time of peak landing the surplus catch mainly of *Caranx malabaricus* and *Caranx ignobins* are deep frozen and stored for ensuring the supply and sale during the off season months to obtain high profit.

**Table 6.8.2: State-wise Catch Trend of Carangids**

| *States* | *Years/Production* | | | | *Avarage (2006-2009)* |
|---|---|---|---|---|---|
| | *2006* | *2007* | *2008* | *2009* | |
| **Kerala** | 52613 | 50848 | 50764 | 49817 | **51010.5** |
| **Tamil Nadu** | 17200 | 18440 | 18044 | 14541 | **17056.25** |
| **Goa** | 12244 | 19930 | 16597 | 696 | **12366.75** |
| **Maharashtra** | 10403 | 10173 | 11634 | 9797 | **10501.75** |
| **Andhra Pradesh** | 7596 | 8605 | 8917 | 12129 | **9311.75** |
| **Gujarat** | 4625 | 8053 | 5896 | 5973 | **6136.75** |
| **West Bengal** | 3768 | 2081 | 7490 | 9719 | **5764.5** |
| **Pondicherry** | 5084 | 4597 | 4767 | 2324 | **4193** |
| **Orissa** | 4274 | 3270 | 3371 | 4973 | **3972** |
| **Daman and Diu** | 1371 | 2000 | 1715 | 5470 | **2639** |
| **Andaman and Nicobar** | 1272 | 1360 | 3650 | 3640 | **2480.5** |
| **Karnataka** | 1176 | 1030 | 2117 | – | **1080.75** |
| **Lakshadweep** | 469 | 494 | 475 | 436 | **468.5** |
| **Total Catch** | **122095** | **130881** | **135437** | **119515** | |

## 6.9 BOMBAY DUCK

### Scientific Classification

| | | |
|---|---|---|
| *Class* | : | Teleostomi |
| Sub- Class | : | Actinopterygii |
| Order | : | Myctophiformes |
| Family | : | Harpadontidae |
| Genus | : | *Harpadon* |
| Species | : | ***Harpadon nehereus*** |
| | | ***H. squamosus*** **(recently recorded from Kakinada, A.P.)** |

### STATUS

Bombay duck is a major single species of fish along the northwest coast of India from Ratnagiri in Maharashtra to Gulf of Kutch. It inhabits waters up to 50 – 70 m depth. In terms of production the Bombay duck fishery is very prominent and ranking in between third to ninth place in all India marine fish landing. The average production of Bombay duck during last decade has shown that the fishery contributes about 5.11 per cent to all Indian marine fish landing. The fishery is of utmost importance in two maritime States of India, Gujarat and Maharashtra, where over 98 per cent of the all-India Bombay duck catches are landed.

## DISTRIBUTION

The fish is known for its remarkably discontinues distribution in Indian waters, since, the fish is caught in very high numbers from North of Mumbai to Saurashtra coast of Gujarat, therefore being referred as "Bombay duck". The fish is rare along entire south west coast to south east coast of India and again emerging along West Bengal, Orissa and North Andhra Pradesh coast. The fish has liking to remain in estuaries as can be seen from its distribution at regions of lower salinity such as estuary north of Mumbai, estuary of Narmada, Tapti, and estuaries of West Bengal. The reasons which can be attributed for the discontinuous distribution are:

- ☆ Peculiarity in the distribution and movement of choicest food organisms of fishes.
- ☆ Choice for lower salinity conditions of estuaries and back water.
- ☆ The surface water temperature around 70°F or 27°C isothermal conditions.

## DIAGNOSTIC FEATURES

Bombay duck has elongated and compressed body. The fish is scale less with very soft flabby flesh. Its eyes are small, snout is too short, mouth is very large and teeth of unequal in size. The lower jaw of fish is longer than upper. Dorsal fin contains 10 - 12 fin rays, followed by a prominent adipose fin. Pectoral fin and anal fin have 10-12 and 14- 15 rays respectively. Pelvic fins are very long having about 9 rays. Lateral line, which is extended on top of pointed median lobe of caudal fin. The average length of fish is 10 to 25 cm.

## FOOD AND FEEDING

The fish is aggressive predator and highly carnivorous with preference for shrimps and smallest clupeid fishes. The jaws are therefore equipped with sharp canine teeths.

## GROWTH AND DEVELOPMENT AND REPRODUCTIVE BEHAVIOR

The fish breed throughout the year with intense spawning activity in two peaks *i.e.* July to August and February to March. The prolonged spawning of the fish and higher age for maturity adversely affects the fishery. At the end of the first year the fish attain an average length of 127 mm and at the end of the second year it attains an average length of 210 mm. The regular appearance of the fingerlings stage shows that the recruitment of fish is continuous and during the post monsoon period *i.e.* September-December the appearance is maximum.

## MIGRATION AND SHOALING BEHAVIOUR

The shoaling behavior of the Bombay duck, seem to be influenced by two main factors, the availability of food and the favorable condition of the water temperature. The low surface temperature is the probable cause for the peculiar distribution of the fish species to a great extent than any other factors.

## CRAFTS AND GEARS USED FOR FISHING

The fish is captured as by-catch commodity from shrimp trawler operating at the mid water. The fish can also be captured effortlessly by gill nets in coastal waters of Gujarat. In the estuaries and shallower waters of Maharashtra and Gujarat a special device of bag net locally referred as Dol net is the most important fishing device. In West Bengal the fixed bag net called Behundi Jal is used for the capture of the fish.

In south and southeast coast of Saurashtra, about 400-500 boats operate in the area during the fishing season, each boat carrying 7-9 fishermen. They operate 'Dol' nets 6-12 miles from the coasts in water of 10-15 fathoms deep. The majority of fishermen operate two nets at a time from each boat, but some units operate three nets. The fishermen of Gujarat coast from Kosmba to Kolak, fish for Bombay duck by gill nets along a stretch of 10 miles of coast line in inshore water during the months of June to September. These gill nets are 30 feet long and 3 feet high with a mesh of one inch from knot to knot. The fishermen of Konkan coast and from Kalai (South of Daman) to Baroda operate dol nets of various sizes in waters ranging in depths from 6-10 fathoms. The fishermen of Andhra-Orissa coast harvest Bombay duck in boat seines and fixed bag nets operated by two catamarans.The fishing season for Bombay duck lasts from September to May, with the bulk of landings taking place during October December.

## ANNUAL CATCH TREND

**Table 6.9.1: Year-wise Bombay Duck Landing**

| *Year* | *Production (mt)* | *Year* | *Production (mt)* |
|---|---|---|---|
| **2003** | 139865 | **2004** | 171230 |
| **2005** | 188228 | **2006** | 188293 |
| **2007** | 210670 | **2008** | 234781 |
| **2009** | 196096 | | |

The catch statics indicate a remarkable increase in landings from 7262 tonnes in 1951 to 1,28,618 tonnes in 1956. Further in 1958 and 1959 recorded poor landing of fish. The fishery revived in 1960 and since then it has more or less stabilized around 80,000 tonnes comprising 80 per cent of the catch of immature fish. 80 per cent of total Bombay duck landings come from the west coast of India, which exclusively are realized from the States of Gujarat and Maharashtra.

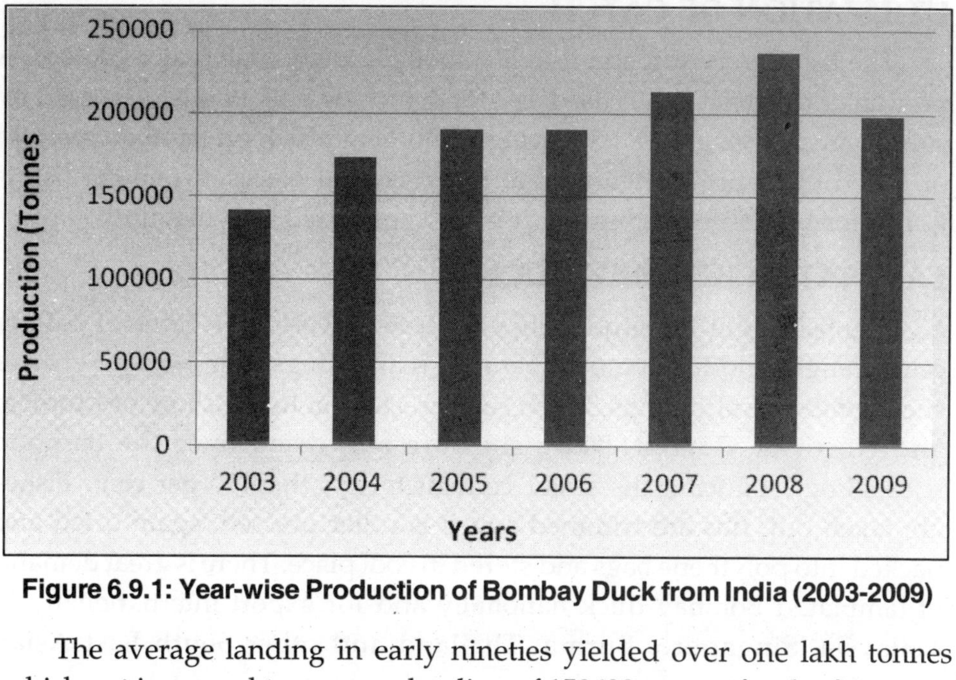


**Figure 6.9.1: Year-wise Production of Bombay Duck from India (2003-2009)**

The average landing in early nineties yielded over one lakh tonnes which got increased to average landing of 153639 tonnes for the five years between 1995 and 1999. The production remained slightly less between 2000 and 2003. The landing was increased to 171230 tonnes in 2004. The next five years from 2005 to 2009 were extremely productive yrars for Bombay duck with the average landing reached up to the peak of 203614 tonnes and the year 2008 yielding so far the highest production of 234781 tonnes for Bombay duck in the country.

## STATE WISE CATCH TRENDS

The state wise average production of Bombay duck from 2006 to 2009 indicates that the state of Gujarat is the highest producer of the fish with the average production of 118900 tonnes. The table indicates that the catch trend of Bombay duck from Gujarat indicated rising trend continuously from 2003 to 2008, except the production in the year of 2009 when the production decreased to about 27 per cent from the previous year. Maharashtra ranks second with the average production of 64372 tonnes. The state of West Bengal, Andhra Pradesh and Orissa ranked at third, fourth and fifth places with the average production of 20919 tonnes, 1845 tonnes and 1086 tonnes respectively. Goa is the lowest contributing state with average production of 12 tonnes.

## UTILIZATION OF CATCH

The fish is very soft and is easily spoiled due to high water content. A portion of the fresh fish is used as a food, but the bulk of it is preserved by sun drying. Drying and salt curing of Bombay duck on bamboo scaffold or raised platform is attempted at many coastal places. When the fish is not fit for human consumption it is also converted into manure.

## LAMINATED BOMBAY DUCK

The fish is cut longitudinally eviscerated, washed in brine of 2-5 per cent strength and hanged over bamboo scaffoldings from hooks. Series of such bamboo scaffoldings can be seen erected on to the shore of Mumbai and North of Gujarat. The fishes are sun dried over the bamboo scaffoldings reducing the water content to less than 10 per cent. Fishes are taken out, fins are trimmed and it is roller pressed, again dried and packed into polythene bags and stored in cool place. There is great demand of laminated Bombay duck nationally and for export internationally to Malaysia, Singapore, Burma, Thailand and other South East Asian countries.

**Table 6.9.2: State-wise Production of Bombay Duck**

| Years / States | Production (tonnes) | | | | | | | Avarage (2006-2009) |
|---|---|---|---|---|---|---|---|---|
| | 2003 | 2004 | 2005 | 2006 | 2007 | 2008 | 2009 | |
| **Gujarat** | 74707 | 90767 | 91916 | 94215 | 114370 | 154709 | 112305 | **118900** |
| **Maharashtra** | 24108 | 44265 | 66614 | 58262 | 70362 | 63570 | 65292 | **64372** |
| **West Bengal** | 39313 | 34349 | 28102 | 32107 | 23410 | 13704 | 14456 | **20919** |
| **Andhra** | 800 | 1077 | 660 | 2420 | 1319 | 1484 | 2158 | **1845** |
| **Orissa** | 751 | 454 | 626 | 1118 | 826 | 1081 | 1317 | **1085** |
| **Daman and Diu** | 149 | 253 | 248 | 61 | 243 | 83 | 332 | **180** |
| **Pondicherry** | 37 | 65 | 62 | 110 | 140 | 150 | 185 | **146** |
| **Goa** | 0 | 0 | 0 | 0 | 0 | 0 | 51 | **13** |
| **Total Catch** | **139865** | **171230** | **188228** | **188293** | **210670** | **234781** | **196096** | |

## 6.10 RIBBONFISHES

### Scientific Classification

| | | |
|---|---|---|
| *Class* | : | Teleostomi |
| *Sub-class* | : | Actinopterygii |
| *Family* | : | Trachiuridae |
| *Species* | : | *Trachiurus lepturus, T. trachiurus, Lepturacanthus savala* |

### STATUS

The fishery contributes about 5.5 per cent to the total marine fish landing in India. There are about 7 to 8 species found in the Indian waters and having low priced food value. *T. lepturus* has been found to be the most common species occurring in Indian Ocean. The fish does not earn good market value even then they are consumed by many people, because of being abundant and cheap. They are specially preferred by common man and considered poor fisherman's food. Recently the export of frozen large sized *L. savala* to China has generated high potential for its fishery.

### DISTRIBUTION

They are widely distributed along the Indian coast. Besides this they are landed at several places of East and West of coasts of India.

Ribbon fish is shoaling fish in the Indian waters the species shoal separately at different places. Along the west coast *T.lepturus* and *L.savala* are prominent in Konkan and Malabar coasts, while along the east coast *L.savala* is known to occur in Gulf of Mannar and *T.lepturus* forms the fishery of Tamil Nadu and Andhra Pradesh.

### DIAGNOSTIC FEATURES

The body of Ribbon fish is a very long, compressed, tape or ribbon like having short head, narrow mouth, strong teeth's in jaws and silvery smooth skin. A high dorsal fin present, running the whole length of the back of the body. Anal fin is absent, the caudal fin consists two bundles of rays, the pectoral fins are small and the pelvic fins are composed of several rays. The fish contains heavy spines along their lateral lines.

## FOOD AND FEEDING

Ribbon fishes are carnivorous and feed mainly on small prawns, small fishes, and larvae etc. from mid water and have sharp canine teeth's in the jaws.

## GROWTH, DEVELOPMENT AND REPRODUCTIVE BEHAVIOR

*T. lepturus* attains first maturity at 41-43 cms length when the fish is more than a year old. It is therefore necessary to increase the age of its first capture to avoid fishing in the first year to safeguard the stock of Ribbon fish against overfishing at higher level of fishing efforts. This fish breeds mainly in monsoon season, peak is from June – July – August. The fish spawns once in a year in the off shore water.

## CRAFTS AND GEARS USED FOR THE FISHING

The fish can be captured by every kind of gear and at every place of column oceanic water. In view of its known diurnal behavior, bottom trawling during day and pelagic trawling or purse seining during night is advocated. Since the fish is caught and trapped with almost every type of gear, unnoticeably therefore it is difficult to draw up the management measures to conserve the stock of ribbon fish. They are also caught by Dol net in coastal waters and also by Gill net.

Fishing season lasts from the end of August to March. During monsoon fishing is recommended since higher standing stock is found at that time along the continental shelf of South West India. It is therefore due to rough weather conditions during monsoon that only large vessels can take this advantage. The main fishing centers for the landing of Ribbon fish are Veraval, Jamnagar, Mumbai, Ratnagiri, Goa, Mangalore, Udupi, Cochin etc. from the west coast and Chennai, Rameshwaram, Tuticorin, Visakhapatnam, Puri, Paradeep etc. from the east coast.

## ANNUAL CATCH TREND

Lowest catch was recorded in the year 1963 with a production of only 16,452 tonnes. The worst poor production years were 1961 to 1965 when the average catch of Ribbon fish production in the country was only about 16,900 tonnes. Highest production was recorded in the year 2000 with the production of about 1,82,743 tonnes. The harvest even though fluctuating, it was at moderate levels fetching annually over 1.0 lakh tonnes between2001to 2005. The ribbon fish landing increased to 1,44,403 tonnes in 2006 and later gradually declined to 1,25,140 tonnes in 2007, to 1,19181 tonnes in 2008,further relatively low to 98,855 tonnes in 2009. The average production of ribbon fish from 2006 to 2009 was 1,21895 tonnes.

**Table 6.10.1: Annual Catch Trend of Ribbon Fish**

| *Year* | *Production (tonnes)* | *Year* | *Production (tonnes)* |
|---|---|---|---|
| **2000** | 1,82,743 | **2001** | 1,27,530 |
| **2003** | 1,11,149 | **2004** | 1,04,719 |
| **2005** | 1,14,968 | **2006** | 1,44,403 |
| **2007** | 1,25,140 | **2008** | 1,19,181 |
| **2009** | 98,855 | | |

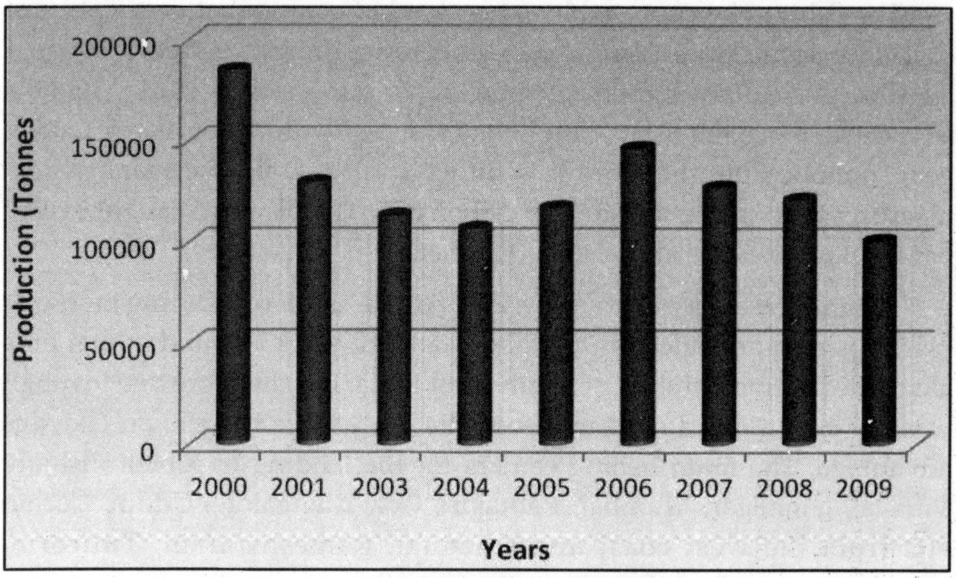


**Figure 6.10.1: Year-wise Production of Ribbon Fishes from India (2000-2009)**

## STATE WISE CATCH TRENDS

Maharashtra is the highest contributing state for the production of Ribbon fish with the average production of 35337 tonnes during 2006 to 2009. The production of Gujrat was more from 2001 to 2005 but in later years from 2006 to 2009 with the exception of the year 2007 it declined to the production than Maharashtra (Table 6.10.2). Gujarat and Kerala

**Table 6.10.2: State-wise Catch Trend of Ribbon Fish**

| *Years* | *Production (tonnes)* | | | | | | | *Avarage (2006-2009)* |
|---|---|---|---|---|---|---|---|---|
| *States* | *2003* | *2004* | *2005* | *2006* | *2007* | *2008* | *2009* | |
| **Maharashtra** | 41844 | 29998 | 33262 | 47455 | 34186 | 29619 | 30089 | **35337** |
| **Gujarat** | 45478 | 45992 | 41175 | 42533 | 35869 | 26986 | 28789 | **33544** |
| **Kerala** | 0 | 0 | 0 | 16533 | 16092 | 16118 | 15911 | **16163** |
| **Orissa** | 6208 | 5580 | 6947 | 8680 | 11628 | 10150 | 5415 | **8968** |
| **Karnataka** | 10854 | 11198 | 13641 | 7616 | 8104 | 16671 | – | **8098** |
| **Andhra Pradesh** | 0 | 3146 | 3924 | 5685 | 5936 | 6453 | 7913 | **6497** |
| **West Bengal** | 2445 | 2950 | 7807 | 8195 | 6440 | 5273 | 5919 | **6457** |
| **Goa** | 1430 | 3178 | 5791 | 5354 | 1368 | 2551 | 558 | **2458** |
| **Tamil Nadu** | 947 | 947 | 947 | 352 | 2553 | 2525 | 2470 | **1975** |
| **Daman and Diu** | 1032 | 980 | 1240 | 1350 | 2000 | 2056 | 1041 | **1612** |
| **Pondicherry** | 911 | 750 | 234 | 588 | 879 | 711 | 688 | **716** |
| **Andaman and Nicobar** | 0 | 0 | 0 | 62 | 85 | 68 | 62 | **69.25** |
| **Total Catch** | **111149** | **104719** | **114968** | **144403** | **125140** | **119181** | **98855** | |

occupy 2nd and 3rd position with the average production of 33,544 and 16,163 tonnes respectively. Along the east coast good landing of Ribbon fish is realized from the states of Orissa and Andhra Pradesh with the average production of 8968 and 6497 tonnes respectively.

## UTILIZATION

Large fishes are preferred for fresh consumption. The smaller ones are mostly suited for sun drying and curing. During peak months the catch is salt cured and scattered for drying on the open beaches. The cured and sun dried Ribbon fish have local as well as export demand in Sri Lanka and Malaysia. Recently *T. leptrurs* and *L. savala* in frozen form have attracted huge demand from China and Japan. Nearly 64 per cent of Ribbon fishes are exported to China, Japan and South East Asian countries by India. The larger Ribbon fish are several times sun dried over bamboo scaffoldings and are also salt cured.

## RECOMMENDATION

During monsoon the maximum movement of fish is in continental waters therefore the mechanized boats of large size which sustain rough wheather conditions can take the advantage of fishing in monsoon months.

## 6.11 HILSA

### Scientific Classification

| | | |
|---|---|---|
| *Class* | : | Teleostomi |
| *Sub-class* | : | Actinopterygii |
| *Order* | : | Clupeiformes |
| *Family* | : | Clupeidae |
| *Species* | : | *Hilsa ilisha* |

## STATUS

Popularly known a Indian Shad, represented by the *Hilsa ilisha*. This fishery is most prominent in the state of West Bengal and other North East Coasts. It is mainly the marine fish of inshore water. It is anadromous, migrating to estuaries, rivers and fresh water bodies for breeding.

## DISTRIBUTION

Hilsa is widely distributed in International waters from Shatt-al-Arab, Tigris, Iran, and Persian Gulf, Sind region of Pakistan, India, Bangladesh and Myanmar. The bulk of landing at International level are realized from Bangladesh 75 per cent, India 20 per cent, and Myanmar 5 per cent.

In India it is found along Arabian Sea, West Bengal with patchy distribution. The high concentration of Hilsa in Bay of Bengal is found all along the Andhra Pradesh, Orissa, with the highest in West Bengal. As being anadromous especially during the breeding time the fish is also known to be harvested from riverine waters of Narmada, Purla, Kali. Krishna, Godavari, Mahanadi, Hugli, Ganga etc.

## DIAGNOSTIC FEATURES

The body of Hilsa is covered by smooth, silvery skin with gold and purple colour spots. Adult fish have no spot. Lower jaw is not projecting beyond the upper. Caudal lobes equal to length of head.

## FOOD AND FEEDING

The fish is mainly the plankton feeder, but sometimes also omnivores. Larvae and young hilsa feed mainly on diatom, Copepod and Daphnia while the older ones feed on Blue Green Algae, Cladocerons, Rotifers, Protozooans, Cructaceans, and Organic Debris etc.

## GROWTH DEVELOPMENT AND REPRODUCTIVE BEHAVIOR

Hilsa is heterosexual. The female attains larger size than males due to higher growth rate. There are no visible signs of sexual dimorphism. They attain maturity when they are one and half year old. The males mature earlier than females. Males mature at 30 cms while female at 35.6 cms of lengths. The minimum size at first maturity for females is between 20 cms while for males it is from 16 to 17 cms. Mating is polygamous type. Fecundity varies according to size, age and weight. However the female is known to release 3 to 20 lakhs eggs at a time. Fertilization is external. The spawning season is from September to October. Spawning is related to tidal action, water flow, availability of food and other natural environmental factors.

### Life Cycle

Hilsa during breeding season migrate to the estuary and riverine waters. They lay eggs mostly in lesser saline of fresh water bodies. The newly hatched larvae find out their nursery ground and reach in size like Chapile called Jatka. Jatka are able to tolerate fresh water or saline water initially but rush later to the coastal water. After they enter into the sea, reach in adult stage and within two years they are ready for breeding.

## MIGRATION AND SHOALING BEHAVIOUR

The fish is a classical example for exhibiting migration for breeding, spawning and feeding. The migration is anadromous type with the mature fish migrate upstream into rivers (fresh water) from sea during their spawning season. Male ascend to the spawning ground earlier than females. After spawning the Hilsa return to the sea. The newly hatched larvae and juvenile which are also called 'Jatka' migrate to sea later on.

During migrations upstream the fish congregate but they have never been observed to form very dense schools as found in other pelagic fishes like Sardines. During winter months however they form very large school at the entrance of the high estuary.

## CRAFT AND GEAR USED FOR FISHING

A wide variety of gears are used for the capture of Hilsa mostly the boat seines. At some places even specially designed gill nets are used for the capture in coastal waters. In the waters of Continental Shelf drift gill nets are also used. The bulk of the fishery is constituted by fish in size range of 260 mm to 480 mm.

## ANNUAL CATCH TREND

The annual catch (1999-2003) increased from 21086 tonnes in 1999 to 44, 734 tonnes. The production between 2006 and 2009 has indicated unsteady trend with the high of 25,743 in 2006 to the low of 19,833 tonnes in 2009 and average of 22,596 tonnes.

**Table 6.11.1: Annual Catch Trend of Hilsa**

| *Year* | *Production (tonnes)* | *Year* | *Production (tonnes)* |
|---|---|---|---|
| **2006** | 25743 | **2007** | 21480 |
| **2008** | 22330 | **2009** | 19833 |

## STATEWISE CATCH TREND

West Bengal is the highest contributing state for the production of Hilsa with the production of 16072 tonnes, 9431 tonnes, 11744 tonnes and 10560 tonnes in 2006, 2007, 2008 and 2009 respectively and average production of 11952 tonnes while during the same time Orissa and Andhra Pradesh are in 2nd and 3rd position with the average production of 3765 and 2968 tonnes respectively.

**Table 6.11.2: State-wise Production of Hilsa**

| States | Years/Production | | | | Avarage (2006-2009) |
|---|---|---|---|---|---|
| | 2006 | 2007 | 2008 | 2009 | |
| **West Bengal** | 16072 | 9431 | 11744 | 10560 | **11952** |
| **Orissa** | 3630 | 4029 | 4146 | 3256 | **3765** |
| **Andhra Pradesh** | 2668 | 3687 | 3904 | 1613 | **2968** |
| **Gujarat** | 2471 | 3240 | 1701 | 1616 | **2257** |
| **Maharashtra** | 0 | 0 | 0 | 2161 | **540** |
| **Daman and Diu** | 706 | 703 | 340 | 250 | **500** |
| **Andaman and Nicobar** | 117 | 196 | 295 | 280 | **222** |
| **Tamil Nadu** | 65 | 154 | 192 | 87 | **124** |
| **Pondicherry** | 14 | 40 | 8 | 10 | **18** |
| **Total Catch** | **25743** | **21480** | **22330** | **19833** | |

## PROBLEMS IN HILSA FISHERIES

In past few years, the population of Hilsa has been steadily declining, all due to the human being upsetting the natural balance through overfishing of the stock. Hilsa is an anadromous fish which mean it lives in ocean but travels to rivers to spawn and after spawning it travels back to sea. There are many literatures citing the example of occurring and production of Hilsa upstream the Ganges as far up to Allahabad and Kanpur. In sixties record production of Hilsa of over 60,000 tonnes was obtained from Buxar (Bihar). However due to construction of Farakka dam the fish is not able to reach to the stretches of Gangetic system to breed. Even the opening of some passage of Farakka dam could not restore the migratory pattern of the fish in Ganges. The closing of the migratory route for the fish to the potent fishing ground of Ganges has resulted into finding their passage for breeding within the state into nearby inland water areas or their migration to the river stretches in Bangladesh.

Presently in West Bengal the fish is under heavy exploitation as adults when they travel from sea to river, similarly as juveniles on their way back to the sea. As being basically oceanic species and similarly due to complexities involved in the understanding of its breeding, biology, physiology and migration behavior, the culturing or rearing of Hilsa is difficult. It therefore requires some urgent management measure like imposing the blanket ban jointly by India and Bangaladesh on commercial fishing of Hilsa during the time of breeding which may help in their conservation. India also could learn from Bangladesh in limiting harvesting of Hilsa by implementing judiciously the minimal size of harvesting. There are similar regulations as issued by West Bengal Government too but the implementation and adherence to these by coastal fishermen is not worthy to be mentioned. In future people participation, consumer's motivation to conserve this species, strict enforcement and vigilance at the fishing site and marketing places may help in conserving this valuable fish stock (IANS, 2012).

The important fishing centers of West Bengal are Shankarpur in Midnapur district, Freserganj in South 24 Parganas, Barge Jetty at Namkhau, Digha, Diamond harbor etc.

## 6.12 BARRACUDAS

### Scientific Classification

| | | |
|---|---|---|
| *Class* | : | Teleostomi |
| *Sub-class* | : | Actinoptergii |
| *Order* | : | Perciformes |
| *Family* | : | Sphyraenidae |
| *Species* | : | *Sphyraena barracuda* |
| | | *S. obtusata* |
| | | *S. jello* |
| | | *S. forsteri* |
| | | *S. sphyraena* |

There are more than twenty species of barracudas belongs to the genus Sphyraena which means "Pike like fish" in Latin.

### DISTRIBUTION

Internationally the barracudas are known to occur in tropical and subtropical parts of World Ocean. Worldwide there are 26 species of the fish. The fish is widely spread in the Indian, Pacific, East and West Atlantic and Caribbean Sea. In Indian Ocean the fish is widely occurring and the fishery is supported by *Sphyraena obtusata, S. barracuda, S. jello* and *S. forsteri.*

## DIAGNOSTIC FEATURES

Barracudas are elongated fish, Pike-like appearance, therefore also known as "Sea-Pike". The fish are of different sizes with prominent sharp-edged, fang-like teeth's, set in sockets of their large jaws which give the fish a fearsome look. They have developed, a highly efficient body, perfectly adopted as a successful predator of the ocean. Their bodies are elongated and slender, perfect for sneaking through the reefs when hunting. They have large mouth and a pair of powerful jaws. The lower jaw juts out slightly and have unequally sized fang-like teeth's which have earned them the nick name "Tiger of the Sea". They have two extensively separated dorsal fins and a forked tailfin which makes them fast swimmers. In terms of coloration barracudas are dark green, dark to blue grey or silver on top, fading into white (Chalky white) on the belly with whitish tips on their dark violet caudal fins.

## FOOD AND FEEDING

Hunting for food is a serious business for barracudas and due to their sharp eyesight and powerful jaws they are one of a few predators towards the top of the food chain. Known to be extremely opportunistic, they often camouflage near Sea grass to ambush unsuspecting prey and move fast (over 40 km/hour) through coral reefs hunting for food. When attacking they do so with a single clean bite of deadly consequence. They mainly feed on smaller fishes such as Snappers, Grunts, Mullets and Breams. The cannibalism is also part of barracuda culture. Their powerful jaws can also attack on larger fish; since they can chop the bigger fish in half, so ultimately anything that seems edible may be fair game for them.

## GROWTH, DEVELOPMENT AND REPRODUCTIVE BEHAVIOR

There does not exist a great deal of documented information about where and when the spawning occurs. It is believed to be between April and September. During the breeding season, the females spawn a few times, releasing about 5000 to 300000 of eggs each time. Like most fish, barracudas leave fertilized eggs floating in the open waters until they hatch.

### Life Cycle

Soon after hatching, barracuda larvae settle in shallow estuaries where vegetation offers both protection and food to the larvae for round a year until they grow into juveniles. Upon entering adulthood, they move to deeper water in areas with reefs and remain there for the rest of their lives.

## MIGRATION AND SHOALING BEHAVIOUR

Generally adult barracudas are considered to be solitary when it comes to hunting. Most young barracudas tend to gather in large schools, sometimes in numbers up to hundreds or even thousands. Schooling offers young fish protection from predators on the basis of safety in numbers. Often when a predator attacks a school, the school would form a confusing tornado, preventing any one barracuda being fixed upon as prey in the eye of the predator. For hunting purposes, the many eyes of the school normally cooperate in finding food. Although a large school means a smaller division of food among them, it actually benefits in terms of protection and food detection for them. The larger species such as *S. barracuda* are solitary and not found in schools.

## CRAFT AND GEAR USED FOR FISHING

The larger fish are caught by hooks and line. They can also be captured by bottom-set-gill-nets and drift gill nets. The smaller one also form good quantum of fishery from the trawl gear.

## ANNUAL CATCH TREND

In India in spite of their good potential the production of Barracudas is less, even among the pelagic fisheries its rank is very low.

The annual catch trend improved remarkably from the low production of 4000 tonnes in 1988 to highest 18575 tonnes in 2001. The average production of Barracudas from 1990 to 2005 was 14,040 tonnes and contributed about 1.1 per cent to the pelagic fish landing from India. Many times the production is still below than this annual production level, may even less than 10,000 tonnes. The average production between 2003 and

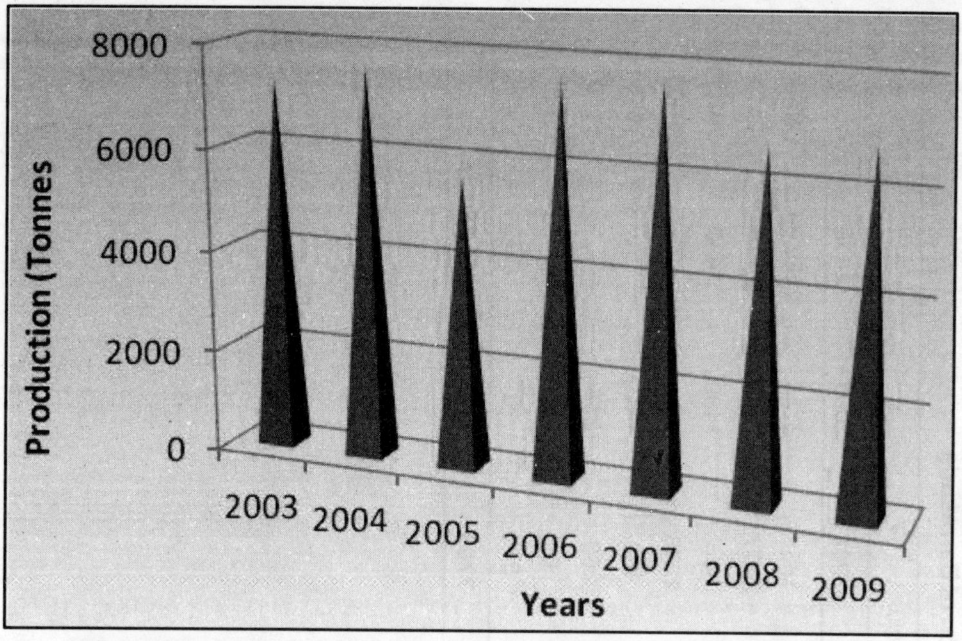


**Figure 6.12.1: Annual Landing of Barracuda from India (2003-2009)**

2005 was just 6,872 tonnes. In 2006 to 2009 the average production of barracuda slightly improved to 7232 tonnes.

**Table 6.12.1: Annual catch trend of Barracuda.**

| *Year* | *Production (tonnes)* | *Year* | *Production (tonnes)* |
|---|---|---|---|
| **2003** | 7310 | **2004** | 7621 |
| **2005** | 5685 | **2006** | 7630 |
| **2007** | 7705 | **2008** | 6739 |
| **2009** | 6856 | | |

## STATEWISE CATCH TREND

Tamil Nadu is the highest contributing state for the production of Barracuda with the average production of 2,574 tonnes during 2003 to 2009, followed by Kerala and Andaman and Nicobar at 2nd and 3rd position with the average production of 2,171 and 1,017 tonnes respectively. The state of Andhra Pradesh ranks fourth but in 2007 it was the highest producer of Barracuda in the country.

**Table 6.12.2: State-wise Production of Barracuda**

| *Years* | *Production (tonnes)* | | | | | | | *Avarage (2006-2009)* |
|---|---|---|---|---|---|---|---|---|
| *States* | *2003* | *2004* | *2005* | *2006* | *2007* | *2008* | *2009* | |
| **Tamil Nadu** | 2562 | 2562 | 2562 | 4054 | 1838 | 2136 | 2269.88 | **2574** |
| **Kerala** | 1940 | 1582 | 1656 | 2233 | 2177 | 2156 | 2118 | **2171** |
| **Andaman and Nicobar** | 1277 | 1277 | 376 | 514 | 634 | 1489 | 1430 | **1017** |
| **Andhra Pradesh** | 880 | 816 | 563 | 563 | 2248 | 0 | 0 | **1405** |
| **Pondicherry** | 537 | 1304 | 460 | 786 | 483 | 612 | 750 | **658** |
| **Karnataka** | 0 | 0 | 0 | 0 | 263 | 328 | – | **148** |
| **West Bengal** | 0 | 0 | 0 | 0 | 0 | 0 | 275 | **69** |
| **Daman and Diu** | 74 | 40 | 40 | 43 | 50 | 18 | 13 | **31** |
| **Total Catch** | **7310** | **7621** | **5685** | **7630** | **7705** | **6739** | **6855.88** | |

## 6.13 ELASMOBRANCHES

### STATUS

The Elasmobranches fishery includes those of sharks, Rays and Skates which are characterized by the possession of cartilaginous skeletons. Elasmobranches fish are essentially marine in nature, but some varieties are encountered in fresh water also. The history of existence of this group of fishes especially the sharks is since from prehistoric time dates back to more than 400 million years old.

### DISTRIBUTION

The elasmobranches internationally indicate rather cosmopolitan distribution that is in tropical, subtropical and temperate cold water of the world oceans. The elasmobranches are widely distributed in Indian waters along both west and east coast of India with the prominence of occurrence in Gujarat, Maharashtra, Tamil Nadu, Andhra Pradesh and Orissa states.

### DIAGNOSTIC FEATURES

Unlike most teleost, members of elasmobranches have no swim bladders. The rough skin which is one of the characters of this group is due to covering of the hard tooth like placoid scales which help to reduce drag and resistance in water. The fishes from the group have five to seven pairs of gill clefts opening individually to exterior. The fishes have rigid dorsal fin. The teeth are very sharp and exist in several series along both the jaws and get continuously replaced. The upper jaw is not fused to the cranium and the lower jaw is articulated with the upper. This group contains fishes with several shapes and sizes most sharks have a torpedo like streamlined body where as skates and rays have flattened bodies. The elasmobranches lead their life in various types of habitats. Some found in coastal inshore waters, some in surface pelagic waters of deep sea, some perform extensive migration while few live like skates and rays in the deep waters to at least 3000 meters.

The elasmobranches are renowned for their highly tuned senses which make them incredibly successful in their environment. Their sense of smell is very sensitive and most species have large nostrils that allow a large volume of water to flow continually over olfactory organs. Some surprisingly use hearing also a very important activity and have well developed ears which do not have any external sign except for two tiny holes behind their eyes. Hearing is often the first sense to detect prey at long distance and is used in conjunction with a special sensory organ called the lateral line which in the line of pressures detectors that runs down each side of their body. These detect changes in water pressure that might result from struggling prey. A special sense organ which is found around the snout and mouth is known as the Ampullae of Lorenzini which detect electric field given off by prey. Many sharks have good eye sight and great white shark can even see when his head is out of water. When combined all these sense make elasmobranches good hunters and helps explain how they have manage to survive for 400 million years.

## FOOD AND FEEDING

They are the top order carnivores while venturing in the ocean from coastal inshore water, offshore and deep waters. The presence of sharp, pointed canine teeth along both the jaws indicates them to be the ferocious feeder, tearing and crushing the prey.

## REPRODUCTIVE CHARACTERISTICS

Most of the elasmobranches with the exception of certain skates are viviparous, having internal fertilization and they give birth to young one. The male and female are distinguished by having two extensions of modification of pelvic fins as claspers in males and a prominent genital opening at lower ventral side in females. These claspers are used by males during reproduction to internally fertilize the female. The young one develops inside the body of mother in much the same way as in mammals. The mother often undergoes the pregnancy period for anywhere up to two years depending upon the species. This form of reproduction can be further divided into two categories. The first is aplacental viviparity where the developing young are nourished either by a yolk ball or by absorbing secretion from mother (histotropy), by eating extra eggs (oophagy) or even by eating their siblings (embryophagy). The other form is placental viviparity where by after using their yolk ball the young develop placental connection with the mother.

Some species of shark such as lesser spotted dog fish (*Scyliorhinus canicula)* and all skates are oviparous and lay egg cases on sea bed or wrapped around the sea weed. After the fertilization of eggs, the young develops within the egg cases whilst being nourished by a ball yolk. These egg cases often washed upon the beaches and are commonly known as mermaid's purse. The egg purse then ruptures during hatching and young one are released in water.

## FISHERY

The elasmobranches fishery in India is dominant along the west coast of India. The bulk of catch realizing from the states of Gujarat, Maharashtra and Karnataka from the west coast and the states of Tamil Nadu, Andhra Pradesh and Orissa from the east coast respectively. The group collectively comprise of the fishery of sharks, skates and rays respectively.

## FISHERY OF SHARKS

Table 6.13.1 provides the group wise and species wise details of elasmobranches occurring in Indian waters.

From immoral time sharks have been the object of amusement. At certain times they are even considered as dreaded monster of the sea because of the dangers of attacking on bathers, fisherman and even damaging their boats. The appearance of open mouth full of sharp teeth and black fins gives fearsome feeling to unarmed people taking bath in the shallow waters. Internationally of all the 350 species of sharks only less than 35 species are aggressive and attack human beings, boats and other objects. About 49 species of sharks belonging to the five orders are namely Hexanchiformes, Squaliforms, Orectolobiformes, Laminiformes and Carcharhiniformes. There are collectively 14 families known to exist in Indian waters. The maximum about 30 species are known to occur from order Carcharhinformes.

## HABITAT DISTRIBUTION

Even though the major species of sharks occur in marine environment some may enter bays, lagoons and estuaries. *Carcharhinus leucas* and *Carcharhinus gangelicus* migrates up into the rivers, lakes which have connection to the sea. Although the maximum species of sharks are demersal such as dog sharks (*Scoliodon laticudus, S. walbeehmii*), cat sharks (*Chiloscyllium griseum*) etc, some found in pelagic inshore water such as

**Table 6.13.1: Number of Shark Species Occurring in the Indian Waters**

| *Order* | *Family* | *Common Name* | *Scientific Name* |
|---|---|---|---|
| Hexanchiformes | Hexanidae | Cowsharks | |
| Squaliformes | Echinorhinidae | Bramble sharks | *Echinorhinus brucus* |
| Orectolobiformes | Hemiscyllidae | Bamboo sharks | |
| | Stegostomatidae | Zebra shark | |
| | Ginglymostomatidae | Nurse shark | |
| | Rhiniodontidae | Whale shark | *Rhiniodon typus* |
| Laminiformes | Alopidae | Thresher/Fox shark | *Allopias vulpinus* |
| | Laminidae | Mackerel shark (Great White shark) | *Carcharodon carcharias* |
| Carcharhiniformes | Scyliorhinidae | Cat shark | *Chiloscyllium griseum* |
| | | lesser spotted dogfish | *Scyliorhinus canicula* |
| | Porscyllidae | Finback cat sharks | |
| | | Small shark (pygmy ribbontail catshark) | *Eridacnis radcliffei* |
| | Leptocharidae | Barbeled hounds | |
| | Hemigaleidae | Weasel shark | |
| | Carcharhinidae | Tiger shark | *Galeocerdo cuvier* |
| | | White tip shark | *Carcharhinus longimanus* |
| | | Bull shark | *Carcharhinus leucas* |
| | | Whitecheek shark | *Carcharhinus dussumieri* |
| | | Dog shark | *Scoliodon laticulus* |
| | | Ganges shark | *Glyphis gangeticus* |
| | | Speartooth shark | *Glyphis glyphis* |
| | | Pondicherry shark | *Carcharhinus hemiodon* |
| | Sphyrnidae | Hammer headed shark | *Sphyrna lewini, S. tudus* |

*Sphyrna lewini, Sphyrna tudes* and few are epipelagic such as oceanic white tip shark (*Carcharhinus longimanus*), Thresher shark/Fox shark (*Alopias vulpinus*) etc. The sharks have evolved a life history strategy very similar to that of marine reptile and mammals. The life of shark is characterized by slow growth during the adult fish, late reproduction and the production of a few but well developed young ones which is quite different then found in teolests.

## SIZE AND SHAPES

Sharks exhibits different ranges of size but are much larger than teolests. The size range is very large ranging from the size of 24 cms in the smallest shark *Eridacnis radcliffei* to the largest whale shark *Rhiniodon typus* which is the largest fish in the world reaching to about 1500 cms.

In the Indian waters 14 species attain length ranging between 24 and 100 cms; 10 attain 101 and 200 cms; 5 attain 201 to 300 cms; 8 attain 301 to 400 cms; 3 attain 501 to 600 cms and 1 the largest is whale shark. The maximum lengths of 6 species, which contribute major fisheries along the Indian coast, range from 60 to 309 cm.

The shape of sharks is also varied having long slender streamline body with thick fleshy dorsal, pectoral and caudal fin to attain demandingly fast speed needed for preying as in the case of most carchichniformis like White Shark (*Carcharhinus dussumieri*), Tiger Shark (*Galeocerdo cuvieri*) etc. The caudal fin in Dog Shark and some of the smallest shark is forked. In most of the shark the front portion gets extended as snout and the cleft of the mouth is forwardly ventrally placed. The Hammer Headed sharks are a group of shark in the family sphyrnidae, so named for the unusual and distinctive structure of their heads, which are flattened and laterally extended into a hammer shaped Cephalofoil. Most of the hammer head sharks are placed in the genus sphyrna. The Cephalofoil carry mutually exclusive function such as sensory reception, maneuvering and prey manipulation. Now it is recently found that the hammer like shape of the head may have evolved to enhance animal vision by positioning of the eyes mounted on the sides of sharks and the distinctive hammer head (along both Cephalofoils) give the shark 360° vision in the vertical plain so that they can see above and below them all times. The hammerheads are found worldwide in warmer waters along coastline and continental shelves. Unlike most sharks hammerhead usually swims in schools during the day and becoming solitary hunter at night. The hammerhead ranges from 0.9 to 6 meters (3 to 20 feet) and weigh from 3 to 580 kg. Although several hammer headed species are quite large, they are more slender and streamlined compared to the other large sharks which undoubtedly increased their speed and maneuverability in the water. Hammerheads have disproportionately small mouth and seem to do a lot of bottom hunting.

## REPRODUCTION

Among sharks occurring in Indian waters 29 species are viviparous, 7 are ovoviviparous and 13 are oviparous. The pattern of oviphagus (egg eating) embryos exists in temperate sharks. Despite the variation in the life pattern there are a few common features. All the viviparous shark produce limited number of well developed young one. The tiger shark (*Galeocerdo cuvieri*) and the hammer headed shark (*Sphyrna species*) have the capacity to produce more than 80 and 30 young ones/brood respectively however most shark produce limited number of young ones like *Carcharchinides* produce only 2 to 4 young ones/broods once or twice a years. Unlike the teolests which have fragile early life stages, the young one of sharks are released in well developed stage with better chances of survival individually. The Bull shark (*C. leucas*) releases the young ones of 56 to 81 cm length which are about 20 per cent of maximum length of shark. Even though the smallest shark *E. radcliffei* produce one or two young ones per brood, but the young ones of 11 cms forms about 46 per cent of maximum length of the fish.

There are instances of oviparity breeding in sharks which is considered primitive to viviparity. The female releases the egg or ova in a capsule which get fertilized outside. The transitional phase of ovo-viviparity is found in Whale Sharks.

## FISHING AND FISHING GEARS

Sharks are subjected for heavy fishing due to its high demand for extraction of oil, skin, fins, teeth etc. The targeted fishing of sharks is followed for the capture of large varieties. Whale sharks *R. typus* are intentionally caught using harpoon while migrating to Saurashtra coast during January – March every year. There has been intense fishing of sharks and elasmobranches through derogatory use of harpoons, hook and lines, long lines since 1990 which has resulted into the depletion of their stock. The Government of India implemented in 2001 under schedule I of the Wildlife Protection Act 1972, imposed ban on fishing of 4 species of sharks they are Whale Shark (*R. typus)*, Pondicherry Shark (*C. hemiodon*), the Gangetic Shark (*Glyphis gangeticus*) and Spear toothed shark (*G. glyphis*) for the conservation of this important community.

## FISHERY OF BATOIDS (SAW FISH, RAYS, SKATES AND ELECTRIC RAYS)

The Batoids is represented by suborder Pristiforms (Saw fish), Rajiformes (Skates), Myliobatiformes (Rays) and Torpedinoformes (Electric rays).

### Pristiformes

The saw fishes are shark-like in form, having tails used for swimming and have small pectoral fins than most of the batoids. The pectoral fins are attached above the gills as in all batoids, giving the fishes a broad headed appearance. They have flat snout that is modified into a long blade, possessing a series of strong teeth on each side. The snouts are up to 1.8 meters (6 feet) long and 30 cms (1 foot) wide are used for slashing and impaling small fishes and to probe in the mud for embedded animals. They are found in seas frequenting between sandy shores and estuaries, they may enter sometimes in rivers also. Some species reach a total length of 6 meters (20 feet). About 6 species are known to occur in warm seas, of these *Pristis monodon* and *Pristis causpidatusie* are prominent in Indian waters.

### Difference between Skates and Rays

The skates and rays are flat bodied elasmobranches both look much alike and share a number of common traits. The difference between skates and rays are that the rays are kite shaped and have streamlined tails with one or more venomous barbs while skates tend to be roundish or triangular in shape with heavier, fleshier tail that have small fins towards the end but it do not contain a barb. Rays and skates also defend themselves differently. The stinging barb on the ray's tail is an effective weapon. When needed the barb comes out of the thin skin, pierced within the victim and releases the venom. Skates don't have barbs, relying instead on thorn-like formations and tails to deter predators.

### Rajiformes (Skates)

They are also referred as Skates. They are represented by five families namely Anacanthobatidae (Smooth Skates), Rajidae or Rhinidae (brown mouth guitar fish), Rhinobatidae (Guitar fish), Rhynchobatidae (Wedge fishes). They are characterized by the large pectoral fins extending to snout and backward, stopping abruptly at the base of slender tail. They have small fins towards the end of the tail in contrast to the rays; skates produce eggs, which are large oblong in shape with dark leathery shells having a tendril at each corner by which the egg become fastened to seaweed or other objects. Skates lack the long, slender barbed spine that distinguishes sting rays. The most wide spread skates belong to the genus Raja of the family Rajidae. In the Indian waters the most prominent ones are *Rhinobatus granulates* (Granulated shovelnose ray), *Rhinobatus obtusus, Rhinobatus armatus, Raja mamillidens* (Prickly Skates) and *Rhynchodonbatus djiddensis* (Guitar fish).

### Myliobatiformes (Rays)

They are represented by about 10 families based on either shape or habitat of species namely Dasyatidae (Whiptail sting rays), Gymnuridae (Butterfly rays), Hexatrygonidae (six gill sting ray), Myliobatidae (Eagle rays), Platyrhinidae (Thorn backs), Plesiobatidae (Deepwater sting ray), Potamotrygonidae (River sting rays), Urolophidae (Round sting rays), Urotrygonidae (American round sting rays), Zanobatidae (Pan rays), Mobulidae (Manta rays or Devil rays).

They have flattened disc like body mostly kite shaped. They have wing like pectoral fins which extend forward along the sides of the head above the gill openings. Many rays propel themselves with their pectoral fins and taking in water for respiration through large openings called spiracles on the upper surface of head rather than through mouth. The ray's tail is whip like generally long slender that usually has a barbed spine connected with a poison gland. This spine is capable of inflicting serious wounds and is a dangerous weapon when the tail lashes. They are all found in warmer seas.

About 15 species are known to occur in the Indian waters. The most dominant ones belong to *Dasyatis* genera. They are *Dasyatis bleekeri* (White Tail Sting Ray), *D. kuhill* (Blue Spotted Sting Ray), *D. zugei* (Pale-Edged Sting Ray) and *D. imbricate*. The other are *Actobatus flagellum, Aetobtus narinari* (Spot Edged Ray), *Rhinoptera javanica* (Javanose Cow Ray), *Manta birostris* (Gaint Devil Ray), *Himantura fluviatilis* and *Urogymnus asperinus*.

They are bottom dwellers and are carnivorous feeding on various fishes, invertebrates, sometimes damaging commercially valuable shellfish beds. Mantra ray feed on plankton and small animals. Unlike skates possibly all rays are viviparous bear living young one. Fertilization is internal, the male introducing sperm into the female by means of special copulatory organs called claspers, that are the modified edges of the pelvic fins. The young one develops into placental link with mother, which after the specific period of pregnancy gives birth to young ones in open waters.

### Torpedineformes (Electric Rays)

They are also called electric ray, characterized by having electrical organs in their pectoral fin disc that generate electric current. They are used to immobilize the prey and for defense. The current is strong enough to stun humans and the ancient Greek and Roman used these fish to treat ailments such as headaches. They are represented by two families namely Narcinidae (Numb fishes) and Torpanidae (Torpedo electric ray). In Indian waters the prominent species are *Narcine india* and *Tygom zuge*. They are not preferred for human consumption.

## ANNUAL CATCH TREND

**Table 6.13.2: Annual Catch Trend of Elasmobranch**

| *Year* | *Production (tonnes)* | *Year* | *Production (tonnes)* |
|---|---|---|---|
| **2003** | 63266 | **2004** | 79825 |
| **2005** | 61056 | **2006** | 80385 |
| **2007** | 86369 | **2008** | 71799 |
| **2009** | 72123 | | |

The elasmobranches are one of the important groups of demersal fishery of India. Even though the production pattern of elasmobranches indicates the increasing trend however its share to the demersal fish production has reduced over the years. It was found that the share of elasmobranches to the total demersal landing from India decreased from 20.6 per cent in 1961 to about 8.6 per cent in 2004. The critical examination of the catch pattern of the demersal fish group and fishing methods employed has revealed that the contribution of elasmobranches to the total demersal fish landing reduced from the time of inception of bottom trawl fishing in India during mid sixties. It is because of always varying habitat of elasmobranches which are the freely venturing commodities in the ocean from deeper waters to pelagic inshore waters and does not primarily form the part of harvest of the trawl gear. It was because of more emphasis towards the employment of trawl gear and perhaps the non-adoption of other demersal fishing methods the production of elasmobranches group declined from mid sixties.

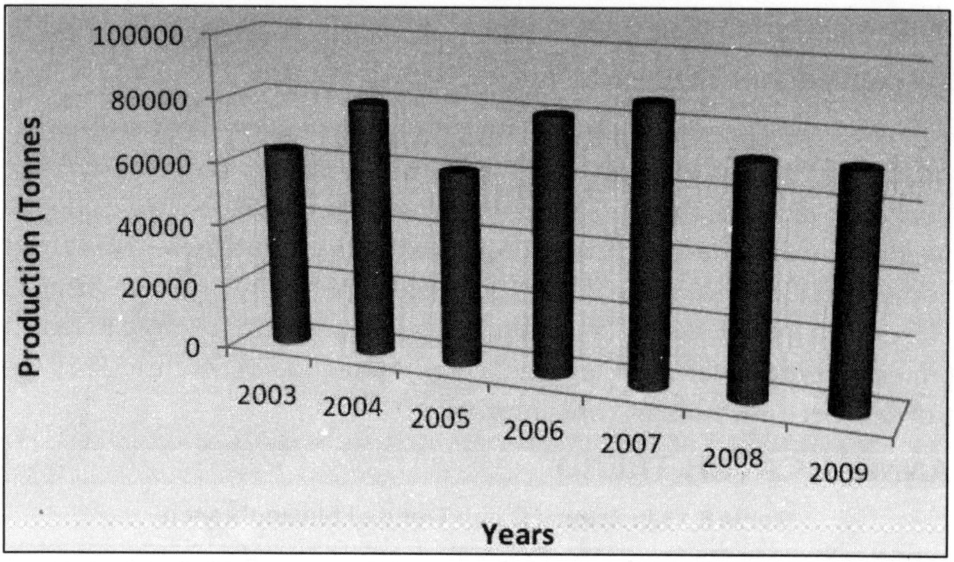


**Figure 6.13.1: Year-wise Landing of Elasmobranches from India (2003-2009)**

In India the elasmobranches mainly the sharks were subjected to heavily targeted fishing and were over exploited due to the use of derogatory fishing methods in the times during late fifties to sixties. It may be also that due to the implementation of conservation methods introduced after 1972 banning the targeted fishing to avoid overexploitation of sharks by the use of hooks and lines, long lines and harpoons the share from the elasmobranches group declined to the total demersal fish production for India. The production pattern of demersal fishery in India from 2001 to 2004 suggested that among the elasmobranches the shark group is the most prominent one contributing about 5 per cent, followed by the rays about 3.7 per cent to the total demersal fish landing from India. The production trend was fluctuating with the landing of 63,266, 79,825 and 61,056 tonnes for the years 2003, 2004 and 2005 respectively. The production significantly increased to 80,385 and 86,369 tonnes in the years 2006 and 2007. The year 2008 and 2009 yielded about 71,799 and 72,123 tonnes of elasmobranches.

## STATEWISE CATCH TREND

The habitat distribution and harvest pattern of elasmobranches in India from 2001 to 2004 suggests that the sharks are the dominant group along the North-West coast of India (Gujarat and Maharashtra) followed by the North–East coast (Orissa and West Bengal), South-East coast (Tamil Nadu and Andhra Pradesh) and minimum from South-West coast (Karnataka and Kerela). The rays sequentially contribute highly from the region of South-East coast followed by North-East coast and rather poorly from North-West and South-West coast of India. The average production pattern between 2006 and 2009 suggested that the state of Tamil Nadu is the largest producer of elasmobranches with the average production of 18719 tonnes followed by the state of Gujarat at the second place having the averaging landing of 17614 tonnes, the state of Andhra Pradesh acquires the third position with the average landing of 15923 tonnes while the state of Maharashtra occupies the fourth rank with the average landing of 8183 tonnes.

## UTILIZATION OF CATCH

Sharks are very valuable fishes owing to the high demand of every part of their body. Shark liver oil which is rich source of vitamin A and help in fighting and curing dreaded disease like cancer. Dried shark fins used for rendering the fin rays widely used in China for the preparation of holya oriental cuisine soup and beverage. In 2002 about 250 tonnes dried shark fins valuing about Rs. 12 crore were exported from India. Dried shark fins have great demand in China, Singapore and Hong Kong, Malaysia etc. Jaws, teeth's and bones rendered for obtaining ornaments and jewelry, these items are also exported from India at expensive prices.

**Table 6.13.3: State-wise Yearly Production of Elasmobranch**

| *Years* | *Production (tonnes)* | | | | | | | *Avarage (2006-2009)* |
|---|---|---|---|---|---|---|---|---|
| *States* | *2003* | *2004* | *2005* | *2006* | *2007* | *2008* | *2009* | |
| **Gujarat** | 14624 | 11117 | 14725 | 16004 | 26194 | 12216 | 16044 | **17614** |
| **Kerala** | 2628 | 3024 | 3149 | 3287 | 3213 | 3208 | 00 | **2427** |
| **Maharashtra** | 7406 | 5207 | 5746 | 8188 | 10217 | 7583 | 6745 | **8183** |
| **Karnataka** | 2548 | 2172 | 2590 | 2811 | 929 | 1834 | 00 | **1393** |
| **Tamil Nadu** | 20244 | 20244 | 20244 | 22334 | 19405 | 16539 | 16598 | **18719** |
| **Andhra Pradesh** | 1674 | 23827 | 6253 | 16106 | 14134 | 16193 | 17261 | **15923** |
| **Goa** | 1016 | 1603 | 1871 | 988 | 1007 | 1019 | 1329 | **1086** |
| **Orissa** | 5814 | 4923 | 4409 | 6671 | 4142 | 4194 | 4764 | **4943** |
| **Daman and Diu** | 1377 | 1138 | 935 | 725 | 957 | 571 | 431 | **671** |
| **Andaman and Nicobar** | 395 | 395 | 71 | 2227 | 2956 | 3016 | 2927 | **2781** |
| **West Bengal** | 4118 | 4730 | 127 | 123 | 1988 | 4133 | 4827 | **2768** |
| **Pondicherry** | 1290 | 1313 | 715 | 841 | 1158 | 1246 | 1156 | **1100** |
| **Lakshadweep** | 132 | 132 | 221 | 80 | 69 | 47 | 41 | **59** |
| **Total Catch** | **63266** | **79825** | **61056** | **80385** | **86369** | **71799** | **72123** | |

Even though owing to the high content of urea and peculiar flavor shark meat is not relished as food. A method has been recently reported to eliminate the urea content from shark flesh completely by salting the fish in the ratio of 1:4 (salt:fish), desalted for 24 hours in 5 per cent brine, again salted in the ratio of 1:6 (salt:fish) for another 24 hours, then dried in sun, reducing the urea content in the fish to a great extent. At present in India the salting and drying is done and marketed locally as wet-cured or dry cured product. Dry –cured cartilaginous fish finds good markets in Sri Lanka, Burma and Singapore. In addition to this in 2002 about 150 tonnes of frozen shark meat were exported mainly to China and South East Asian market fetching the foreign exchange earnings of about Rs. 5.0 million annually for the country.

## 6.14 PERCHES

### Scientific Classification

| | | |
|---|---|---|
| *Class* | : | Teleostomi |
| Sub- Class | : | Actinopterygii |
| Order | : | Perciformes |
| Family | : | Lutjanidae, Serrinidae, Lethrinidae |
| Species | : | *Epinephelus lanceolatus, E. coioides, E. akarr, E. boenack, E.tauvina, Promicrops lanceolatus, Lutjanus campechanus, L. malbaricus* |

This group includes major and minor Perches. The major perches which are generally large sized belonging to the families of Lutjanidae (also called Snappers), Serrinidae (rock perch/cod or groupers) and Lethrinidae (Pig face breams). The small sized minor perches belong to the families of Nemipteridae, Piracanthidae, Sparidae, Acanthuridae and Siganidae. All along the Indian coasts there are over 40 species of rock perch or groupers, about 18 species of snappers and about 10 species of pigface breams.

## GROUPERS

The word 'Grouper' believed to be come from the Portuguese name, garoupa for the fish. The main genera comprise of Epinephalus. The other genera include Anyperidon, Cromileptes, Dermatolepis, Gracila, Salopita and Triso. Fish belonging to Genus Plectropomus are referred to as coral groupers.

## DISTRIBUTION

Groupers are widely distributed in all tropical parts of world oceans from the region of Persian Gulf to the region of Middle East to Arabian Sea and Bay of Bengal shoring India, area of Indian Ocean to Indo Pacific Archipelago, in the Pacific from Philippines to other South East Asian Countries and down to Australia and New Zealand.

All along the Indian coasts, but the groupers prominently form the commercial fisheries of South West coast of India. The fish is bottom dweller of rocky and coral reef areas. The rocky wedge bank area extending from Kovalam to Kanyakumari and the Quilon bank are one of the most preferable habitats of the fish. The groupers are also located all along the South West coast of India extending from 8° N (Kanyakumari) to 13° N (Mangalore). This area is shallow rocky having irregular ridges where in crevices these perches are found.

## DIAGNOSTIC FEATURES

The groupers are large and Epinephelus species are indeed the largest among them. They have stout body and large mouth. They are not built for long distance fast swimming, in fact are more sluggish. They can be quite large and length from 20 to 231cms, some times over a meter or also more and weights up to 100 – 400 kg or more. The largest one is the giant grouper *Epinephelus lanceolatus.*

## FOOD AND FEEDING

Groupers are carnivorous and swallow prey rather than biting pieces off it. They do not have many teeth on the edges of their jaws but have heavy crushing tooth plates inside the pharynx. Their mouth and gills form a powerful sucking system that sucks their prey in from a long distance. Some species prefer to ambush their prey, while other species are active predators. The groupers feeds on variety of fishes, large crustaceans and cephalopods, the large head and mouth of groupers enable them to engulf large amount of prey and presence of inwardly curved teeth help them to seize the prey firmly and preventing its escape from the mouth.

They also use their mouths to dig into sand to form their shelters under the big rocks, jetting it out through their gills. Their gill muscles are so powerful that, it is nearly impossible to pull them out of a cave if they feel attacked and extend the muscles to lock themselves in.

## GROWTH DEVELOPMENT AND REPRODUCTIVE BEHAVIOR

It is found that the groupers are protogynous hermaphrodites. It means the fish while still growing change its own sex. The female which are generally smaller than male bears oocytes, after leading life as female it degenerate the oocytes and bear functional testis.

As in *Epinephelus coioides,* which matures as female to 25 – 30 cm length (up to 2-3 years old) meanwhile the spawning also occurs with the fecundity averaging to 0.85 million ova for a fish of 35 cm to 2.90 million ova for fish of 62 cm. However when the fish grows its transition starts as male from about over 65 cms size and it remains as male till the maximum growth of 95 cms. In *E. akarr* the fish matures as female at 45 to 50 cm length, further the transition to male starts at about 74 cms length and develop ripe testis. There are instances of intersex condition also as in some cases found to be at 66 to 72 cms length when the fish contains both female and male gonadal tissues. The groupers spawn several times in a year.

The fishery management practices are difficult to implement for groupers because of its protogynous type of reproduction. It is because sometimes the larger female does not transform into male, also due to broader range of age of sexual transition to females taking more time than age for their transition as males. The males are lesser than females in population. It is therefore now more pertinent to know about biological characteristic and the stock assessment of grouper and major perches from the Indian coast.

Therefore combined these reasons may result into the occurrence of insufficient or inadequate ratio of female to male in numbers due to large numbers of females than males or vice versa which may adversely affect breeding and spawning. Since the inducement of sex is exogenous type due to imbalancement of numbers of female to male the right synchronization or timing of courtship and breeding gets affected. The stock of groupers is also most vulnerable because of targeted fishing for capturing larger groupers which are mostly males. Hence the capture of even a small number of males (which are already less in number than female) would result in the overexploitation of stock and risk of halting of progeny to grow further due to existence of few number of males. There is great export demand of larger grouper therefore the problem of overfishing for this fish is more compounding.

## SNAPPERS

Snappers belongs to the family of Lutjanidae, are prized food fish. The fish is distributed widely in tropical parts of world oceans. Red snapper (*Lutjanus campechanus*) is found to be common from tropical Atlantic waters from Gulf of Mexico to Northwards along the Coastal United States from the region of Carrabian Islands to little south along Latin America to Honduras, Colombia, Venezuela and North Brazilian Coast. International distribution also suggests the presence of snapper in tropical waters of Pacific from Philippines to the Australian and New Zealand coast.

In India even though the Red Snapper is not found, the other species are found all along the shallower reef area of South West Coast of India in region of Quilon bank and Wedge Bank of Kanyakumari and Gulf of Mannar. The important species which is most sought for is *Lutjanus malbaricus,* also called as Blood Red Snapper, which is a high class table fish and has high commercial demand in the Indian market.

## DIAGNOSTIC FEATURES

The snapper have laterally compressed body having medium to large scales, a spiny dorsal fin. Most of the snapper have attractive coloration. The coloration of Blood Red Snapper *L. malbaricus* is red with more intense pigment on back. They form large schools having fishes of similar size around creeks and reefs.

## FOOD AND FEEDING

They are carnivore and feed on creatures found in shallow reefs. The choicest items are small to medium fishes, squids, octopus, crabs and other crustaceans. They have short, sharp needle like teeth but they lack the prominent upper canine teeth.

## GROWTH, DEVELOPMENT AND REPRODUCTIVE BEHAVIOR

Snappers attain sexual maturity at two to five years of age by the length of 39 cm. The common adult length is 60 cm but may reach 100 cm.

The preferred habitat of snapper changes as it grows and matures due to increased need for cover and changing food habits. Newly hatched snapper are spread out over large areas of benthic habitat, and then they move to low relief habitat, such as shallow rocky areas and oyster beds. As they reach one year of age they move to intermediate relief habitats and finally when they become grown as adult of large size they move to high relief areas with room for more individuals.

## CRAFTS AND GEARS USED FOR FISHING

In the shallower part of coastal oceans the anglers follow sport or recreational fishing. Fishing is also done using lines with hooks using the bait of favored food.

## ANNUAL CATCH TREND

**Table 6.14.1: Annual Catch Trend of Perches**

| *Year* | *Production (tonnes)* | *Year* | *Production (tonnes)* |
|---|---|---|---|
| **2003** | 70162 | **2004** | 79876 |
| **2005** | 79851 | **2006** | 181079 |
| **2007** | 146629 | **2008** | 132403 |
| **2009** | 98399 | | |

Perches collectively are very important commodity of demersal fish landing from India. Among them the Pigface breams contribute the highest of 5.3 per cent followed by Groupers 4.5 per cent, Snappers 0.9 per cent and other perches 6.5 per cent to the demersal landing from India. They are thus by share the third largest component of the demersal fisheries of the country. The production of perches in eighties and nineties ranged between 50, 000 and 65,000 tonnes. The turn of the century witnessed the

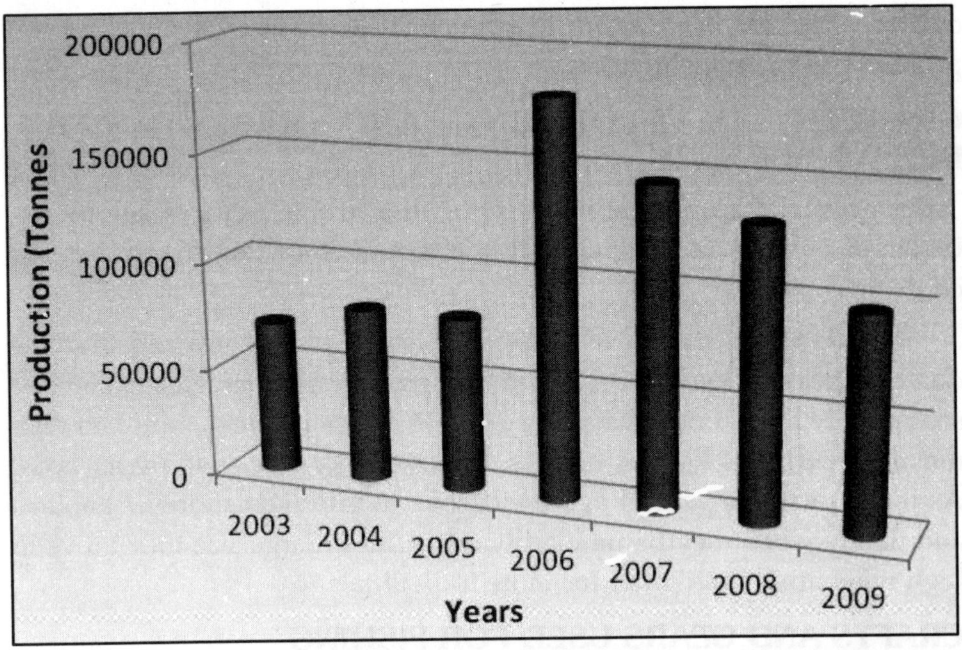


**Figure 6.14.1: Annual Production of Perches from India (2003-2009)**

substantial increase into the landing of perches as evident from the average landing of 76,626 tonnes from 2003 to 2005.

The years from 2006 to 2009 were extremely productive years with the all time highest landing of 1,81,079 tonnes in 2006. The average landing of perches from 2006 to 2009 excelled to 1,39,237 tonnes.

## STATEWISE CATCH TREND

The state wise annual landing of total perches from 2003 to 2009 and the average landing pattern between 2006 to 2009 suggested the state of Kerala to be the leading and highest producer with the average landing of 32302 tonnes, followed by the state of Tamil Nadu at second place with the average landing of 27262 tonnes and the state of Gujarat at third place with the average landing of 18756 tonnes. The state of Andhra Pradesh from the east coast contributed maximum with the average landing of 11027 tonnes. The state of Karnataka for which the landing between 2003 and 2005 were not available turned out to be a surprise package with the overwhelming production between 2006 to 2008, in fact it turned out to be the first and largest producer of the total landing of perches overtaking the production from the state of Kerala in the year

**Table 6.14.2: State-wise Production of Perches**

| *Years* | *Production (tonnes)* | | | | | | | *Avarage* |
|---|---|---|---|---|---|---|---|---|
| *States* | *2003* | *2004* | *2005* | *2006* | *2007* | *2008* | *2009* | *(2006-2009)* |
| **Kerala** | 28956 | 30373 | 30333 | 33662 | 32224 | 32214 | 31107 | **32302** |
| **Tamil Nadu** | 19062 | 19062 | 19062 | 26709 | 26819 | 28785 | 26736 | **27262** |
| **Gujarat** | 8417 | 10572 | 16275 | 14539 | 23666 | 15367 | 21454 | **18756** |
| **Andhra Pradesh** | 800 | 5791 | 5320 | 8509 | 10318 | 10595 | 14688 | **11027** |
| **Andaman and Nicobar** | 9062 | 9062 | 3019 | 4365 | 4808 | 0 | 0 | **2293** |
| **Karnataka** | 0 | 0 | 0 | 19443 | 33760 | 32794 | 0 | **28665** |
| **West Bengal** | 470 | 470 | 359 | 4480 | 5397 | 5677 | 0 | **3888** |
| **Orissa** | 887 | 1116 | 2310 | 2241 | 2997 | 2623 | 2997 | **2714** |
| **Pondicherry** | 1963 | 1939 | 1181 | 2285 | 2273 | 2240 | 0 | **1699** |
| **Goa** | 83 | 769 | 1379 | 2427 | 950 | 276 | 0 | **913** |
| **Maharashtra** | 150 | 432 | 324 | 1436 | 1588 | 299 | 579 | **975** |
| **Daman and Diu** | 150 | 128 | 112 | 778 | 1612 | 1306 | 604 | **1075** |
| **Lakshadweep** | 162 | 162 | 177 | 205 | 217 | 227 | 234 | **221** |
| **Total Catch** | **70162** | **79876** | **79851** | **181079** | **146629** | **132403** | **98399** | |

2007 and 2008 with the production of 33,760 and 32,794 tonnes respectively. Therefore Karnataka by virtue of the average production between 2006 and 2008 earned the second position in total perches landing from the country. There has been fairly handsome landing of perches from the Andaman and Nicobar Island and Pondicherry especially in the years from 2003 to 2007. The states of Goa and Maharashtra also have shown good improvement into the production of perches from 2004 to 2007.

## UTILIZATION

The perches are high valued fishes and are exported in live condition to the different countries since it command very high price in the foreign market. There are also reports of culturing the groupers in USA and some other foreign countries. A live grouper fry for aquaculture practices command a price of 1 US dollar, fingerlings 3 US dollar and table size adult of 600 gm 20 US dollar. India exported few consignments of groupers in live or fresh chilled condition in 1996 – 1997 but later discontinued the export due to various constraints (Ayyappan, 2006). More recently there have been also attempts of cage and pond culturing and breeding of Greasy Grouper *Epinephelus tauvina* at the regional centre CMFRI Visakhapatnam, which is a major species and not available in sufficient numbers but commands excellent live market in India (CMFRI Bulletin 41, 2013)

# 6.15 SCIAENIDS

## Scientific Classification

*Class* : Teleostomi

*Sub-class* : Actinoptergii

*Order* : Perciformes

*Family* : Sciaenidae

*Genus* : *Otolithes, Protonibea, Johnius, Nibia, Johineops, Kathala, Atrobucca* etc.

*Species* : *Atrobucca niba, Johnius aneus, J. belengari, J. carutta, J. dussumieri, Johineops sina, Kathala axillaris, Nibea maculate, N. soldado, Otolithes biauritus, O. brunneus, O. cuvieri, O. ruber, Protonibea diacanthus* etc.

## STATUS

Sciaenids belong to the family Sciaenidae commonly called as drums, croakers or hardheads. They are found worldwide and are typically benthic carnivores. Internationally this family consists of about 275 species in about 70 genera. However, they are prominent in tropical waters of Indian Ocean. In the Indian Ocean the group represents dominant varied diversity with about 17 genera and 34 species, having the size range between 20 cms to over 150 cms.

The larger varieties which are over 1 meter in length commonly called Koth are represented by three species *Otolithes biauritus, O. brunneus* and *Protonibea diacanthus.* They form the prominent fisheries of North West coast of Kutch and Kathiawar coast. The medium sized 50 cms to less than one meter are represented by 6 species mainly *johnieops dussumieri, Otolithes ruber, Nibea soldado* etc. The other Sciaenids which are smaller than 50 cms are about 25 species represented mainly by *Johnius aneus, J. belengari, J. dussumieri, J. carutta, Johnieops sina, Ototithes cuvieri, Nibea maculata, Kathala axillaris and Atrobucca nibe.*

The Sciaenid contribute about 18.4 per cent to the total demersal marine fish production of India.

## DISTRIBUTION

Internationally they are known to live in warm temperate and tropical waters and are best represented in major rivers in South East Asia, North East South America, The Gulf of Mexico and the Gulf of California. They are mostly confined to the inshore waters up to 50 m depth with only some large species like *Protonibea dicanthus* reported up to 70 meters of depth. The possessing of closed type of swim bladder where the exchange of air is through the waii oi uie bladder helps them adjust in the desired range of depth. The Sciaenids are active swimmers in the coastal waters. They are widely distributed all along the west coast of India with high concentration along the North east to Northwest coast of India where it forms the commercial fisheries, contributing about 36.6 per cent and 29.5 per cent of demersal fish landing of the regions respectively. (Ayyappan, 2006).

## DIAGNOSTIC FEATURES

A sciaenid has a long dorsal fin reaching nearly to the tail and a notch between the rays and spines of the dorsal fin, although the two parts are actually separate. They produce throbbing or drumming sounds which also is called as croaking mechanism which involves the beating the abdominal muscle against the swim bladder. Drums are somberly coloured usually in shades of brown with a lateral line in each side that extends to the tip of caudal fin. The anal fin usually has two spines while the dorsal fins are deeply notched or separate. Most species have rounded or pointed caudal fin. The mouth is low and usually inferior.

## FOOD AND FEEDING

The Sciaenid which are benthic carnivores feed on invertebrates and smaller fish. The post larvae and juveniles feed mainly on copepods, amphipods, prawns and acetes. The adults of small to medium sized sciaenid feed mainly on benthic crustaceans and polychaetes and to smaller extent on gastropods, fishes and detritus. Sometimes pelagic crustaceans, ptreropods and salps are also consumed. The adults of the larger sciaenid like *P. dicanthus, O. biauritus* feed mostly on fishes (65 per cent), crustacean and molluscs form the rest of the diet.

## GROWTH, DEVELOPMENT AND REPRODUCTIVE BEHAVIOR

Some medium sized croakers which are bottom dwelling fishes living primarily in estuaries, bays and muddy river banks. Some of them ascend into riverine waters. Most of these fishes avoid clear waters such as coral reefs and oceanic islands, with a few notable exceptions like Reef Croaker and Spotted Drum.

Two patterns with respect to spawning are identified among the Sciaenid, those which have shorter or restricted spawning of 3- 4 months spawning between June to September and November to February along the North West to South West coast of India as found in *J. sina,* and *J. dussumieri.* In other group the spawning is prolonged for about 6 or 7 months, as in *J. carutta* from January to August; *J. aneus* from January to July and *N. maculata* from March to August along the South East coast of India. The fecundity of Sciaenid is generally high which is prominent in *O. rubber* and *J. dussumieri* from 44,621 to 1,79,659 and 1,42000 to 2,25988 respectively.

## CRAFTS AND GEARS USED FOR FISHING

Most of the croakers form the benthic community of inshore waters. In India therefore most of the shrimp fishing trawlers which operates in shallow continental waters also as by-catch harvest substantial quantity of croakers. Therefore the principal gears which can be employed for the harvest for croakers are bottom water operating trawl net and gill net etc.

Even though the fish is found all along the west and east coast of India, the principal species of croakers form the major fishery of west coast of India. *Johnius dussumieri* is harvested from October to May from the Maharashtra coast to Gulf of Munnar. *J. soldado* which is found distributed along Kerala and Karnataka coast, the fishing season extend from October to March. The medium sized *Sciaena aneus* and *daysciaena albida* are caught from October to March. The blotched croaker *Nibea maculata* also is captured in high number from October to March from Tamilnadu Coast. The tiger toothed croakers *Otolith rubber* which is found in abundance from Kerala to Maharashtra coast also has the high fishing season from October to March. The large croaker 'Ghol' *Protonibea dicanthus* which form the major commercial fisheries of Gujarat and Maharashtra coast *i.e.* the North West coast of India has the fishing season extending from August to March. Therefore for the most of the croakers the peak fishing season is from October to March.

## ANNUAL CATCH TREND

Internationally, most of the Sciaenid are reported from Western Indian Ocean (FAO fishing area 51) and North West Pacific (FAO fishing area 61).The sciaenids are the most major and the dominant demersal fish resource of India. The annual landing is always invariably over one lakh tonnes. The landing of the Sciaenid between 2006 and 2009 indicated overwhelming production with the low of 226486 tonnes in 2007 to highest landing of 249465 tonnes in 2009.The average production of Sciaenid in this duration was 237877 tonnes.

**Table 6.15.1: Annual Catch Trend of Sciaenids**

| *Year* | *Production (tonnes)* | *Year* | *Production (tonnes)* |
|---|---|---|---|
| **2006** | 235176 | **2007** | 226486 |
| **2008** | 240383 | **2009** | 249465.63 |

## STATEWISE CATCH TREND

The average landing of Sciaenid from 2006 to 2009 indicated the state of Gujarat to be the leading producer occupying the first position with the production of 149576 tonnes, followed by West Bengal and Maharashtra at 2nd and 3rd positions with the average production of 22468 and 20079 tonnes respectively.

**Table 6.15.2: State-wise Production of Sciaenids**

| *States* | *Years/Production* | | | | *Avarage (2006-2009)* |
|---|---|---|---|---|---|
| | *2006* | *2007* | *2008* | *2009* | |
| **Gujarat** | 161385 | 135947 | 139311 | 161660 | **149576** |
| **West Bengal** | 7239 | 19366 | 37385 | 25881 | **22468** |
| **Maharashtra** | 21627 | 21720 | 14530 | 22439 | **20079** |
| **Tamil Nadu** | 10584 | 10900 | 11817 | 12693 | **11498** |
| **Orissa** | 12241 | 12125 | 9713 | 11538 | **11404** |
| **Kerala** | 9879 | 9700 | 9643 | 9522 | **9686** |
| **Andhra** | 5693 | 5808 | 6060 | 4082 | **5411** |
| **Daman and Diu** | 988 | 7032 | 4194 | 1144 | **3339** |
| **Karnataka** | 2377 | 1570 | 4471 | – | **2104** |
| **Goa** | 2404 | 1938 | 2780 | 00 | **1780** |
| **Pondicherry** | 759 | 380 | 479 | 507 | **531** |
| **Total Catch** | **235176** | **226486** | **240383** | **249466** | |

# 6.16 SILVER BELLIES

## Scientific Classification

| | | |
|---|---|---|
| *Class* | : | Teleostomi |
| *Sub-class* | : | Actinoptergii |
| *Order* | : | Perciformes |
| *Family* | : | Leiognathidae |
| *Genus/Species* | : | *Leiognathus bindus, L. brevirostris, L. dussumieri, L. equlus, L. jonesi, L. daura, L. berbis, L. splendens, L. lineolatus, L. elongates, L. novaeehollandiae, L. fasciatus, L. leuciscus, L. interruptus, L. blochii, Gazza minuta, Secuter insidiator, S. ruconius* |

## STATUS

The silver bellies constitute one of the most important inshore fisheries forming about 4 per cent of the total marine fish catch of India. It is essentially round the year a coastal fishery and range up to about 30 m of depth. In the Indian waters they are represented by 3 genera, *Leognathus* being the most prominent one represented by 16 species which include *Leiognathus bindus; L. brevirostris* (also called as Pony fish), *L. dussumieri, L. equlus, L. jonesi, L. daura, L. berbis, L. splendens, L. lineolatus, L. elongatus, L. novaeehollandiae, L. fasciatus, L. leuciscus, L. interruptus, L. blochii.* The other two genera are Gazza and *Secutor* are represented by *Gazza minuta, Secutor insidiator and S. ruconius* species.

## DISTRIBUTION

The international distribution suggest that silver bellies are dominant in Red Sea, Persian Gulf, East of Africa, Indian Ocean, Western Pacific from Taiwan to Indonesia, Gulf of Thailand, Timor sea, Arafur sea, Fiji North to the Ryuku Island, South of Australia.

Silver bellies even though found all along the Indian coast they are abundant only along the south east coast of India around Gulf of Mannar and Palk Bay. Except *L. elongates, L. blochii, L. indicus* and *L. splendens* all the fishery of silver bellies are dominant in Gulf of Mannar and Palk Bay.

## DIAGNOSTIC FEATURES

They are small, laterally compressed with the blend of silvery colouration on ventral side, therefore are most appropriately referred as silver bellies. They are also distinguished by highly extensible mouths and presence of a mechanism for locking spines in the dorsal and anal fins, especially prominent in Pony fish (*L. brevirostris*). In *Secutor, L. aureus* and some other species of *Leiognathus* mouth is protruding forward and not downward, have small slender pointed, uniserial teeth on jaws. The membrane between jaws and cheeks are densely pigmented with a black line between anteroventral margin of eye and lower articulation when mouth closed. Lateral line is incomplete ending at some distance below the dorsal fin. In some other species of *Leognathus* the mouth is protusible downwards. In *G. minuta* the jaws are equipped with sharp canine teeth.

## FOOD AND FEEDING

The feeding habit of silver bellies is varied especially governed by the nature of their mouth. The silver bellies have adapted to different feeding strategies for species compatibility and sustainability due to their presence in large numbers of species in the restricted area of Gulf of Mannar and Palk Bay. In *Secutor* species and some species of *Leiognathus*, whole mouth is protrusible upwards the food is mainly plankton. For other *Leiognathus* species with mouth protrusible downwards, the food comprise of benthic organisms like gastropods, bivalves, polychaets and crustaceans which form the major food. *G. minuta* by having the presence of canine tooth are carnivores and feed on crustaceans and small fishes. Thus the silver bellies to a very large extent, avoid competition for food.

Species like *L. jonesi* undertakes the diurnal vertical migration. The 0 year class (< 60 mm) of fish occupies column water in daytime and descends to bottom in the night. The adults (> 60 mm) remain in bottom during daytime and ascend to the column/surface in night. At bottom they feed on benthos and at column/surface they feed on plankton. The three dimensional feeding strategy (benthic, column and estuarine) is a strategy evolving a successful group without much of feeding competition between them. Predation is also reported to be very marginal for the silver bellies.

## LIFE PATTERN

The silver bellies are short lived fishes and live for not more than 2 years, rarely 3 years. They are small size fishes barring *L. equlus*, which attains maximum length of 260 mm. the size of the different species in the fishery ranges from 40 to 150 mm.

## REPRODUCTIVE BEHAVIOR AND SPAWNING

The silver bellies attain first maturity by an age of a year. For *L. brevirostris* 50 per cent maturity for the males and females were estimated to be 79 and 81 mm. The females predominates the male. The spawning is prolonged in *S. insidiator, S. ruconius, L. dussumieri and L. splendens* but the restricted spawning is reported in *Gazza minuta. L. dussunieri* and *L. splendens* spawn throughout the year with two distinct peaks from April to May and November to Decembers. The restricted spawning for *G. munuta* occurs from August to January and for *L. bindus* from December to February. The spawning occurs in inshore deep waters and the young ones move to the inshore nursery grounds or for some species in the estuaries. The fecundity ranges from 7000 to 27000 in *L. splendens*, 5000 to 13000 in *S. insidiator* and 12000 to 27000 in *G. minuta*.

## CRAFTS AND GEARS USED FOR FISHING

The best suitable gears for the capture of these fishes are the trawl nets followed by boat seine and shore seines. It is also reported to be the major contributor to the trawl by-catch.

## ANNUAL CATCH TREND

Silver bellies are important demersal fish resource of India, contributing about 8.1 per cent of total demersal fish landing from the country during 2000 to 2004. The production was fairly high, yielding about 54479; 58091; and 61471 tonnes respectively for the years 2003, 2004, and 2005. However declining and fluctuating trend was observed between the years of 2006 and 2009, when the average production of 52525 tonnes was obtained.

**Table 6.16.1: Annual catch trend of Silver bellies**

| *Year* | *Production (tonnes)* | *Year* | *Production (tonnes)* |
|---|---|---|---|
| **2003** | 54479 | **2004** | 58091 |
| **2005** | 61471 | **2006** | 51752 |
| **2007** | 55613 | **2008** | 51486 |
| **2009** | 51248 | | |

## STATEWISE CATCH TREND

The state of Tamil Nadu acquired the first position as evident from the average landing of 29341 tonnes during 2006 to 2009; however it was extremely high about 37512 tonnes during 2003 to 2005.

The state of Kerala occupies the second rank with the average landing of 5437 tonnes. The state of Karnataka ranked at third place with average production of 3330 tonnes. The production from the state of Orissa from the east coast and the state of Goa from the west coast indicated fairly rich and substantial landing of fish. The production of Silver bellies indicated good potential from the state of Maharashtra especially in the years of 2007 and 2009.

**Table 6.16.2: State-wise Production of Silver Bellies**

| *Years* | *Production (tonnes)* | | | | | | | *Avarage (2006-2009)* |
|---|---|---|---|---|---|---|---|---|
| *States* | *2003* | *2004* | *2005* | *2006* | *2007* | *2008* | *2009* | |
| **Tamil Nadu** | 37512 | 37512 | 37512 | 24967 | 29583 | 30631 | 32182 | **29341** |
| **Kerala** | 5992 | 5114 | 5292 | 5577 | 5427 | 5408 | 5336 | **5437** |
| **Karnataka** | 3754 | 4704 | 5565 | 4781 | 3956 | 4584 | – | **3330** |
| **Andhra Pradesh** | 1181 | 2949 | 3027 | 2305 | 2688 | 2770 | 1378 | **2285** |
| **Goa** | 1533 | 2740 | 2046 | 3187 | 1664 | 1688 | 1975 | **2128** |
| **West Bengal** | 384 | 390 | 3987 | 3650 | 3159 | 380 | 216 | **1851** |
| **Pondicherry** | 1815 | 1875 | 1263 | 1751 | 1486 | 1711 | 1728 | **1669** |
| **Andaman and Nicobar** | 662 | 662 | 217 | 2376 | 2450 | 2624 | 2635 | **2521** |
| **Orissa** | 1035 | 1440 | 1684 | 1788 | 1444 | 1665 | 2214 | **1778** |
| **Maharashtra** | 611 | 650 | 811 | 1347 | 3587 | 0 | 3564 | **2124** |
| **Daman and Diu** | 0 | 55 | 67 | 23 | 169 | 25 | 20 | **59** |
| **Total Catch** | **54479** | **58091** | **61471** | **51752** | **55613** | **51486** | **51248** | |

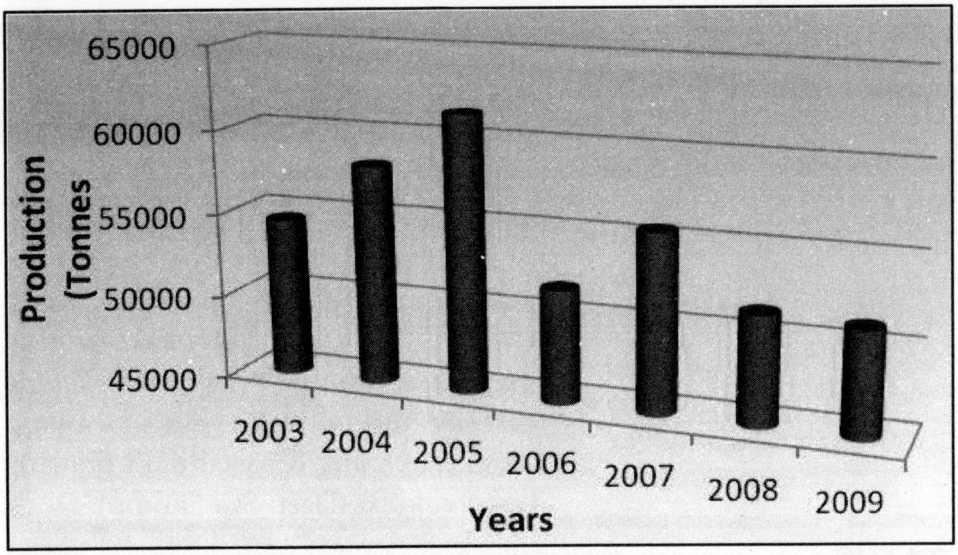


**Figure 6.16.1: Annual Catch Trend of Silver Bellies from India (2003-2009)**

## 6.17 PENAEID SHRMPS AND OTHER PRAWNS

### Scientific Classification

| | | |
|---|---|---|
| *Class* | : | Teleostomi |
| *Order* | : | Decapoda |
| *Suborder* | : | Malacostraca |
| *Family* | : | Pinninae |
| *Genus/Species* | | *Fenneropenaeus indicus* (Indian White Shrimp), *Penaeus semisulcatus* (Green Tiger Shrimp or Flower Shrimp), *Penaeus monodon* (Giant Tiger Shrimp), *Penaeus penicillatus* (Red-tail Shrimp), *Fenneropenaeus merguiensis* (Banana Shrimp), *Marsupenaeus japonicus* (Kurma Shrimp), *Metapenaeus dobsoni* (Flowertail Shrimp), *Metapenaeus monoceros* (Speakled Shrimp), *Metapenaeus affinis* (Jingra), *Metapenaeus kutchensis* (Ginger Shrimp), *Metapenaeus brevicornis* (Yellow Shrimp or Prawn), *Metapeneopsis stridulans* (Fiddler |

Shrimp), *MetaPeneopsis andamanensis* (Deep Sea Shrimp), *Parapenaeus longiceps* (Flaming Prawn), *Parapeneopsis stylifera* (Kidding Prawn, Tiny Prawn), *Parapeneopsis hardwickii* (Spear Prawn), *Parapeneopsis alcocki* (Red-ring, Deep Sea Penaeid Prawn), *Parapeneopsis sculptilis* (Rainbow Prawn), *Parapeneopsis uncta* (Uncta Prawn), *Trachysulambria curvirostris* (Rough Prawn), *Solanocera crassiocornis* (Coastal mud prawn), *Solanocera choprai* (Coastal mud prawn), *Aristeus alcocki* (Deep Sea Shrimp)

## STATUS

The penaeid shrimp is one of the most sought seafood commodity in India due to its phenomenal commercial demand for export. India is one of the leading exporters in the world for penaeid shrimp. A retrospect of India's marine fisheries development during the last four decades would reveal that it witnessed intense increase in exploitation of penaeid shrimps. The production of penaeid shrimp was enhanced with the inception of trawling in India. The earlier results of production proved to be extremely overwhelming especially from early seventies to late eighties. However due to constant pressure of targeted fishing form the lower and marginal waters of continental shelf up to maximum 70 meters of depth has resulted into catastrophic decline into the landing of penaeid shrimp. India, which was once the leading producer of shrimp a few years ago has suffered a setback in production and presently it is rated behind the other Asian countries like China, Taiwan, Indonesia and even Thailand. The recent record of export earnings (Figure 5.5 and 5.6) would suggest that the impact of this valuable resource of shrimp is truly enormous for the country. Hence it should be an earnest endeavour of one and all from harvesters to the users to ensure that this valuable resource is not unduly declined through overexploitation. If the conservation methods for this stock to sustain high production are not taken promptly it would be a reality of famous saying- "The story of killing the goose laying the golden eggs".

## DISTRIBUTION

The biodiversity of Prawn/Shrimps decreases markedly at increasing latitudes. In India the high concentration of Penaeid Shrimp is found along the west coast, therefore the bulk of the landing of penaeid shrimp is realized from the states of Kerala, Maharashtra and Gujarat.

## DIAGNOSTIC FEATURES

The body is typically robust, and can be divided into a cephalothorax (head and thorax fused together) and a pleon (abdomen). The body is generally slightly flattened side-to-side. The largest species, *Penaeus monodon*, can reach a mass of 450 grams and a length of 336 millimeters.

## FOOD AND FEEDING

Penaeid shrimp are detritus and macro zooplankton feeder and also feed on available carnivore materials. During early juvenile stage in backwater they thrive on organic detritus materials which are rich in nutrients.

## LIFE CYCLE

The life cycle of all penaeid shrimp with the exception of *Parapeneopsis stylifera* is held in two phases with shoreward migration of larvae and seaward migration of adult.

The fertilized eggs spawn in open surface water, while passing through several instars larval stages, they migrate to shoreward side in back water area or sheltering in estuary. The back water happens to be the nursery area with organically rich water where they grow rapidly to adolescent stages. After reaching to adolescent stage of about 70 -75 mm they permanently migrate to oceanic niches to earn gonadal development and breed to continue or repeat the same cycle.

## SIZE AND GROWTH

a) *P. semisulcatus, F. indicus and P. monodon*: Grow into total length of 250, 270 and 300 mm respectively.

b) Smaller species such as *P. stylifera, M. dobsoni and S. crossiocornis*: Grow into total length of 46 - 145 mm, 31 – 115 mm and 55 – 125 mm respectively.

## CRAFTS AND GEARS USED FOR FISHING

Trawling is the principal fishing method employed for the exploitation of penaeid shrimps. Usually the fishing vessels between 36 to 48 feet operate the trawl gear with the cod and mesh size between 18 and 20 meters operate at the depth between 40 to 70 meters to accomplish the fishing of penaeid shrimp in the Indian waters. The trawling which had been single day fishing shifted to multiday fishing from late eighties onwards out of the quest of landing more and more shrimp and earn handsome profit.

The important fishing centers for Penaeid shrimp from the west coast are Sassoondock, Versova and New Ferrywarf from Mumbai; Alibagh, Harnai, Ratnagiri, Malvan and Vengurla (Maharashtra); Panjim (Goa); Karvar, Mangalore, Malpe (Karnataka); Kozhikode, Cochi, Shaktikulangara and Neendakara (Kerala). In fact the two fishing centers of Shaktikulangara and Neendakara from Quilone district in Kerala are the prominent fishing centers which produce about 19 per cent of total shrimp landing in the country. The important fishing centers for Penaeid shrimp from the east coast are Mandapam, Tuticorin, Chenai, Visakhapatnam, Kakinada etc.

## STATUS/ANNUAL CATCH TREND

**Table 6.17.1: Annual Catch Trend of Penaeid Shrimp**

| *Year* | *Production (tonnes)* | *Year* | *Production (tonnes)* |
|---|---|---|---|
| **2003** | 215033 | **2004** | 171641 |
| **2005** | 175889 | **2006** | 213677 |
| **2007** | 198612 | **2008** | 189155 |
| **2009** | 191772 | | |

Penaeid shrimp constitute the backbone of seafood export industry as the major foreign exchange earner. Frozen shrimps contribute about 70 per cent of the total export value of our country and the share of capture fisheries is about 59 per cent by volume. During the last 45 years, the penaeid shrimp landings increased to about 5 fold from 32,000 tonnes in 1960 to 1,71,641 tonnes in 2004. The single day operation of trawling during the day time till eighties, the fishing was intensified to intensive multi-day operation in deeper grounds to meet with persistent demand of

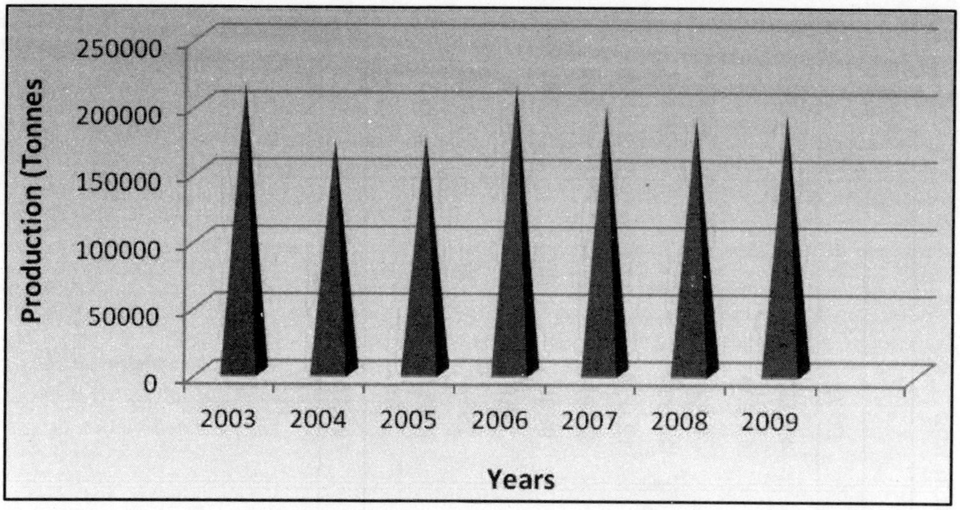


**Figure 6.17.1: Annual production of Penaeid Shrimps from India (2003-2009)**

export. The penaeid shrimp contribution in the edible crustacean landings of the country during the 10 year period (1995 – 2004) amounted to 53 per cent.

The all India penaeid shrimp production from 2003 to 2009 varied between 1,71,641 tonnes in 2004 to all time 2,15,033 tonnes in 2003, after a low of about 1,75,889 tonnes in 2005 the production noticeably increased to 2,13,677 tonnes in 2006, the years of 2007, 2008 and 2009 yielded about 1,98,612, 1,89,155 and 1,91,772 tonnes of Penaeid shrimps respectively. The average production of Penaeid shrimp between 2006 and 2009 was 1,98,304 tonnes. In addition to all penaeid species *A. alcocki* popularly known as red-ring is the most sought deep sea shrimp by exporters with an average of 2,00,481.33 tonnes between 2006 and 2009.

## STATEWISE CATCH TREND

During the years between 1995 -2003 about 74 per cent of penaeid catch was landed along the west coast. The highest catch was from Maharashtra state with 26.7 per cent landing and the shrimp landing from Kerala, Gujarat and Karnataka was 24 per cent, 16.7 per cent and 5.05 per cent respectively. Along the east coast the prominent states are Tamil Nadu and Andhra Pradesh with the share of 11.65 per cent and 9.1 per cent respectively.

**Table 6.17.2: State-wise Catch Trend of Penaeid Shrimp**

| *Years* | *Production (tonnes)* | | | | | | | *Avarage (2006-2009)* |
|---|---|---|---|---|---|---|---|---|
| *States* | *2003* | *2004* | *2005* | *2006* | *2007* | *2008* | *2009* | |
| **Kerala** | 53437 | 53469 | 47752 | 51,479 | 49,022 | 49,353 | 48456 | **49,578** |
| **Maharashtra** | 45442 | 30507 | 44227 | 48,461 | 47,836 | 43,299 | 41311 | **45,227** |
| **Tamil Nadu** | 21079 | 21079 | 21079 | 45,579 | 28,100 | 26,991 | 30026 | **32,674** |
| **Andhra Pradesh** | 1160 | 25969 | 17062 | 22,161 | 24,987 | 28,824 | 31847 | **26,955** |
| **Orissa** | 5715 | 9129 | 9417 | 12,126 | 12,108 | 12,056 | 11310 | **11,900** |
| **Gujarat** | 46330 | 7037 | 12199 | 11,477 | 12,686 | 9,299 | 12195 | **11,414** |
| **West Bengal** | 13050 | 13000 | 12000 | 11001 | 12855 | 9600 | 8532 | **10,497** |
| **Goa** | 2284 | 6665 | 10599 | 6065 | 8642 | 7458 | 5577 | **6,936** |
| **Pondicherry** | 2398 | 2348 | 1387 | 1690 | 1674 | 1559 | 1712 | **1,659** |
| **Andaman and Nicobar** | 560 | 560 | 108 | 550 | 586 | 591 | 632 | **590** |
| **Daman and Diu** | 47 | 33 | 59 | 88 | 116 | 125 | 174 | **126** |
| **Total** | **191502** | **169796** | **175889** | **210,677** | **198,612** | **189,155** | **191,772** | |

Contrary to earlier times (before 2003) when the state of Maharashtra was the leading producer, the production pattern of penaeid shrimp from 2006 to 2009 indicated that the state of Kerala ranks first with the average production of 49,578 tonnes, followed by the state of Maharashtra at second place with the average production of 45,227 tonnes, the state of Tamil Nadu occupies the third position with the average landing of 32,674 tonnes and the state of Andhra Pradesh ranks fourth with the average landing of about 26,955 tonnes.

## IMPLEMENTATION OF MANAGEMENT MEASURES FOR THE RESTORATION OF SHRIMP STOCK

The intensive studies regarding recruitment harvest and the population dynamics has revealed that the stocks of penaeid shrimp in the Indian water for all major species of commercial importance have already reached to the maximum sustainable yield. This amply proves the fact that at most places the shrimp fishery is on brink of disaster. If its targeted fishing from coastal continental water is not checked it will further sustain the damage beyond any chance of recovery. It is therefore imperative to implement stringent management measures to conserve and recover the glory of yester years. The fishing efforts must be substantially reduced by reducing the number of trawlers meant for shrimp fishing and introduction of off fishing days. In order to avert the harvest of juvenile stock the cod-end mesh size be increased from 15 mm to 20 mm presently being used, to at least 25 mm. Employment of mini trawl operation for capture of juveniles of *P. stylifera* and *M. dobsoni* along coastal waters and use of Thalluvalai along the Tuticorin – Pamban coast for the harvest of juvenile tiger shrimp must be immediately stopped. There is heavy exploitation of penaeid shrimp from their nursery grounds of backwaters and estuaries by local people through the use of scoop or stake net. The suitable enforcement of laws and their implementation are necessary to prevent or ban the easy lifting and indiscriminate fishing of shrimp juveniles from the backwaters and estuaries.

The ban also must be imposed on export of juvenile shrimps to prevent their fishing. Marine fishing regulations and earmarking of fishing area for the operation of different vessels and gears must be adhered and strictly followed to avert the overexploitation of most valuable resource of penaeid shrimp from the Indian waters.

## 6.18 NON-PENAEID SHRIMPS

### Scientific Classification

| | | |
|---|---|---|
| *Class* | : | Crustacea |
| *Order* | : | Decapoda |
| *Suborder* | : | Malacostraca |
| *Genus/Species* | : | *Acetes indicus, A. johni, A. sibogae, A. erythraeus, A. japonicas, Nematopalaemon tenuipes, Exhippolysmata ensirostris* |

### STATUS

Non-penaeid prawns are one of the important fishery resources of India contributing to 5.8 per cent of total marine fish production. The fishery comprises of multispecies, mainly supported by minute species of genus *Acetes, Nematopalaemon* and *Exhippolysmata*. The resource is characteristic of the northwest coast, which accounts for almost 85 per cent of the total non-penaeid prawn production in the country. In Maharashtra and Gujarat, the non-penaeid prawns account for 10.8 per cent and 12.6 per cent of the total marine fish landings in these states.

The species belonging to the genus *Acetes* are called paste shrimp, but locally they are called Jawala in fresh and Kolim in dried form, in both Marathi and Gujarati. Similarly, the *Nematopalaemon tenuipes* (spider prawn) is known as Karandi in fresh and Ambad in dried state. The *Exhippolysmata ensirostris* (hunter shrimp), is called Bhoba and Ghobi in Marathi and Gujarati respectively.

### DISTRIBUTION

The non-penaeid shrimp support the commercially important fisheries from marine water as well as estuarine and near shore coastal seas along both north east and north west regions. The bulk of the landing of non-penaeid shrimp is realized from the states of Maharashtra, Gujarat and Kerala.

### DIAGNOSTIC FEATURES

Like penaeid shrimp, the body is divided into a cephalothorax (head and thorax fused together) and a pleon (abdomen). The body is generally slightly flattened side-to-side.

## FOOD AND FEEDING

*Acetes indicus* feeds mainly on detritus consisting of fibrous and granular material of phytoplankton and zooplankton origin. In addition to detritus and diatoms the *Nematopalaemon tenuipes* feeds mainly on the planktonic crustaceans. *Exhippolysmata ensirostris* is highly predaceous and feeds on *Acetes*, polychaetes and young ones of fish and shrimps.

## SIZE AND GROWTH

a) *Acetes indicus*: Attain a total length of 8-38 mm. Males and females exhibit differential growth rates of 6.15 mm and 5.96 mm per month respectively.

b) *Nematopalaemon tenuipes*: A male reaches 57 mm and females reaches 64 mm respectively in total length at the completion of one year.

c) *Exhippolysmata ensirostris*: Attains 92.8 mm at the end of one year.

## REPRODUCTIVE BEHAVIOR AND SPAWNING

*Acetes indicus* breeds almost throughout the year in the shallow coastal waters showing peak spawning activity during September-January period. The males with spermatophores in genital coxae and females with mature ovaries occur as they attain a total length of 15 -17 mm. The females lay 4,300-10,300 eggs. The smallest mature individual of *Nematopalaemon tenuipes* is 36 mm in length but 50 per cent females become mature at 54 mm in total length. The fecundity varies from 242 - 3648 eggs. The females undertake breeding migrations to offshore waters and accordingly the sex-ratio shows progressive dominance of males in the inshore waters and females in the offshore waters. The females spawn 5 - 6 times during March-October period. *Exhippolysmata ensirostris* is a hermaphrodite and breeds throughout the year with peaks during May-September and December-January. The ovotestes produce sperms as well as large yolky eggs when the prawns attain 40 - 45 mm size. The fecundity ranges from 476 -13260 eggs in individuals varying from 45 - 99 mm in total length.

## CRAFTS AND GEARS USED FOR FISHING

The non penaeid resource is mainly caught by the traditionally used fixed bag nets, locally called "dol nets" along the northwest coast. In Gujarat, the fishing operation done by trawl nets with reduced mesh size (from 25 mm to 12 -15 mm) and is responsible for the enormous landings of the resource. In Maharashtra, on the contrary the trawlers catch only *N. tenuipes*. In the Gangetic delta of West Bengal *Acetes indicus* and *N. tenuipes* are caught in bag nets, while in Krishna and Godavary estuaries of Andhra Pradesh at least five species of *Acetes* are caught along with *Macrobrachium spp.* by a multitude of indigenous gears.

In Maharashtra as well as in Gujarat, the non-penaeid shrimps showed two peaks of fishing, in October-November and in April-May, but in Andhra Pradesh there is only one peak during July. Along the Gujarat-Maharashtra coast, *A. johni* occurs during October-November in large quantities, *A. indicus* forms the bulk of the catch in March-April, *N. tenuipes* in May-June and *E.ensirostris* during June-August and December-January periods.

## ANNUAL CATCH TREND

**Table 6.18.1: Annual Catch Trend of Non-Penaeid Shrimp**

| Year | Production (tonnes) | Year | Production (tonnes) |
|---|---|---|---|
| **2003** | 87722 | **2004** | 146681 |
| **2005** | 140066 | **2006** | 141342 |
| **2007** | 131493 | **2008** | 134802 |
| **2009** | **129089** | | |

The non-penaeid shrimp production is significantly increased from 2003 with 87,722 tonnes to 2006 with 1,41,342 tonnes and after that there is a decreasing trend of production up to 2009. The average production of non-penaeid shrimp between 2003 and 2009 was 1,30,171 tonnes.

## STATEWISE CATCH TREND

Prior to 1988, Maharashtra accounted for 78 per cent and Gujarat 11.4 per cent of the non-penaeid prawn landings in the country. But thereafter, shrimp trawlers in Gujarat started commercial exploitation of *Acetes spp.* on large-scale.

The production pattern of non-penaeid shrimp from 2006 to 2009 indicated that the state of Maharashtra ranks first with the average production of 59,548 tonnes, followed by the state of Gujarat at second place with the average production of 40,064 tonnes, the state of Andhra

**Table 6.18.2: State-wise Catch Trend of Non-Penaeid Shrimp**

| *Years* | *Production (tonnes)* | | | | | | | *Avarage (2006-2009)* |
|---|---|---|---|---|---|---|---|---|
| *States* | *2003* | *2004* | *2005* | *2006* | *2007* | *2008* | *2009* | |
| **Maharashtra** | 56965 | 68634 | 67696 | 54792 | 57017 | 57741 | 68644 | **59548** |
| **Gujarat** | 9150 | 48194 | 51480 | 53147 | 42567 | 31143 | 33400 | **40064** |
| **Andhra Pradesh** | 1061 | 12185 | 6732 | 9834 | 11745 | 13412 | 10356 | **11337** |
| **Karnataka** | 464 | 0 | 0 | 12742 | 8800 | 16542 | 0 | **9521** |
| **West Bengal** | 7950 | 7000 | 6000 | 5527 | 6329 | 6400 | 3832 | **5522** |
| **Tamil Nadu** | 4671 | 4671 | 4671 | 1369 | 1059 | 6091 | 8041 | **4140** |
| **Orissa** | 2771 | 1529 | 1390 | 1725 | 1749 | 1317 | 2755 | **1886** |
| **Kerala** | 3364 | 2923 | 1714 | 1798 | 1689 | 1731 | 1714 | **1733** |
| **Pondicherry** | 1072 | 1328 | 190 | 316 | 398 | 357 | 298 | **342** |
| **Daman and Diu** | 126 | 89 | 138 | 77 | 122 | 68 | 49 | **79** |
| **Andaman and Nicobar** | 128 | 128 | 55 | 15 | 18 | 0 | 0 | **8** |
| **Total** | **87722** | **146681** | **140066** | **141342** | **131493** | **134802** | **129089** | |

Pradesh occupies the third position with the average landing of 11,337 tonnes.

## UTILIZATION OF CATCH

The non-penaeid shrimp have assumed greater importance in the diet of fish eating population of Maharashtra. But in Gujarat, enormous quantities landed by trawlers are mostly reduced to fish meal. The Acetes spp. due to their small size and delicate nature get rapidly decomposed, therefore they are sundried and generally consumed by the poor people. *N. tenuipes* has market acceptance in fresh and as well as in dried forms. Peeled meat of somewhat larger species like *E. ensirostris* is salted and dried or consumed fresh.

## 6.19 FISHERY OF MOLLUSCS

The mollusca are a large phylum of invertebrate organisms, around 85,000 species of mollusca are recognized and which are next to only largest representing phylum arthropods. However mollusca are the largest marine phylum, comprising above 23 per cent of all the marine organisms. Mollusca also are the most varied group having different sizes, shapes and habitat types. The size range may vary from few millimeters to more than 15 meters like giant squids and weighing more than 500 kg. Majority of the species even though are marine but found in different habitats from the sea shores to the depth of abyssal zone. They are also extremely diverse in distribution in tropical and temperate regions and can be found at all latitudes. There diversity can be judged from the fact that within the tropical environment molluscs occupy every trophic level, from the extent of primary producers to top carnivores.

Three classes among mollusca which dominate the fisheries of world oceans are Bivalvia, Cephalopoda and Gastropoda.

### I) BIVALVIA

### Scientific Classification

*Class* : Bivalvia

*Order* : Protobranchia, Filibranchia, Eulamellibranchia, Septibranchia

The presence of bivalve can be traced as fossils from the time of early Cambrian period of more than 500 million year ago. They include Clams, Oysters, Mussels and Scallops. The organisms are enclosed in the shell having one edge by flexible ligament that in conjunction with interlocking teeth on each of the valve forms the hinge. The shell is made of calcium carbonate and is typically bilaterally symmetrical with the hinge lying in sagittal plate. Bivalves do not have head or radula. The gills have evolved into ctenidia, which are sophisticated organs for feeding and breathing. Most bivalve busy themselves in sediment of the sea bed or sea floor or attach themselves to rocks or other hard surfaces with the help of clump of horny thread called byssus given as extensions from their foot. A few bore in wood clay and live inside these substances. Even though mostly sessile for most of part of their live, some bivalve such as the scallop can also swim.

## FOOD AND FEEDING

Majority of bivalves are filter feeders using their gills to capture particulate food such as phytoplankton from the water.

## DEVELOPMENT AND REPRODUCTIVE BEHAVIOR

The sexes are usually separate but the hermaphroditism is also known in some. The gonads are located close to the intensive and either open into the nephridia or through a separate pore into the mantle cavity. The ripe gonads of males and females release sperm and eggs into the water column. Spawning may take place continually or be triggered by environmental factors such as day length, water temperature or the presence of sperm in water. Fertilization is usually external. Typically there is short stage lasting few hours or days before the egg hatch into trochophore larvae. These later develop into veliger larvae which settle on rock or any solid substrate and metamorphosis into juvenile known as spat. In edible oyster the larval stage (veliger) is up to 20 days. On $21^{st}$ day it settles on to the sea rock or any solid substrata as spat.

## SPECIES CONTRIBUTION

The class bivalve includes clams or cockles, oysters and mussels. The detail of species wise representation of the class is given in Table 6.19.1.

**Table 6.19.1: Species-wise Representation of the Class Bivalvia**

| Group | Scientific Name | Common Name |
|---|---|---|
| Clams or Cockles | *Meritrix casta, Meritrix meritrix* | Yellow clam |
| | *Katalysia opima* | Baby clam |
| | *Villorita cyprinoides* | Black clam |
| | *Paphia malbarica* | Short neck clam or Textile clam |
| | *Mesodesma glabaratum* | |
| | *Donax sp.* | Surf clam |
| | *Synetta scripta* | Big black clam |
| | *Anadara granosa* | Cockle |
| | *Tridacna sp, Hippopus hippopus* | Giant clam |
| Mussels | *Perna viridis* | Green mussel |
| | *Perna indica* | Brown mussel |
| Pearl Oyster | *Pinctada fucata* | Indian pearl oyster |
| | *Pinctada margeritefera* | Black lip pearl oyster |
| Edible oyster | *Crassostrea cuculata or Saccostrea cuculata* | Rock oyster |
| | *Crossostrea madrasensis, Crossostra rivularis* | Indian Backwater oyster |
| | *Placenta placenta* | Windowpane oyster |

## FISHERY

Bivalve fishery is mostly a small scale activity at the primitive subsistence level in inshore, backwaters, estuaries, bays and lagoons. The fishery is still at many places by hand picking for clams. Clams are picked by local people when the water recedes during low tide in the backwater estuaries and beaches. The use of scoop net or rectangular to semicircular iron frame with nylon net of 30 mm mesh size is used for lifting clams from the inshore waters. The use of hand dredge is also common for obtaining more harvest. The use of mechanized and canoe to reach the fishing site to accomplish fishing and then to return back is common to the fishermen of Vembanad lake. In Kakinada Bay a special craft 'Shoe Dhone' is used which carry entire fishermen family and the fishing can be performing for 3 to 4 consecutive days.

The specialized divers perform fishing by diving at the site of pearl oyster bed and remove them by hammer and chisel. The clams dominate the fishery of bivalve with the share of about 75 per cent followed by oysters 14 per cent and mussels 6 per cent and windowpane oyster 5 per cent respectively. The annual average production of clam production is about 60,000 tonnes, oysters 20,000 tonnes and mussels about 15000 tonnes.

Fishery of bivalves although is practiced along both west and east coast of India, it is slightly more dominant in west coast of India. Along the west coast of India the bulk of harvest is realized from the states of Kerala. The other which contribute substantially to the production are Karnataka, Gujarat and Maharashtra states. The major production of clams in Kerala is contributed by *Villorita cyprinoids, Paphia malbarica, Meretrix castra, Katalysa opima* etc. The other which accounts for the production of bivalves is edible oyster *Crassostrea madrasensis* and *Saccostrea coculata* and mussels *Perna viridis and Perna indica.* The total production of bivalve from Kerala was average about 58760 tonnes.

In Kerala the major centers for clams production are Vembanad and Ashtamuda lake especially for the fishing of *Villorita cyprinoids (Black clams) and Paphia malbarica* (Short neck clams) respectively where the estuarine ecosystem has helped to sustain the production of clams. Vembanad Lake, the largest estuarine system in Kerala has been estimated the production of 33980 tonnes which was about 55 per cent to the total production of clams in 2000.

In Karnataka the major fishing of bivalve is represented by clams *Meritrix casta, Villorita cyprinoids, Paphia malbarica*; by oysters *Crassostrea madrasensis and Saccostrea cuculata* and mussels by *Parna viridis.* The total landing of bivalve from Karnataka state was averaged about 12750 tonnes. The important sites of production of bivalve from Karnataka are mainly concentrated in the extensive estuarine system of Aghanashini, Kalinadi, Coondapur, Mulki and Gurupur.

The state of Gujarat is exclusively dominated by edible oyster like *Crassostrea gryphydes, Crassostrea rivularis; Placenta placenta* a windowpane oyster and the pearl oyster *Pinctada fucata*. The production of bivalve in Gujarat was averaged about 4202 tonnes. The fishery of windowpane oyster and pearl oyster is form Gulf of Kutch and the edible oyster from the rest of the coastal area of Gujarat.

In Maharashtra the average total annual production of bivalves is about 2035 tonnes. The Ratnagiri coast, the main fishing region in the state is dominated by clams, *paphia sp.* and *moretrix castra* with the average production of about 12000 tonnes annually. It also supports the average annual production of 780 tonnes of green mussels (*Parna viridis*) and 55 tonnes of oyster collectively reported by *C. gryphydes, C. rivularis* and *S. coculata.*

Among the east coast the bivalve resource are rich in the estuarine ecosystem of Tamil Nadu and Pondicherry. The important sites are Kakinada Bay and Krishna Delta. The region accounts for the average annual production of 2098 tonnes and reported by *Meritrix casta, M. meritrix, P. malbarica, Crossostrea madrasensis, S. cuculata, P. viridis, P. indica* and *Pinctada fucata.*

Andhra Pradesh rests next along the east coast with the annual average production of 1278 tonnes and represented by clams such as *Anadara granosa, Geloina bengalensis, Meritrix casta, Meritrix meritrix, Paphia malbarica* and the rare *Anadara rhombea.* The other bivalve includes edible oyster *Crossostrea madrasensis,* the mussel *P. viridis* and windowpane oyster *Placenta placenta.* The information on bivalve fishing from Orissa and West Bengal are not available.

## PRODUCTION TREND

The fishery of bivalves in India is at the most subsistence level mainly followed on the basis of handpicking (for calms), exploitation by the use of hammer and chisel from back and inshore water. However the bivalves have shown considerable prospects for its culture. The rake culture, raft culture have indicated remarkable potential for increase in the landing of oysters, mussels etc. The fishery of pearl oyster still is dependent on their collection and exploitation by divers.

The fishery of calms is most resounding from South-West to South-East coast of India from the region of Kerala, Kanyakumari, Tamil Nadu and Andhra Pradesh. The leading producers are Kerala, Andhra Pradesh and Tamil Nadu. The edible oysters are exploited at highest level from Andhra Pradesh and Tamil Nadu respectively. The states of Gujarat and Kerala from the West coast also add their share to good production of oysters. The recent findings have shown tremendous prospects of culture of edible oysters form the back waters of Maharashtra, Goa and Karnataka.

Mussels are predominantly produced from west coast of India with highest share of landing from Kerala followed by Karnataka and Maharashtra. The windowpane oysters are harvested at highest level from Andhra Pradesh followed by Gujarat. The occurrence of natural beds of Pearl oysters exists exclusively in Gulf of Munnar and Palk Bay from east coast and Ran of Kutch from the west coast. The fishery of pearl oyster is mostly exploited in these waters from skilled divers.

## UTILIZATION OF CATCH

The bivalves are considered as food for poor fishermen and coastal folks which largely depend on collecting clams, edible oysters and mussels from the back waters for their livelihood.

However, the bivalve fished in recent times are utilized for the human consumption in the form of smoked and canned oysters which has considerable demand in Indian market.

In recent times there has been increasing demand of export of bivalve from the country especially for calms, oyster and mussel meat. The average annual foreign exchange earning by country during 1991 – 2003 was amounting to Rs. 13 crores from the export of about 1990 tonnes of products like frozen, smoked, dried meat and sea shells, collectively from bivalves and gastropods.

The shells of bivalves are also important resource for the manufacturing of cement, calcium carbide, sand lime bricks and lime. The lime shell is used as manure in coffee plantation, as mortar in building construction, in the treatment of effluent, as a pesticide by mixing copper sulphate and in glass, rayon, polyfibre, paper, and sugar industries.

The shells of bivalves are also used for making attractive sculpture, ornamental shell craft industry. Lastly but not least the pearls extracted from the natural pearl oysters commands very high price in the international market.

## II) CEPHALOPODS

### Scientific Classification

*Class* : Cephalopoda

*Order* : Sepiodea, Teuthoidea, Octopoda.

These are exclusively marine mollusc comes under the category of Coleoidea. They are highly advanced and specialized therefore known to be the most intelligent invertebrates. They have eyes and other senses that rival those of human beings. There are over 800 species known in international waters. The group mainly comprise of squids, cuttlefishes and octopuses. They are characterized by bilateral symmetry, a prominent head and set of armed tentacles, a modified form of primitive molluscan foot. They have ink gland and ink is ejected to protect the animal from predation or to confuse the predator and resist it form attack. They are perhaps most fastest venturing invertebrates in ocean, capable to make rapid stride in water column and are even able to dart rapidly back form the same position. This may be possible due to the undulations from their muscular body. They can also change the texture, shape and colour of the body and if these camouflage techniques do not work, they can still disappear in the cloud of ink they eject. Cephalopods are also fascinating

**Table 6.19.2: Different Species of the Class Cephalopoda**

| *Order* | *Species* | *Common Name* |
|---|---|---|
| Sepiodea | *Sepia elliptica* | Golden cuttlefish |
| | *S. prashadi* | Hoded cuttlefish |
| | *S. aculeate* | Needle cuttlefish |
| | *S. pharaonis* | Pharaoh cuttlefish |
| | *S. brivimana* | Short club cuttlefish |
| | *S. inermis* | Spineless cuttlefish |
| Teuthoidea | *Loligo duvauceli* | Indian squid |
| | *L. uyil* | Little squid |
| | *Lolioulus investigatoris* | Investigater squid |
| | *Thysantoteuthis rhombus* | Diamond squid |
| | *Doryteuthis sp.* | Needle squid |
| | *Sepioteuthis lessoniana* | |
| | *Symplectoteuthis oualainiensis* | Oceanic squid |
| Octopoda | *Octopus vulgaris* | Common octopus |
| | *Octopus doiffusi* | Marbled octopus |
| | *O. lobensis* | Lobed octopus |
| | *O. membranaceous* | Web foot octopus |
| | *Cistopus indicus* | Old woman octopus |

because they have three hearts that pump blue blood. They are found in all oceans of the world from tropics to the poles and from intertidal to the abyss. Most of the cephalopods like squids and cuttllefishes have photophores diffused all along their body which help them for orientation and visual detection of prey in deeper waters.

Cephalopods are represented by three orders namely sepiodea, teuthoidea and octopoda. The order sepiodea comprise of all cuttlefishes in addition to the common characters of cephalopods mentioned above, they internally reduced shell called as cuttlebone located dorsally in the musculature. They are also characterized by presence of ten tentacles retractile into pockets from circum oral appendage. Arms have suckers. The body is flappy, highly masculine and sides are flattened to assist in rapid swimming. They have photophores differed all along their body. Fin lobes are posteriorly free. The important species found in the Indian waters are *Sepia elliptica* (golden cuttlefish) *S. prashadi* (Hoded cuttlefish), *S. aculeate* (Needle cuttlefish), *S. pharaonis* (Pharaoh cuttlefish), *S. brivimana* (Short club cuttlefish) and *Sepiella inermis* (Spineless cuttlefish). They are found all along the west and east coast of India.

The order teuthoidea include all wide ranging squids. They also have reduced internal chitinous rod shaped shell called as pen. Here also there are ten oral appendages of which eight are sessile arms and two are contractile tentacular arms suckers are stalked with or without hooks. In squids fin lobs on lower side are fused. Eyes are large without lids but either covered with a transparent membrane with a minute pore (Myopsida) or are completely open to the sea without a pore (Oegopsida). Spuids are wide ranging from smallest *Loligo uyil* to largest giant squid *Architeuthis* which may attain length of over 10 meters and can weigh up to 200 kg. In the Indian waters they are represented by *Loligo duvauceli* (Indian squid), *L. uyil* (Little squid), *Lolioulus investigatoris* (Investigater squid), *Thysantoteuthis rhombus* (Diamond squid), *Doryteuthis sp.* (Needle squid) *Sepioteuthis lessoniana, Symplectoteuthis oualainiensis* (Oceanic squid).

Octopuses come under the order Octopoda. They are characterized by eight arms but no tentacles. Suckers are set directly on arms but are without chitinous rings and stalks. The shell is either vestigial or absent. Fins are absent. The octopuses usually oriented from their circular head, followed by the arms. Head has prominently large eye. They are able to change their colour smartly to match with the surroundings which helps them to be invisible for predating. Similarly it helps in praying when invisible by pouncing on the prey. They are also wide ranging from small to quite large in shape. Unlike squids and cephalopods they do not have consumable value. There are about 5 species occur in the Indian waters represented by *Octopus vulgaris* (Common octopus); *Octopus doiffusi* (Marbled octopus); *O. lobensis* (Lobed octopus); *O. membranaceous* (Web foot octopus) and *Cistopus indicus* (Old woman octopus).

## FOOD AND FEEDING

All adult cephalopods are carnivores of top order feeding mainly on fish. The diet of smaller one may include some invertebrates also. The cannibalism in some of the species is also common. Cephalopods also happen to be the food choice for tunas, billfishes and whales.

## REPRODUCTIVE CHARACTERS

In *L. duvauceli* and *Sepia pharaonsis* the females grow faster then males while in *Sepia aculeate* males grow faster than females. The spawning seems to be prolonged. The squids come in large numbers for spawning along the shore. After mating the female carry with her the fertilized eggs and migrate to the rocky shallow subtidal for laying fertilized eggs. In most species the female die after the spawning is accomplished. Indian squid *Loligo duvancelo* spawn throughout the year along both the coast but the peak spawning along the west coast is observed during post monsoon months.

For *Sepia pharaoni* the peak spawning season along both the coast is from October to April. The squid *Sepioteuthis lessoniana* which is mostly native of east coast the intensive spawning season is from January to June. *Sepia aculeate* is a proliferic breeder, the spawning is mostly coastal habitat based. Along Waltair it breeds twice from January to April and from July to December; along Mandapam in the east coast the same species breeds first between February to April and then between July to August. Along the west coast *Sepia aculeate* breeds thrice in a year. Along Kochi coast it breed April, July and December while along Mumbai coast it breeds first during February to March and later in September to November.

## CRAFTS AND GEARS USED FOR FISHING

The demand for the capture of cephalopods especially the squids and cuttlefishes in India became high from early eighties onward; it became more intense in late eighties and nineties due to sudden escalation of its export demand at the international market. This lead to the targeted fishing of these important seafood commodities from some Indian waters especially North-West, South-West coastal areas. The large trawl gears are operated in different maritime areas of the country for the capture of cephalopods, by purse seiners in Karnataka, seine netting and even cast net in knee deep coastal waters.

## ANNUAL CATCH TREND

Even though cephalopods are fished from Indian maritime areas from very early times, the production remained at very low level up to seventies. However firstly due to the great demand for this group from international market and later due to shortage of penaeid shrimp owing to overexploitation of stock from continental waters, the attention for fishing was diverted for fishing of cephalopods from late eighties and nineties. The production showed remarkable increase crossing over 100000 tonnes mark in 1994 and remained at high level even in later years. The cephalopods are actively fished early part of this century and even now. It is now considered to be the most important exploited marine fish resource of the country contributing between 4 per cent and 5 per cent of all India marine fish production.

**Table 16.19.3: Annual Catch Trend of Cephalopods and Other Molluscs**

| Years | Production of Cephalopods (tonnes) | Production of other Molluscs (tonnes) |
|---|---|---|
| **2003** | 84032 | 607 |
| **2004** | 67684 | 7234 |
| **2005** | 75319 | 5612 |
| **2006** | 91403 | 2221 |
| **2007** | 74973 | 5492 |
| **2008** | 75494 | 2415 |
| **2009** | 57996 | 2963 |

The production of cephalopods for the five year period from 2003-2007 varied between highest of 87350 tonnes in 2003 to lowest of 69292 in 2004. The average production of cephalopods during this period was 78750 tonnes. Even though, the production of cephalopods increased after 2004 onwards up to 2007. These are indications that the sustainable effect of its fishing in recent times influenced its stock from the Indian waters. The recent rapid increase in production warrants close monitoring of this short lived resource from the viewpoint of judicious management. It has also been suggested that the most effective means of managing cephalopod fisheries is by regulating fishing effort, which will reduce the risk recruitment and overfishing. The present ban on trawl fishing during the monsoon in different maritime states is a one such measure which must be followed further.

Wide fluctuations in the production of other molluscs were observed between minimum of 607 tonnes in 2003 and maximum of 7,234 tonnes in 2004. Thereafter the landings have shown the declining trend with the average production of just 3740 tonnes between 2005 and 2009.

## STATEWISE CATCH TREND

The major share to the landing of cephalopods was realized from the west coast of India accounting for over 80 per cent of landing with sequentially high level of contribution from the states of Gujarat, Kerala, Maharashtra and Karnataka states. The statewise average percentage landing of cephalopods for the five year period indicated the state of Gujarat is the leading with the highest share in production of 33.65 per cent followed by Kerala 19.91 per cent, Maharashtra 16.29 per cent, Karnataka 12.63 per cent and Tamil Nadu 11.96 per cent respectively in the order. Even though the state of Gujarat has shown sustainably high production and Kerala with an average good production followed next the state of Maharashtra, Karnataka and Kerala have shown remarkably wide fluctuation in the production of cephalopods.

The state wise landing from 2006 to 2009 for other molluscs have indicated that the state of Pondicherry to be the proud leading producer with the average production of 1,262 tonnes, while the states of Andhra Pradesh and Gujarat attained the second and third rank with the average production of 995 tonnes and 691 tonnes respectively.

## UTILIZATION

In India major emphasis for cephalopods landing and export was laid specially after the decline of shrimp production and export sustained

## Table 6.19.4: State-wise Yearly Production of Cephalopods

| *Years* | *Production (tonnes)* | | | | | | | *Avarage (2006-2009)* |
|---|---|---|---|---|---|---|---|---|
| *States* | *2003* | *2004* | *2005* | *2006* | *2007* | *2008* | *2009* | |
| **Gujarat** | 29302 | 21437 | 29590 | 31839 | 20526 | 19301 | 17090 | **22189** |
| **Kerala** | 17754 | 15891 | 14172 | 15465 | 14909 | 14879 | 14538 | **14948** |
| **Maharashtra** | 12816 | 7410 | 13125 | 13765 | 17512 | 12!86 | 13450 | **14228** |
| **Karnataka** | 13200 | 9277 | 9169 | 14775 | 9624 | 16404 | 0 | **10201** |
| **Tamil Nadu** | 9169 | 9169 | 7338 | 11102 | 7532 | 5963 | 6633 | **7807** |
| **Andhra Pradesh** | 421 | 479 | 1089 | 1603 | 3661 | 3851 | 4036 | **3288** |
| **Goa** | 829 | 2486 | 73 | 1919 | 330 | 2201 | 1595 | **1511** |
| **Orissa** | 370 | 1319 | 497 | 544 | 535 | 578 | 545 | **550** |
| **Pondicherry** | 2933 | 1593 | 829 | 778 | 1263 | 1532 | 1474 | **1262** |
| **Daman and Diu** | 541 | 216 | 266 | 370 | 318 | 107 | 68 | **216** |
| **Andaman and Nicobar** | 0 | 0 | 0 | 21 | 26 | 24 | 41 | **28** |
| **Total Catch** | **87335** | **69277** | **76148** | **92181** | **76236** | **77026** | **59470** | |

**Table 6.19.5: State-wise Yearly Production of Other Molluscs**

| Years | Production (tonnes) | | | | | | | Avarage (2006-2009) |
|---|---|---|---|---|---|---|---|---|
| States | 2003 | 2004 | 2005 | 2006 | 2007 | 2008 | 2009 | |
| **Gujarat** | 607 | 732 | 1237 | 558 | 2209 | 0 | 0 | **691.8** |
| **Karnataka** | 0 | 0 | 0 | 0 | 620 | 0 | 0 | **155** |
| **Andhra Pradesh** | 0 | 6361 | 4364 | 847 | 813 | 858 | 1465 | **995.8** |
| **Goa** | 0 | 141 | 0 | 11 | 568 | 0 | 0 | **144.8** |
| **Orissa** | 0 | 0 | 11 | 27 | 19 | 25 | 24 | **23.75** |
| **Pondicherry** | 0 | 0 | 0 | 778 | 1263 | 1532 | 1474 | **1262** |
| Total Catch | 607 | 7234 | 5612 | 2221 | 5492 | 2415 | 2963 | |

during late eighties. Even though there is little internal demand for cephalopods and consequently almost all the catch is exported due to high international demand.

The export by quantity picked its highest mark in 1995 when cephalopods formed about the 45 per cent of total quantity export from the country having the annual average growth rate of 24 per cent. In term of value cephalopods which averaged at 15 per cent in nineties, later increased in 2003 to earn Rs. 800 crores of revenue for the country. Category wise the squid products earned more demand than cuttlefish products. The products of export include dried, frozen holed, filleted tentacles, rings, row, wings, IQF, bones and ink. Octopus even though earned comparably less demand; it has shown rising trend in export from 1994 onwards. The main markets for export of Indian cephalopods are Europe, Japan and China.

The everlasting rising demand of cephalopods with almost cent percent export potential warrants, careful monitoring, immaculate management practices and rational exploitation of the stock in order to earn the sustainably high potential yield in future.

# *Chapter 7*
# MANAGEMENT OF MARINE FISHERIES RESOURCES

The presence of marine fisheries sector looks gloomy mainly due to stalemate in marine fish landing. The marine fish production in the span of 11 years from 1997-2008 with the exception of few years (2006-2007, 2007-2008) when it was over 3.0 MMT has been hovering between 2.69 to 2.94 MMT with the average of 2.87 MMT. The situation of this ineptness of marine fisheries sector was mainly arouse due to heavy exploitation of continental waters up to 50 meters resulting into the extreme decline of the production and relatively very limited effort made in over the years for the diversification of fishing into the extended waters.

It is therefore noteworthy and highly necessary to identify the critical gaps and constraints ailing the fisheries and the implementation of immaculate management measures pertinent to excel the prospect of marine fisheries sector in the country.

## Current Gaps and Constrains from Marine Fishery Sector

- ✰ Lack of reliable data base relating to resources.
- ✰ Non availability of suitable fish yield models for multi-species fisheries from marine ecosystem.

- ✰ Lack of use of sophisticated gears for fishing.
- ✰ Lack of large ocean going vessels.
- ✰ Non adoption of targeted and selective fishing.
- ✰ Over exploitation of coastal fisheries.
- ✰ Lack of knowledge of marine biodiversity, database conservation and management.
- ✰ No advent to fishing from open, deep sea offshore waters.
- ✰ Apprehension for adoption of mariculture, coastal brackish water aquaculture.
- ✰ Concept of diversification in aquaculture practices unadopted.
- ✰ Unplanned and unregulated development of fish/shrimp farms.
- ✰ Linkages between research and development machinery are weak.
- ✰ Gaps in upgradation and promotion of the concept of fish processing and value addition.
- ✰ Weak marketing and distribution for marine fishes.
- ✰ Inadequate manpower, lack of specialized training in marine capture and culture fisheries.

## Promotional Measures Required for Marine Fisheries Resource Management

- ✰ Upgradation of most correct data base system for marine fishery resources.
- ✰ Intensive monitoring of exploited marine fish stocks.
- ✰ Routine scientific voyages and survey in Arabian Sea, Indian Ocean and Bay of Bengal to estimate depth wise and species wise potential of marine fishes.
- ✰ Stock assessment of commercially important marine species from prominent fishing centers using modern technologies of sonar and fish finders.
- ✰ Marine biodiversity, database conservation and management.
- ✰ Catchment ecology in relation to fisheries.
- ✰ Intensification of exploitation of oceanic deep sea resources from offshore fishing grounds.

- ☆ Regulation of fishing efforts, effort rationalization and closed fishing seasons.
- ☆ Gear, area and temporal restrictions and mesh size regulation to prevent over fishing vis-a-vis growth and recruitment.
- ☆ Promoting tuna long lining, offshore purse seining, oceanic squid jigging, offshore midwater and deepwater trawling etc.
- ☆ Upgradation of fishery forecast linked oceanographic parameters.
- ☆ Finding new virgin grounds for marine fishing.
- ☆ Enhancement of coastal stock through sea-ranching.
- ☆ Creating artificial fish habitats in inshore fishing grounds and marine parks for conservation of endangered marine fish species.
- ☆ Promotion of coastal brackish water and mariculture activities.
- ☆ Scientific management of coastal shrimp/fish farms.
- ☆ Development of pearl culture technology.
- ☆ Upgradation of avenues of fish processing.
- ☆ Countrywide distribution of marine fishes.
- ☆ Utilization of by-catch by conversion into value added products.

# INDEX

## G



## I



## L



## M